ASPECTS OF TOURISM 21
Series Editors: Chris Cooper (*University of Queensland, Australia*),
C. Michael Hall (*University of Otago, New Zealand*)
and Dallen Timothy (*Arizona State University, USA*)

Nature-based Tourism in Peripheral Areas
Development or Disaster?

Edited by
C. Michael Hall and Stephen Boyd

CHANNEL VIEW PUBLICATIONS
Clevedon • Buffalo • Toronto

Library of Congress Cataloging in Publication Data
Nature-based Tourism in Peripheral Areas: Development or Disaster?
Edited by C. Michael Hall and Stephen Boyd.
Aspects of Tourism: 21
Includes bibliographical references and index.
1. Ecotourism. I. Hall, Colin Michael. II. Boyd, Stephen W. III. Series.
G156.5.E26N28 2005
338.4'791–dc22   2004016905

British Library Cataloguing in Publication Data
A catalogue entry for this book is available from the British Library.

ISBN 1-874541-001-7 (hbk)
ISBN 1-874541-000-9 (pbk)

Channel View Publications
An imprint of Multilingual Matters Ltd

UK: Frankfurt Lodge, Clevedon Hall, Victoria Road, Clevedon BS21 7HH.
USA: 2250 Military Road, Tonawanda, NY 14150, USA.
Canada: 5201 Dufferin Street, North York, Ontario, Canada M3H 5T8.

Typeset by Florence Production Ltd.
Printed and bound in Great Britain by the Cromwell Press.

Nature-based Tourism in Peripheral Areas

ASPECTS OF TOURISM
Series Editors: Professor Chris Cooper, *University of Queensland, Australia*
Dr C. Michael Hall, *University of Otago, Dunedin, New Zealand*
Dr Dallen Timothy, *Arizona State University, Tempe, USA*

Aspects of Tourism is an innovative, multifaceted series which will comprise authoritative reference handbooks on global tourism regions, research volumes, texts and monographs. It is designed to provide readers with the latest thinking on tourism world-wide and in so doing will push back the frontiers of tourism knowledge. The series will also introduce a new generation of international tourism authors, writing on leading edge topics. The volumes will be readable and user-friendly, providing accessible sources for further research. The list will be underpinned by an annual authoritative tourism research volume. Books in the series will be commissioned that probe the relationship between tourism and cognate subject areas such as strategy, development, retailing, sport and environmental studies. The publisher and series editors welcome proposals from writers with projects on these topics.

Other Books in the Series
Marine Ecotourism: Issues and Experiences
    Brian Garrod and Julie C. Wilson (eds)
Classic Reviews in Tourism
    Chris Cooper (ed.)
Progressing Tourism Research
    Bill Faulkner, edited by Liz Fredline, Leo Jago and Chris Cooper
Managing Educational Tourism
    Brent W. Ritchie
Recreational Tourism: Demand and Impacts
    Chris Ryan
Coastal Mass Tourism: Diversification and Sustainable Development in Southern Europe
    Bill Bramwell (ed.)
Sport Tourism Development
    Thomas Hinch and James Higham
Sport Tourism: Interrelationships, Impact and Issues
    Brent Ritchie and Daryl Adair (eds)
Tourism, Mobility and Second Homes
    C. Michael Hall and Dieter Müller
Strategic Management for Tourism Communities: Bridging the Gaps
    Peter E. Murphy and Ann E. Murphy
Oceania: A Tourism Handbook
    Chris Cooper and C. Michael Hall (eds)
Tourism Marketing: A Collaborative Approach
    Alan Fyall and Brian Garrod
Music and Tourism: On the Road Again
    Chris Gibson and John Connell
Tourism Development: Issues for a Vulnerable Industry
    Julio Aramberri and Richard Butler (eds)

For more details of these or any other of our publications, please contact:
Channel View Publications, Frankfurt Lodge, Clevedon Hall,
Victoria Road, Clevedon, BS21 7HH, England
http://www.channelviewpublications.com

Contents

Acknowledgements

The University of Otago at Dunedin, in the South Island of New Zealand, is the world's southernmost university. It should therefore perhaps be of no great surprise that the study of tourism in peripheral regions is one of the major research foci of the Department of Tourism based at the university. Peripheral areas, by virtue of the level of their economic development and their distance from national and international economic cores, tend to have a high level of dependence on resource-based industries. Traditionally these have tended to be potentially renewable natural resources such as timber and fisheries, and agriculture, as well as non-renewable resources such as minerals. More recently, the natural resources of the periphery, and their relative lack of economic development and landscape change have come to serve as the basis for the development of tourism as a means of economic development and, in some cases, as a means of alternative development that may serve to conserve the natural resource base while extracting use value from it. However, almost paradoxically, the relative lack of development and accessibility seems to attract tourists and, in many cases, only serves as an economic and political stimulant for the provision of infrastructure, access and more people. Thereby potentially damaging the very resources that attracted visitors in the first place. Nature-based tourism therefore, from some perspectives, can potentially be disastrous in as much as it offers development.

The purpose of this book is not to romanticise nature, tourism or the people who live in the periphery. Rather this edited book represents an opportunity to bring together a number of case studies and reviews that highlight some of the difficulties of managing nature-based tourism resources and the desire for economic development in an increasingly competitive world for both people and capital. The chapters have been developed either in conjunction with the research and extension activities of the research team at the University of Otago and its partners, or have been especially invited for this volume. Nevertheless, the New Zealand component remains significant in an international setting because, rightly or wrongly, New Zealand is often seen as an international benchmark for best practice, with respect to many aspects of the management of nature-based tourism in peripheral areas (e.g. see Lusseau, Chapter 16, this volume). However, the problems that New Zealand faces, particularly with respect to the management and regulation of tourism activities are clearly to be found in other jurisdictions. The studies in the book also provide a basis for examining and comparing nature-based tourism in different environments as well as in countries and locations in the developed and less-developed world. Such studies are extremely useful, as they highlight not only previously poorly recognised, yet critical, aspects of tourism in peripheral areas, such as health (see Musa, Chapter 8, this volume) but also the interplay of tourism with other development concerns, such as education (see Schreyens, Chapter 12, this volume). Moreover a central message of this volume, is that nature-based tourism and tourism development, needs to be located not just within the context of the success or otherwise of tourism, but, far more importantly, within the wider regional development context and broader economic, social, political and environmental concerns. From such a perspective, it then becomes readily apparent that, in some cases, the best form of tourism development may well be no tourism at all. The editors would like to thank all the authors for their contribution as well as the assistance of other members of the Department of Tourism at the University of Otago: Anna Carr, David Duval, James Higham, Donna Keen, Brent Lovelock, Eric Shelton and Hazel Tucker. A special thanks for administrative assistance also goes to Frances Cadogan and Melinda Elliott, as well as Monica Gilmour. Other acknowledgements are due to Nick Cave, Hoodoo Gurus, Joe Jackson, Jethro Tull, Rufus Wainwright and Melissa Williams who assisted enormously in the final editing stages and Jody Cowper, for her invaluable support, as well as all the staff at Channel View.

Dunedin

January 2004

Contributors

Stephen Boyd, Department of Tourism, University of Otago, Dunedin, New Zealand.

Ludovic Dupuis, Department of Social and Economic Geography and Spatial Modeling Center, Umeå University, Kiruna, Sweden.

Elizabeth Fredline, Research Development Unit, RMIT Business, RMIT University, Melbourne, Victoria, Australia.

Warwick Frost, Department of Management, Monash University, Berwick, Victoria, Australia.

C. Michael Hall, Department of Tourism, University of Otago, Dunedin, New Zealand.

Margaret Johnston, School of Outdoor Recreation, Parks and Tourism, Lakehead University Thunder Bay, Ontario, Canada.

Brent Lovelock, Department of Tourism, University of Otago, Dunedin, New Zealand.

Hildegard Lübcke, Nature Guides Otago, 6a Elliffe Place, Dunedin, New Zealand.

David Lusseau, Lighthouse Field Station, University of Aberdeen, Cromarty, Scotland.

Dieter K. Müller, Department of Social and Economic Geography, Umeå University, Umeå, Sweden.

Ghazali Musa, Faculty of Business and Accountancy, University Malay, Kuala Lumpur, Malaysia.

Mark Orams, Coastal–Marine Research Group, Massey University at Albany, Albany, New Zealand.

Robert Payne, School of Outdoor Recreation, Parks and Tourism, Lakehead University, Thunder Bay, Ontario, Canada.

Dorothy Queiros, Tourism Group, Business School, University of Hertfordshire, Hatfield Campus, Hatfield, England.

Kevin Robinson, 608 North Rd, Invercargill, New Zealand.

Roslyn Russell, RMIT Business, RMIT University, Melbourne, Victoria, Australia.

Jarkko Saarinen, Department of Geography, University of Oulu, Oulu, Finland.

Regina Scheyvens, Massey University, Palmerston North, New Zealand.

Eric Shelton, Department of Tourism, University of Otago, Dunedin, New Zealand.

Philippa Thomas, School of Tourism and Hospitality, La Trobe University, Victoria, Australia

Filipo Tokalau, Department of Economics, University of the South Pacific, Fiji.

Nicholas J. Westwood, Department of Tourism, University of Otago, Dunedin, New Zealand.

Brian Wheeller, NHTV Breda University of Professional Education, Breda, Holland

Deon Wilson, Department of Tourism Management, University of Pretoria, Hatfield, Pretoria, South Africa.

Part 1: Introduction

Chapter 1
Nature-based Tourism in Peripheral Areas: Introduction

C. MICHAEL HALL AND STEPHEN BOYD

Nature-based tourism is undoubtedly one of the most significant areas of research in tourism studies today. Nature-based tourism includes tourism in natural settings (e.g. adventure tourism), tourism that focuses on specific elements of the natural environment (e.g. safari and wildlife tourism, nature tourism, marine tourism), and tourism that is developed in order to conserve or protect natural areas (e.g. ecotourism, national parks). Drawing upon the landscape and environment traditions within geography in particular, as well as broader environmental studies in the social and physical sciences, nature-based tourism research has grown to include not only discussions of the complex relationships between tourism and the physical environment in rural and natural areas but also social, economic and political relations (e.g. Cater & Lowman, 1994; Hall & Johnston, 1995; Butler & Boyd, 2000; Holden, 2000; Newsome *et al.*, 2002). Undoubtedly, much research has also focused on ecotourism as a subset of nature-based tourism (e.g. Fennell, 1999; Weaver, 2001). Indeed, the development of specialist journals such as the *Journal of Ecotourism* and the *Journal of Tourism in Marine Environments* is testimony to the amount of research being undertaken in this field. So what then can yet another book add to what might appear to be an already congested field?

Despite the growth of research and publications on tourism in natural areas, our understanding of the role and effects of tourism in natural areas is surprisingly limited. Arguably, the majority of studies have examined the impacts of tourism and recreation on a particular environment or component of the environment rather than over a range of environments. There is substantial research undertaken on tourism with respect to rainforest, reefs and dolphins and whales for example, and very limited research undertaken on what are arguably less attractive environments, such as deserts, or animals such as warthogs, even though they may also be part of wildlife viewing tourism. This is not to deny that research or particular environments or species are unimportant, rather it is to high-light the huge gaps that exist in our knowledge of tourism. But perhaps most importantly, nature-based tourism needs to be seen within the broader natural, socio-cultural, political and economic systems within which it is embedded and which determine its development.

Therefore, this book seeks to contribute to our understanding of nature-based tourism in what is the main environment in which it occurs, namely that of peripheral areas, and the issues that arise out of specific natural resources being utilised for the development of tourism for what are primarily economic reasons. Importantly, this book explicitly takes the position that regional development through tourism is established not only by the stock of its human-made capital (e.g. transport and energy infrastructure, housing, production of goods), or of its natural capital (wilderness, natural resources, national parks, green space, high value species), but also by its human capital (professional skill, training, indi-vidual knowledge, education) and social capital (subjects' ability to co-ordinate their own actions and choices in view of common goals) (Ostrom, 1990; Fukuyama, 1995). Human and social capital, therefore, become crit-ical requirements for sustainable nature-based tourism development as they are not the consequence of development, but rather its prerequisite. A region is rich if it has human capital and social capital because these are the means by which other forms of capital are produced and specific aspects of the natural environment turned into tourism resources. Never-theless, the relative absence of human and social capital also becomes one of the development challenges of many peripheral areas.

Peripheral areas are characterised by a number of interrelated features that impact on the development of nature-based tourism, as well as other industry sectors (Botterill *et al.*, 1997; Buhalis, 1997; Hall & Jenkins, 1998; Jenkins *et al.*, 1998):

(1) Peripheral areas tend to lack effective political and economic control over major decisions affecting their well-being. They are particularly susceptible to the impacts of economic globalisation and restructur-ing through the removal of tariffs and the development of free-trade regimes (Jenkins *et al.*, 1998). In addition, the political and economic decisions made by corporations whose headquarters lie elsewhere and political institutions in the capital or at the supranational level may lead to a situation where 'organisations and individuals within the periphery often feel a sense of alienation, a feeling of governance from afar and a lack of control over their own destiny' (Botterill *et al.*, 1997: 3).

(2) Peripheral areas, by definition, are geographically remote from mass markets. This not only implies increased transportation costs to and from the core areas but may also increase communication costs with suppliers and the market as well.

(3) Internal economic linkages tend to be weaker at the periphery than at the core thereby potentially limiting the ability to achieve high multiplier effects because of the substantial degree of importation of goods and services (Archer, 1989).

(4) In contemporary society migration flows tend to be from the periphery to the core. This is a major issue for many peripheral and rural regions because of the impact that this can have not only on the absolute population of a given area but its profile as well. For example, migration outflows tend to be younger people looking for improved employment and education opportunities for both themselves and/or their children. The loss of younger members of communities can then have flow-on effects in terms of school closures thereby further reinforcing such a vicious cycle of out-migration. In addition, out-migration can also lead to a loss of intellectual and social capital. However, for some peripheral areas new forms of in-migration may occur with respect to retirement and second home development, although this will tend to be with respect to older age groups. In some situations, although such developments may inject economic and human capital into peripheral areas, it may also place further strain on health and social services (Hall & Müller, 2004). As Troughton (1990: 25) noted with respect to the Canadian situation:

> In many areas, even of viable agriculture, villages and towns are stagnating or in decline due to losses of populations, and, in turn, of basic functions such as transportation links, schools, doctors, and churches, as well as rural industry. The situation is generally worst in physically poor and/or isolated 'marginal' areas, where outmigration has been highest and dependency in all senses is most pronounced. The only exception is in the rural-urban fringe zone, close to urban centres, where repopulation by exurbanites is universal.

(5) Botterill et al. (1997) have argued that peripheries tend to be characterised by a comparative lack of innovation as new products tend to be imported rather than developed locally.

(6) Because of the economic difficulties experienced by peripheral regions, the national and local state may have greater interventionist role than in core regions (Hall & Jenkins, 1998). This is illustrated through the establishment of local economic development agencies, the development of special grant schemes for peripheral areas as in the case of the European Union, and/or agricultural subsidy programmes (Jenkins et al., 1998).

(7) Information flows within the periphery and from the periphery to the core are weaker than those from the core to the periphery (Botterill et al., 1997). Such information flows may have implications for political

and economic decision-making undertaken in core regions as well as broader perceptions of place given the difficulties that may exist in changing existing images of the periphery (Hall, 1997).

(8) Peripheral regions often retain high aesthetic amenity values because of being relatively underdeveloped in relation to core areas. Such high natural values may not only serve as a basis for the development of nature-based tourism but may also be significant for other types of tourism and leisure developments, such as those associated with vacation homes (Hall & Müller, 2004). 'Ironically, the very consequences of lack of development, the unspoilt character of the landscape and distinctive local cultures, become positive resources as far as tourism is concerned' (Duffield & Long, 1981: 409).

Arguably, the peripheral nature of many of the areas in which nature-based tourism occurs is surprisingly not often explicitly recognised in many studies of nature-based tourism. Instead, we argue it is an important, if not essential, dimension of tourism in natural areas. Although it may sound something of a tautology to note that nature-based tourism tends to occur in areas with high natural values, it does serve to highlight the extent to which nature-based tourism tends to occur away from urban areas. Naturalness is a concept that has aesthetic and biophysical dimensions. Naturalness is a relative concept that may be quantified in terms of factors such as, for example, the extent of non-indigenous plant and animal species. Naturalness, sometimes also termed primitiveness, has played an important part in the developed of better understanding of the associated concepts such as wilderness, particularly with respect to the conduct of wilderness inventories (Lesslie & Taylor, 1983, 1985). Another concept that has also been utilised in evaluating the relative qualities of natural environments is that of remoteness from human settlement and access points such as roads (Helburn, 1977). Remoteness can be measured in terms of various dimensions of distance such as Euclidean distance or time distance. The concepts of naturalness and remoteness may therefore be combined to provide a two dimensional continuum approach to identifying remote areas with high natural values that are usually termed as wilderness (Figure 1.1) (Hall, 1992; Hall & Page, 2002).

Such a continuum approach can be further expanded to highlight the key elements of nature-based tourism in peripheral areas (Figure 1.2). Three dimensions are identified: naturalness, accessibility and trip numbers. The concept of naturalness has been discussed above. Accessibility is used as an equivalent term for remoteness, but it is argued that it better conveys the significance of connectivity between trip generation and destination that comprises the travel experience. As Gould (1969: 64) recognised, 'Accessibility is . . . a slippery notion . . . one of

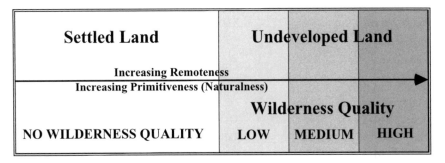

Figure 1.1 The wilderness continuum

Source: Hall (1992)

those common terms that everyone uses until faced with the problem of defining and measuring it'. Accessibility has both a social dimension and a physical dimension. The social dimension refers to the socio-cultural sanctions that surround travel as well as the legal ability to travel. Physical accessibility refers to 'the ability of people to reach desti-nations at which they can carry out a given activity' (Mitchell & Town, 1976: 3) and 'the inherent characteristic, or advantage, of a place with respect to overcoming some form of spatially operating source of fric-tion, for example time and /or distance' (Ingram, 1971: 101). Figure 1.2 primarily uses the concept of accessibility in physical terms although the social dimensions of travel clearly also underlies people's ability to move. The final dimension, that of trip numbers, recognises that there is a distant decay effect with respect to the number of trips undertaken from a central point whether this be at the level of individuals (i.e. from 'home') or a collective point such as a cosmopolitan area or urban centre.

Several important issues emerge from Figure 1.2 that highlight the difficulties of developing nature-based tourism in peripheral areas. First, given that naturalness is by definition determined in part by the level of human settlement and impact, to increase numbers of visitors may therefore reduce the natural qualities that attracted visitors in the first place. Second, the improvement of access, so important a role for tourism and overall economic development, may also potentially result in the loss of natural values. Third, and as a result of the first two observa-tions, nature-based tourism in peripheral areas therefore has a difficult balancing act between achieving regional development objectives and retaining high levels of naturalness, if these are regarded as significant values to maintain. Moreover, the figure also highlights the relative nature of the peripheral area concept. Significant changes in access to main urban centres can serve to substantially redefine the perceived peripherality of locations. Such changes can occur through changes in

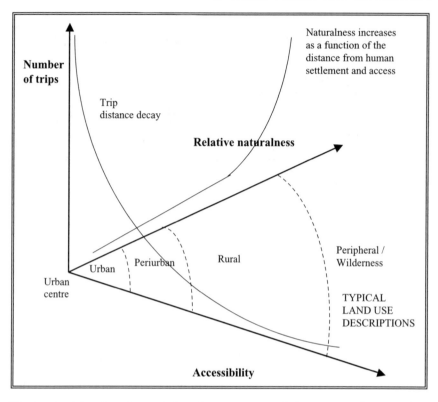

Figure 1.2 Tourism in peripheral areas: accessibility, naturalness and
        trip distance decay

Source: after Hall (2003, 2005)

transport technology, the development of new transport gateways (e.g.
shipping ports and airports) as well as new or improved transport
infrastructure (e.g. new railways or roads, or upgrading of rail and road-
ways). More than ever therefore nature-based tourism in peripheral areas
needs to be seen within the context of the wider regional development
objectives and management strategies of the areas in which such tourism
development occurs.

Tourism and Regional Development in Peripheral Areas

Tourism has long been utilised as a mechanism for regional development. There is a longstanding, widespread, but arguably erroneous
perception that tourism offers salvation from local economic crises
(e.g. Clout, 1972). Indeed, optimism over the potential employment and

economic benefits of tourism 'owes much to a policy climate that has been uncritical over a range of issues' (Hudson & Townsend, 1992: 50). According to Hall and Jenkins (1998) this is not surprising because few strong theories, concepts or studies exist to guide the sustainable long-term development, role and management of tourism in rural and peripheral areas. Indeed cautionary comments regarding tourism development in peripheral areas have existed for almost as long as government has promoted tourism development. For example, as Baum and Moore observed in the United States in the 1960s:

> there are and there will be increasing opportunities for recreation [and tourism] development, but this industry should not be considered to be a panacea for the longstanding problems of substantial and persistent unemployment and underemployment besetting low-income rural areas . . . The successful development of a particular recreational [and tourism] enterprise or complex of enterprises requires the same economic considerations as the planning and development of economic activities in other sectors. (Baum & Moore, 1966: 5)

Similarly, as the Canadian Council on Rural Development (1975: 5) reported:

> Tourism and recreation demands for rural resources can provide income and employment opportunities for rural people and therefore assist in a 'stay' option for those who prefer rural living. The supply and demand relationship however remains a controlling factor underlining that tourism and recreation are not a panacea to the economic problems of depressed areas but that they can be an important supplement to existing economic activities . . . benefits are likely to accrue only to those with the necessary imagination, managerial skills and financial capability. Other factors identified which determine the degree to which rural communities can be expected to benefit from tourism and recreation are: the diversity of recreational facilities available; accessibility to markets; and the retainment locally of tourist expenditures.

Nevertheless, such observations remain in the minority with respect to local and central government's enthusiasm for tourism development in peripheral areas (Hall & Jenkins, 1998; Jenkins *et al.*, 1998). However, many of the expectations for long-term economic development generated by government support for tourism in peripheral areas have often failed to come to fruition. Several reasons can be posited for this. Perhaps most importantly is the tendency by both government development agencies and tourism researchers to fail to see tourism within the larger development context. Most significantly, while recent government programmes have sought to address peripheral problems and imbalances by way of local and/or regional tourism development programmes; simultaneously, many governments have adopted restrictionist economic policies, which have compounded the difficulties of peripheral areas adjusting to economic and social restructuring (e.g. by way of centralisation of health and transport services). In such instances policy makers appear to be struggling with national versus local priorities (e.g. the restructuring and deregulation of agriculture and other industries versus subsidy provision), a point that also raises the issue of conflict in the values and objectives of the nation state as opposed to the local state (Jenkins *et al.*, 1998).

A second reason for the relative lack of success of tourism development in peripheral areas are that policy makers are also confronted with inadequate (and sometimes misleading) information on peripheral area issues, and therefore have a restricted capacity to identify appropriate policy instruments to select, promote and support industries and other productive capacities as viable and sustainable alternatives. Indeed, a number of industries, and not just tourism, appears to present opportunities to diversify the economic base of peripheral areas, and to stem the leakage and transfer of labour and capital (and thus community services and infrastructure) from peripheral economies. Nevertheless, some forms of tourism development and a focus on specific markets may actually preclude other development alternatives that may be more extractive in nature. Indeed, in some cases of maximising economic development in the periphery the best form of tourism may well be no tourism at all.

A third reason for perceived policy failure is that the initial expectations for tourism as a means of regional development were too high. Arguably this is particularly the case with nature-based tourism, which, almost by definition, tends to be very small scale, often highly seasonal, and fails to attract the large numbers of tourists characterised by mass pleasure tourism. Indeed, policy realism often appears to be lacking with respect to nature-based tourism. Nevertheless, at a local scale such developments can still be extremely significant, allowing population and lifestyle maintenance and possibly even a small amount of growth, although not the dramatic improvements that many regions and their politicians seek.

One of the greatest difficulties in developing tourism in peripheral areas is understanding the factors by which tourism firms chose to locate as well as the means by which governments can intervene in assisting the location of private firms. Clearly, if tourist firms are publicly owned then some of the commercial pressures that influence firm location can be resisted. However, given contemporary philosophies regarding the appropriate role of the state with respect to firm ownership then even 100% owned public firms will often need to provide a return to government.

Table 1.1 illustrates some of the external factors than influence the location of tourism firms (Hall, 2003, 2005). Arguably the most important factor is access to market. In the case of tourism it is self-evident that if tourists are not able to get to a certain location than any tourist firm will find it hard to survive. Unfortunately, such self-evident propositions are surprisingly little accounted for in many regional development programmes that seek to utilise tourism. For peripheral areas, that by definition are hard to access from core areas of population, in which potential tourism markets exist this is the major drawback in attracting substantial numbers of visitors. Accessibility is important from the perspective of both international and domestic tourism. Exchange rates may also be a significant determinant of the relative cost attractiveness of locations. Although this factor is clearly important in terms of international markets it may also influence potential domestic travel behaviour. In countries with a strong currency it may be relatively cheap to holiday abroad than at home, while the reverse may also apply with respect to the relative attractiveness of domestic holiday locations when a currency is weak. Government intervention has a moderate influence on firm location, as does the provision of business services (including access to and cost of credit), the overall quality of infrastructure provision, and amenity values. Wage rates may also be significant for some internationally competitive destinations and firms that are seeking to minimise labour costs. Factors which have only very limited or no influence on the location of tourist firms include access to research, unionisation (indeed in some cases unions may be a disincentive to firm establishment), headquarters function and the provision of skilled labour. Skilled labour is usually only significant for very specialised tourism services in which a high degree of knowledge is required. Significantly, this may be important for some forms of nature-based tourism in which substantial environmental or indigenous knowledge is required for the development of particular product such as guided tours or museums. Destination promotion has only a very limited influence on firm location with other factors predominating. Many firms will have their own promotional channels while information sources, such as the general media, will play a much greater role in determining destination attractiveness than specific destination promotion. Nevertheless, for more specialised types of firms then the provision of very specific and targeted destination promotion may provide leverage for the promotion of their own product and therefore influence firm location.

Given the basic premise then that firm establishment and development lie at the core of regional tourism development how then may the various factors be influenced by government? Tables 1.2 and 1.3 indicate a range of macro and micro regional policy measures that may be used to influence the reallocation of labour and capital. Many of these

Table 1.1 Relative importance of factors in explaining the distribution of the tourism industry

Important	Moderately important	Not important
Accessibility – road – aviation/airports – train – communication (general) – pedestrian Exchange rate	Amenity values Infrastructure Local linkages Business services Wage rates Government intervention – land and premises – land prices and rents – loans, grants and tax reductions – planning – advice and assistance – support from various levels of government Destination promotion (highly targeted and specific, e.g. special interest marketing) Skilled labour	Access to research Industry organisation Unionisation Headquarters function Destination promotion

Source: Hall (2003, 2005)

Table 1.2 Macro-economic policy measures with regional implications

Category	*Regional effect*
Fiscal: Automatic stabilisers	progressive taxes and income support measures, especially unemployment benefit
Discretionary	regional variation in taxes and central government expenditure (including infra-structure and procurement)
Monetary	geographical variation in interest rates and credit control
Import controls and tariffs	protect specific industries, which may be localised
Export controls and tariffs	assist specific industries, which may be localised
Currency exchange rate	affects the competitiveness of domestic production and exports relative to imports
Public investment	differential regional impact

Source: after Armstrong and Taylor (1985); Chisholm (1990) in Hall (2003)

approaches are targeted at peripheral areas under the various European Union objective funds for example (Hall & Jenkins, 1998), with Australia, Canada and the United States also operating similar targeted programmes at the federal level (Jenkins *et al.*, 1998). Clearly, these policy measures will not be tourism specific yet tourism development will often be a beneficiary of regional assistance programmes. Nevertheless, these measures may be utilised directly to assist tourism in peripheral areas.

From the perspective of many regions, assistance in improving accessibility will be a major factor in tourism development. This may include road, rail or airport improvements and, increasingly, providing cheap access for air carriers to what are usually regarded as secondary destinations. Therefore, state intervention can have an enormous part to play in the development of the infrastructure that may bring visitors to peripheral regions. However, from the perspective of the promotion of nature-based tourism opportunities, such measures also pose a paradox with respect to development. In order to promote nature-based tourism it clearly also becomes desirable to conserve the natural resources that serve as the main basis for attracting visitors. This may mean not only the conservation of general amenity values, such as landscape, but may also refer to very specific environment features, such as certain lakes

Table 1.3 Micro-economic regional policy measures

Policies to reallocate labour	
In situ reallocation	occupational training and retraining educational policies journey-to-work subsidies
Spatial reallocation	migration policies housing assistance employment information improvements in efficiency of labour market
Policies to reallocate capital	
Taxes and subsidies: inputs	assistance with capital investment wage subsidies operational subsidies research and development assistance, including new product and product differentition
Taxes and subsidies: outputs	export rebates price subsidies marketing and promotion assistance
Taxes and subsidies: technology	research and development innovation communication access assistance
Improved efficiency of capital markets	loan guarantees export credit guarantees venture capital
Administrative controls	controls on location of investment planning controls reduced administrative controls

Source: after Armstrong and Taylor (1985); Chisholm (1990) in Hall (2003)

and rivers or species. Governments will therefore tend to have not only a development role in peripheral areas but also a regulatory or managerial role. Such considerations of nature-based tourism development require as much an understanding of the development of human and social capital as it will knowledge of the physical environment and individual species and their respective tolerance to visitor impact. Indeed arguably more so, as noted above, as such human and social capital are the prerequisites to sustainable regional development, particularly when it is increasingly recognised that cooperative measures between various stakeholders are required if common resources, such as those nature resources that underlie nature-based tourism are to maintained. Therefore, the remainder of this book focuses on issues of development, management and regulation of nature-based tourism rather than the inherent qualities of nature itself.

The Task of the Book

The remainder of this book is divided into two main sections followed by a short reflective section to conclude. These main sections are divided according to the environment within which nature-based tourism occurs. One group of chapters examines nature-based tourism in wilderness, alpine and sub-polar environments while the other looks at island, coastal and marine environments. This division has been undertaken in order to attempt to illustrate some of the common challenges that exist in particular environmental settings. However, a number of themes also reoccur across the various chapters including the complexity of management tasks, particularly with respect to meeting the needs of various stakeholders; the importance of developing appropriate management regimes; and the value of tourism to peripheral locations in which few other development alternatives may exist. Various chapters, including the reflective chapter by Wheeller (Chapter 17, this volume), also highlight that people lie at the heart of nature-based tourist development and that such development may be full of contradictions, many of which are not easily reconcilable. Nevertheless, the position of the book as a whole is that given the restricted number of development alternatives in the periphery, tourism will be critical. Yet if such development is to succeed,attention must be paid to human and social capital and the wider context of region development. Access must include not only transport accessibility for visitors to the periphery but also access for the periphery to economic capital and the means to improve the quality of human and social capital. Although it is also important to acknowledge

> that for those regions that do successfully embark on the 'high road' to regional economic success, this very success raises new problems in terms of a requirement continuously to learn and anticipate, if not create, market trends. Moreover, if some regions 'learn' and 'win', many more will fail to do so and 'lose'. (Hudson, 2000: 106)

The book uses as its subtitle the notion of development or disaster. Indeed, with nature-based tourism this option may be quite stark. Nature-based tourism relies more directly than other forms of tourism on maintaining the stock of natural capital, usually in peripheral locations. To do this requires an understanding of regional development strategies and the policy, management and regulatory frameworks that surround them. The various chapters in this book provide numerous insights into these frameworks and their operation in various peripheral locations. It is hoped that this collection therefore assists in identifying some of the means by which nature-based tourism can become a development success and, just as importantly, help peripheral regions identify some of the strategies by which they may become winners in an increasingly competitive and complicated global economic and social environment.

References

Archer, B. (1989) Tourism and island economies: Impact analysis. In Cooper, C. (ed.) *Progress in Tourism, Recreation and Hospitality Management* (Vol. 1) (pp. 125–34). London: Belhaven Press.

Armstrong, H. and Taylor, J. (1985) *Regional Economics and Policy*. Oxford: Philip Allan.

Baum, E.L. and Moore, E.J. (1966) Some economic opportunities and limitations of outdoor recreation enterprises. In Cornwall, G.W. and Holcomb, C.J. (eds) *Guidelines to the Planning, Developing, and Managing of Rural Recreation Enterprises* (pp. 52–64). Bulletin 301, Cooperative Extension Service. Blacksburg: Virginia Polytechnic Institute.

Botterill, D., Owen, R.E., Emanuel, L., Foster, N., Gale, T. *et al.* (1997) Perceptions from the periphery: The experience of Wales. In *Peripheral Area Tourism: International Tourism Research Conference*, Bornholm, 8–12 September 1997. Bornholm: Unit of Tourism Research at the Research Centre of Bornholm.

Buhalis, D. (1997) Tourism in the Greek Islands: The issues of peripherality, competitiveness and development. In *Peripheral Area Tourism: International Tourism Research Conference*, Bornholm, 8–12 September 1997. Bornholm: Unit of Tourism Research at the Research Centre of Bornholm.

Butler, R. and Boyd, S. (eds) (2000) *Tourism and National Parks*. Chichester: John Wiley.

Canadian Council on Rural Development (1975) *Economic Significance of Tourism and Outdoor Recreation for Rural Development*. Working paper. Ottawa: Canadian Council on Rural Development.

Cater, E. and Lowman, G. (eds) (1994) *Ecotourism: A Sustainable Option?* Chichester: John Wiley.

Chisholm, M. (1990) *Regions in Recession and Resurgence*. London: Unwin Hyman.

Clout, H.D. (1972) *Rural Geography: An Introductory Survey*. Oxford: Pergammon Press.

Duffield, B.S. and Long, J. (1981) Tourism in the highlands and islands of Scotland: Rewards and conflicts. *Annals of Tourism Research* 8 (3), 403–31.

Fennell, D. (1999) *Ecotourism: An Introduction*. London: Routledge.

Fukuyama, F. (1995) *Trust: The Social Virtues and the Creation of Prosperity*. New York: Free Press.

Gould, P. (1969) *Spatial Diffusion*. Washington, DC: Commission on College Geography, Association of American Geographers.

Hall, C.M. (1992) *Wasteland to World Heritage: Preserving Australia's Wilderness*. Carlton: Melbourne University Press.

Hall, C.M. (2003) Tourism and regional development in peripheral areas. Paper presented at Tourism in Peripheral Areas Conference, Umeå University, Sweden, August.

Hall, C.M. (2005) *Tourism: Rethinking the Social Science of Mobility*. London: Pearson Education.

Hall, C.M. and Jenkins, J. (1998) Rural tourism and recreation policy dimensions. In Butler, R., Hall, C.M. and Jenkins, J. (eds) *Tourism and Recreation in Rural Areas* (pp. 19–42). Chichester: John Wiley.

Hall, C.M. and Johnston, M. (eds) (1995) *Polar Tourism: Tourism in the Arctic and Antarctic Regions*. Chichester: John Wiley.

Hall, C.M. and Müller, D. (eds) (2004) *Tourism, Mobility and Second Homes: Between Elite Landscape and Common Ground*. Clevedon: Channel View.

Hall, C.M. and Page, S.J. (2002) *The Geography of Tourism and Recreation* (2nd edn). London: Routledge.

Hall, D. (1997) Sustaining tourism development in the fragile Balkan periphery of Europe. In *Peripheral Area Tourism: International Tourism Research Conference, Bornholm, 8–12 September 1997*. Bornholm: Unit of Tourism Research at the Research Centre of Bornholm.

Helburn, N. (1977) The wilderness continuum. *Professional Geographer* 29, 337–47.

Holden, A. (2000) *Environment and Tourism*. London: Routledge.

Hudson, R. (2000) *Production, Places and the Environment: Changing Perspectives in Economic Geography*. London: Prentice Hall, Pearson Education.

Hudson, R. and Townsend, A. (1992) Tourism employment and policy choices for local government. In Johnson, P. and Thomas, B. (eds) *Perspectives on Tourism Policy* (pp. 49–68). London: Mansell.

Ingram, D.R. (1971) The concept of accessibility: A search for an operational form. *Regional Studies* 5 (2), 101–7.

Jenkins, J., Hall, C.M. and Troughton, M. (1998) The restructuring of rural economies: Rural tourism and recreation as a government response. In Butler, R., Hall, C.M. and Jenkins, J. (eds) *Tourism and Recreation in Rural Areas* (pp. 43–68). Chichester: John Wiley.

Lesslie, R.G. and Taylor, S.G. (1983) *Wilderness in South Australia*. Occasional Paper No. 1. Adelaide: Centre for Environmental Studies, University of Adelaide.

Lesslie, R.G. and Taylor, S.G. (1985) The wilderness continuum concept and its implications for Australian wilderness preservation policy. *Biological Conservation* 32, 309–33.

Mitchell, C.G.B. and Town, S.W. (1976) *Accessibility of Various Social Groups to Different Activities*. Crowthorne: Transport and Road Research Laboratory.

Newsome, D., Moore, S.A. and Dowling, R.K. (2002) *Natural Area Tourism: Ecology, Impacts and Management*. Clevedon: Channel View Publications.

Ostrom, J. (1990), *Governing the Commons: The Evolution of Institutions for Collective Action*. Cambridge: Cambridge University Press.

Troughton, M.J. (1990) Decline to development: Towards a framework for sustainable rural development. In Dykeman, F.W. (ed) *Entrepreneurial and Sustainable Rural Communities*. Sackville: Rural and Small Town Research and Studies, Department of Geography, Mount Allison University.

Weaver, D. (2001) *The Encyclopedia of Ecotourism*. Oxford: CABI Publishing.

Part 2: Nature-based Tourism in Alpine, Forest and Sub-polar Environments

Chapter 2

Ecotourism and Regional Transformation in Northwestern Ontario

MARGARET JOHNSTON AND ROBERT PAYNE

Introduction

Ecotourism is viewed in many parts of the world as the next wave of community and regional development. Three goals of ecotourism identified by Dawson (2001) are that it should bring benefits to local communities, protect the natural and cultural heritage upon which the tourism is founded, and expect adherence to ethical standards by tourists and operators. As a nature-based form of tourism, ecotourism requires a relatively untouched landscape that is physically accessible to markets and entrepreneurial individuals who can develop the product within accepted parameters. It also needs a supporting regulatory framework and buy-in from the nearby communities. Expectations about the benefits of ecotourism include the potential for robust regional development or regional redevelopment for areas facing decline. Immediately this suggests the potential for conflict in areas where the scale of regional development expectations and needs far exceeds the capacity of ecotourism to deliver. This might be the case particularly in hinterland regions where intensive resource-based consumptive industries have already laid the economic groundwork of regional development.

In the hinterland region of Northwestern Ontario (Figure 2.1), economic transformation of this type rests upon a regional history of natural resource extraction complemented by a tourism history based on hunting, fishing and cottaging. Whether ecotourism will have any lasting impact on the economic development of the region will reflect the ability of local entrepreneurs and local communities to situate ecotourism within their views of what is desirable for themselves and their region, and concomitantly on the ability and desire of all levels of government to support such development through whatever means are necessary. This chapter addresses the context of, and issues arising from,

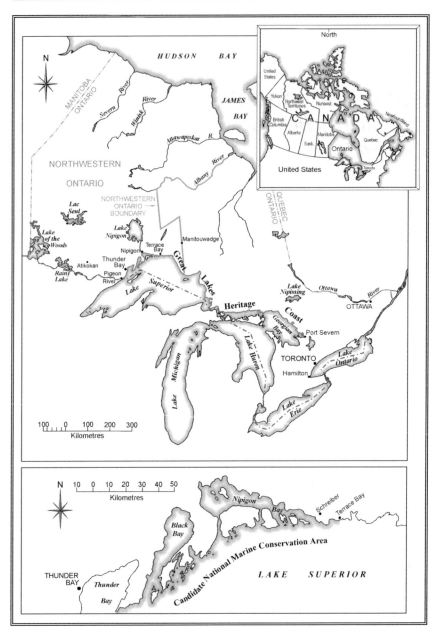

Figure 2.1 Eastern Ontario

increased interest in ecotourism in Northwestern Ontario. It describes the economic background of the region and examines challenges in the shift from a natural resource extraction economy to a broader base. It also identifies the ways in which ecotourism might contribute to economic development through opportunities related to its establishment alongside the traditional largely consumptive and mechanized tourism.

Resource Extraction and Regional Development

Northern Ontario has a long history of resource extraction that began with fur trading and has extended to forestry, mining and hydroelectric development. Regional development has been pinned upon the hopes that exploitation of the resource sector, supported by rail, road and power grid infrastructure, would fuel the economy and engender thriving communities in this economic hinterland. Communities were built to support resource developments and they continue to dot the landscape of rural Northern Ontario (Randall & Ironside, 1996). These communities are subject to ongoing cycles of boom and bust that reflect vulnerability to external forces and internal economic weaknesses. Early on in provincial development the economic heartland was centred in Toronto in Southern Ontario; more recently these communities and the industries within them are influenced by international developments such as changes in markets and in supply that might be occurring half way around the world. Southcott (2000) identified these influences as characteristics of resource Fordism and post-industrialism, economic transformations that have swept through hinterlands and resource economies over the last two decades. Currently in Northwestern Ontario there are 17 communities that fit the label of resource sector of single industry towns, dependent upon forestry, mining and rail transportation. They range in population size from under 500 to around 9000 and are dominated in the region by Thunder Bay, a government, education, retail and manufacturing centre of just over 100,000 people.

Though there have been considerable government and research efforts to understand the relationships between these communities and regional development issues (e.g. Lucas, 1971; Saarinen, 1986; Bradbury & St Martin, 1983; Gill, 1994), the questions that are now being asked reflect this economic transformation and its effects on communities. More recently, the research emphasis on these hinterland resource towns has moved from examining growth and decline within a traditional economic framework to an exploration of the broader sustainability of communities, echoing an international shift in focus (Beckley, 1995; Randall & Ironside, 1996). This focus on sustainability reflects a growing interest in understanding what is needed to enable resource dependent communities to diversify and move beyond the confines of the boom and bust cycle. The ability of communities to adapt is the social and economic foundation of sustainability.

Attributes such as the type of industrial base (Randall & Ironside, 1996) and the extent of government assistance (McBride *et al.*, 1993) influence how communities are able to respond to economic crises associated with the winding down of company operations and eventual closure. However, community sustainability is also affected by other factors that reflect the commitment and attachment of the residents to remaining in the community (Johnston & Lorch, 1996), and the availability and proximity of other resources. Atikokan is one example of a Northwestern Ontario community that was able to survive the closure of its two mines in 1979 and 1980 and emerge with a more diversified economy. The economic base of the community rests upon a now 20-year-old thermal generating plant, a particle board factory, the use of the community for government offices and as a base camp for forestry workers, and the development of a strong tourism outfitting role related to a nearby provincial park (Muirhead *et al.*, 1992; Johnston & Lorch, 1996). The community of Atikokan aggressively pursued development options when it was planning its survival vision following the announced closure of the mines. Similarly, leaders in Manitouwadge, a 50-year-old planned town, hope that tourism will broaden the community's economic base to help it manage the expected loss of mining jobs in early 2005. Residents of Manitouwadge, having already experienced several cycles of boom and bust, have shown considerable persistence and attachment to the community. Though Manitouwadge is not situated in a prime location for tourism growth, being off the main highway, this optimistic view and willingness to stay in a community is vital for future economic development.

Much of the discussion around the potential of tourism development to strengthen local and regional economies does not readily distinguish ecotourism as a specific target. The Ontario government has taken a broad view of nature-based tourism, including ecotourism, and uses the term resource-based tourism. Activities covered are: hunting and fishing, visiting provincial or national parks, birdwatching and wildlife viewing, snowmobiling, cross-country and downhill skiing, nature walking, hiking, swimming and other water-based sports. In 1996, 34% of the total visits to Northern Ontario were for resource-based activities. Of the 3.1 million person-visits nearly two-thirds were made by Ontarians, and the vast majority of these were residents of Northern Ontario (Ministry of Tourism, 1998). Just over a quarter of the visits were by Americans. When compared to all tourists, resource-based tourists had higher than average spending and their impact was felt particularly strongly in the accommodation sector, where nearly 75% of all accommodation establishments are classified as resource-based tourism operations

(Ministry of Tourism, 1998). Resource-based tourism accounted for 2.9% of the north's employment, lower than both mining and related manufacturing (6.6%) and forest products and services (8.1%). All tourism, though, was comparable at 6.4% of employment (Ministry of Tourism, 1998). It is important to note that these are regional statistics, dominated by patterns in Thunder Bay. In the small single-sector communities, dependence on primary employment continues to be high and consequently leaving these communities more vulnerable to transformation. For example, Johnston and Lorch (1996) found that over half of the households in their community survey in Manitouwadge had a direct employment tie to one of the mining companies operating locally.

Ontario's Resource-based Tourism Policy

Although nature-based tourism has long been a feature of Ontario's economy, Ontario government land and resource managers have seldom accorded it the same consideration given to forestry or mining (see McKercher, 1992). During a six-year examination of the environmental effects of timber operations on the natural environment (Environmental Assessment Board, Ontario, 1994), the Ontario government ministry responsible for tourism had so little to contribute about the effects of timber operations on the industry that the Ontario Ministry of Natural Resources (MNR) had to create a 'resource-based' tourism policy to give the appearance that tourism was considered before timber operations commenced. The initial policy was treated with such disdain during the environmental assessment hearings that it was radically revised. The policy that is in place today is meant to 'promote and encourage the development of the Ontario resource-based tourism industry in both an ecologically and economically sustainable manner' (Ministry of Natural Resources, Ontario, 2001: 2).

One supporting principle recognizes that disputes over land and resource allocation will occur and that such disputes will be managed through appropriate means. The principle suggests that tourism remains a *constraint* on timber operations rather than a land use on equal footing with forestry. Another significant outcome of the class EA hearings on timber management was revised legislation governing forestry in Ontario. That legislation, the *Crown Forest Sustainability Act*, demands that forestry, as well as other uses of Ontario's public lands, be sustainable in ecological, economic and social terms. That the Ontario government was moved to implement a large-scale land use planning exercise in Northern Ontario in 1997 to resolve land use conflicts concerning forestry, parks and tourism indicates that, even in its revised form, the resource-based tourism policy was not effective in providing an institutional frame for tourism in Northern Ontario.

Recognizing this deficiency, the Ontario government brought together representatives of forest companies, tourism operators and land and resource managers to develop a strategy to reconcile forestry and nature-based tourism. The resulting strategy (Ministry of Natural Resources, Ontario, 2001) broke new ground in differentiating nature-based tourism into three types: drive-in, semi-remote and remote. These types of tourism recognize the crucial role played by roads in Northern Ontario, for providing access for timber harvesting and for recreation and tourism activities. Roads also adversely affect tourism, where that tourism depends upon roadless conditions to support remote, wilderness-oriented experiences. The strategy describes reconciling forest operations with semi-remote and remote tourism as 'very tricky' (2001: 5). However, the idea that there might be areas that are simply off-limits to forestry operations (an idea put into practice in British Columbia) is not raised.

More recently, in 2002, the Ontario government put forward a more detailed vision of tourism, and especially nature-based tourism, for Northern Ontario. The *Ontario Resource-based Tourism Diversification Opportunities Report* was prepared by a consortium of consultants for the Ontario Ministry of Northern Development and Mines, a ministry that has largely replaced both the Ministry of Natural Resources and the Ministry of Tourism and Recreation as the lead Ontario government actor in Northern Ontario. The report expressly set out to 'identify alternative resource-based tourism product development opportunities beyond the traditional fishing and hunting markets' (Economic Solutions Inc., 2002: i). The report pointed out that, in the view of tourism operators, government regulations were a pervasive barrier to a shift to less consumptive tourism products. However, operators themselves had both knowledge of and interest in such activities.

As an initiative that recognizes the diversification in market tastes from a purely consumptive tourism (i.e. hunting and fishing) to less consumptive products such as 'catch and release' fishing and birdwatching, the report represents an improvement over the former resource-based tourism policy. However, one still must question whether there is an institutional framework available in Northern Ontario that is capable of accommodating this broader appreciation of tourism opportunities. It is worth noting that in the Northwestern Ontario context the word 'remote' does not automatically equate with the kinds of activities that might represent ecotourism. In fact, remote tourism is more likely to involve activities at the consumptive end of the spectrum.

Nonetheless, ecotourism remains an option for existing and new nature-based tourism operators. Though the ecotourist is not well known to operators, there appears to be some interest in understanding the opportunities available, if not for philosophical reasons, then at least for economic reasons. A large ecotourism conference held in Northeastern

Ontario in 2002 was followed by another in Thunder Bay in 2004. With government sponsorship, and participation by researchers, operators and ministry personnel, these conferences represent and probably create an increasing interest in ecotourism in the north.

Integrating New and Traditional Forms of Tourism: Lake Superior North Shore

In recent years, the north shore of Lake Superior has come to be viewed as a unique resource for tourism. A closer look at this part of North-western Ontario is instructive in describing the context of ecotourism development as demonstrated in local views on tourism and in management frameworks. Lake Superior's north shore and islands comprise an area of land and water from Terrace Bay/Slate Islands in the east to Thunder Cape at the foot of the Sibley Peninsula in the west. The imprint of settlement in the region is most visible along the coast, where the Trans-Canada Highway (Highway 17 in Ontario) and the main line of the transcontinental Canadian Pacific Railway join the communities of Terrace Bay, Schreiber, Rossport, Pays Plat, Nipigon and Red Rock. Apart from these communities and isolated pockets of shoreline development, most land in the region is in public hands as Crown land that, in Ontario, the provincial Ministry of Natural Resources is charged with managing in a sustainable manner. Several of the north shore communities are home to large pulp mills, testifying to the importance of the forest industry as employer and as influence in the region. The region has an identity ('the north shore') that is recognized by those living there as well as by other Northern Ontario residents and is used in tourism marketing campaigns that promise wilderness cruising, kayaking, camping and hiking.

The region has been recognized as possessing both outstanding natural beauty and ecological integrity by several agencies. Attention from outside the region has come from Parks Canada, which has selected a candidate National Marine Conservation Area (Parks Canada, 1995: 85) centred on the region (see Figure 2.1). Environment Canada and the US Environmental Protection Agency have identified the region, and especially the islands, as 'A Shoreline Biodiversity Investment Area' (Reid & Holland, 1997: 58). Both recognitions contribute to the growing tourism promotion of the natural heritage aspects of the region.

As part of an effort to provide information for management decision-making, workshops were held with local people to determine their views about increasing tourism's local importance along the north shore (Payne *et al.*, 2001). These discussions revealed three themes:

- concern about host–tourist interactions;
- concern about tourism's environmental impacts; and
- tourism management issues.

The themes illustrate the residents' far-ranging knowledge about the north shore and the islands as well as their uncertainties about the future role of tourism in their lives and in the region. Residents recognize that while increased tourism may bring them benefits, there may also be costs, in terms of environmental degradation, changes in lifestyles and loss of local control.

Host–tourist interactions

People on the north shore recognized that it might be a considerable challenge to balance the demands of the tourism industry with their existing (local) lifestyles. They expected to have access to any facilities and infrastructure that were developed for tourists, and they also expected to participate in economic benefits. They expressed opposition to large-scale, transnational commercial tourism enterprises, which would drain those benefits from the region. The fear was expressed that the Lake Superior shoreline and/or the islands would be rendered inaccessible to them because of private, tourist-oriented development.

Though local people value hunting, fishing and snowmobiling, there is some recognition that tourists may prefer other, less consumptive forms of activity. Several people pointed to the potential for conflict between, for example, kayakers and power boaters. Potential for conflict also was noted in relation to the feeling among local people that tourists cause environmental degradation. Garbage and human waste near known campsites were attributed to existing tourists who, in the view of local people, possess neither the knowledge nor the sensitivity to act more appropriately.

Tourism's environmental impacts

A second major theme reflects the belief held by residents that increased tourism, of any sort, will cause unwanted environmental degradation. Local people realize that large-scale tourism developments will be accompanied by negative environmental effects. However, they recognize that even their preferred smaller-scale versions of tourism development could cause some environmental degradation. Some local people believed that any tourism development should undergo an environmental impact assessment; others felt that tourism should be environmentally sensitive and responsible. Though the concern about environmental degradation was widespread, there was an element of caution that concerns about environmental quality cannot stand in the way of all (tourism) development and that it was necessary to find a workable balance between protection and development.

Tourism management issues

People throughout the north shore stated that tourism must be managed in order to protect the natural environment, to maintain high standards in facilities and operations, to provide tourism benefits for the region, to discourage inappropriate activities and facilities, and to achieve coordination of tourism development. Furthermore, they stated emphatically that local involvement in decision-making was imperative and that local control was highly desirable. Local people outlined a number of ways to achieve this including the status quo, involving user pays groups, creating a regional tourism authority, and creating a north shore regional government.

Though alienation from the southern government is a common theme in the north, residents indicated that they expected senior governments (provincial and federal) to support their decisions concerning tourism development on the north shore and in the islands. The discussions in the region about tourism management incorporate a significant contradiction: regulation implies government, but in the view of local people, governments, especially senior levels of government in Toronto or Ottawa (the national capital), cannot be trusted. Time and time again in discussions, people argued for the regulation of tourism, only to realize with dismay that they were invoking government action, accompanying bureaucracy and the loss of local control. Many felt that entrepreneurs in the tourism business should be capable of regulating themselves. However, even these people seemed to doubt that tourism entrepreneurs, if left alone, would do so.

Local people showed themselves to be very knowledgeable about the north shore and islands of Lake Superior during the discussions. This knowledge is based on their long experience in the region and it substantiates their wishes to remain involved, at the least, in decision-making along the north shore and in the islands. Moreover, it adds credibility to their desire to establish local control over tourism development in the region.

These findings illustrate several common issues confronting sustainable tourism and ecotourism in peripheral areas. Local people exhibit a high degree of customary knowledge about the shore zone and islands. Perhaps most important, however, is the adamant belief among local people that they should have a voice in whatever tourism developments take place on the north shore of Lake Superior. Moreover, if they could find a suitable management structure, they would strongly favour not only a voice but also control over such development. Local people also feel strongly that any future tourism development must be appropriate, in their terms. By this, they mean that tourism development should be small in scale, sensitive in its environmental effects and considerate of their established way of life.

With this background illustrating how people on Lake Superior's north shore feel about tourism development, it is helpful to examine two large-scale initiatives in the area that involve tourism. One, a proposal by Parks Canada for a National Marine Conservation Area on Lake Superior, putting tourism within the context of a marine protected area. The second, the Great Lakes Heritage Coast, emerged from a land use planning exercise orchestrated by the Ontario Ministry of Natural Resources. Of special interest in tracing the outlines of these two initiatives is the treatment accorded local people and their interests along the shore of Lake Superior.

The Advent of the Lake Superior National Marine Conservation Area

One of the key issues occurring on the north shore has been the advent of the National Marine Conservation Area (NMCA). A programme of Parks Canada, the federal agency in Canada responsible for national parks, NMCAs are intended to protect representative examples of marine natural and cultural heritage on Canada's three sea coasts and in the Great Lakes (Parks Canada, 2003). The agency's procedures for establishing parks and other protected areas under its control have changed dramatically in the last 30 years. Scientific assessment, concerning the quality of the natural and cultural heritage available in a candidate area, has certainly been improved. However, the most critical change in establishment procedures has come in Parks Canada's dealings with local people, both aboriginal and non-aboriginal. No federal park or protected area may be established until it has been considered and approved at the local level, usually by a committee of local people representing the full range of economic and social interests in the area. Local discussion of the western Lake Superior candidate NMCA began in 1997, with the formation of a committee composed of people from the north shore communities, representatives of the Ontario provincial government (the Ontario Ministry of Natural Resources) and the NMCA project manager from Parks Canada.

At the outset, local people were ambivalent about the NMCA initiative. Their ambivalence was rooted in a degree of distrust of a distant federal agency, i.e. Parks Canada, in some degrees of uncertainty about what a NMCA would mean for the region and in evident concern that an NMCA designation would attract large numbers of tourists. Parks Canada worked hard to gain the trust of committee members during this initial phase, supplying them with information about its efforts, both successful and unsuccessful, to establish parks and protected areas in other parts of the country. These efforts served to ease people's concerns that they might face expropriation, that their activities might be proscribed or that their aboriginal treaty rights might be extinguished (Parks Canada, 1999).

One issue in particular illustrates how committee members, while coming to appreciate the concept and potential of an NMCA, still were hesitant to preclude other economic development opportunities by approving the NMCA proposal. Falconbridge Inc., an international mining company, holds exploration rights to the area of Nipigon Bay with undetermined hard rock mineral potential. People in the nearby communities of Nipigon and Red Rock were reluctant to forego the economic benefits that might come with a mine, even one with only a 20-year life expectancy. Establishing the NMCA in that area would eliminate any mining activity. Discussions led to the committee agreeing to excise the area of mineral potential from the NMCA, with the qualification that, if, upon exploration, Falconbridge found that a mine was not economically viable, the area of Nipigon Bay would be added to the NMCA. This compromise solution maintains the possibility of jobs and other economic benefits that a mine would bring to the region. Parks Canada's willingness to accept such a solution went far to cement the view that the agency was not intending to establish the NMCA at the expense of local concerns and issues.

In 2001, the committee of local people gave its approval to Parks Canada for the NMCA to proceed. In his letter to the minister responsible for Parks Canada, the committee chair wrote:

> On behalf of the Regional Committee whose principal task has been to examine the feasibility of a national marine conservation area on Lake Superior, it is with great pleasure that I announce that our committee endorses a National Marine Conservation designation with the hope that we can balance preservation and responsible use of the Lake Superior area for present and future generations. (Parks Canada, 2001)

At the time of writing, the negotiations between the province of Ontario and Parks Canada over land transfers have been concluded successfully. However, final declaration of the Lake Superior National Marine Conservation Area has yet to be made by the Canadian parliament.

Parks Canada obtained local support for the NMCA because it recognized and took seriously the concerns of local people about the impacts of NMCA designation upon their lives and livelihoods. Parks Canada held a series of open houses across the region in 1999 to explain the NMCA concept, to hear people's opinions and to collect information. It worked with local people to determine, in a co-operative manner, a proposal for an NMCA that is acceptable to all the interested parties.

Implementing the Great Lakes Heritage Coast Strategy

While local people on Lake Superior's north shore were contending with the prospect of the proposed NMCA, another large-scale project, the Great Lakes Heritage Coast (GLHC), was launched by the Ontario government. The heritage coast project emerged from a major land use planning initiative known as Lands for Life. Lands for Life was intended as a broad planning exercise to reconcile forestry, parks and, to a lesser degree, tourism across the southern portions of Northern Ontario (National Round Table on the Environment and the Economy, Canada, 2003).

The Lands for Life discussions pointed to the ecological, social and economic significance of the shores of Lake Superior, Lake Huron and Georgian Bay and the need to develop a strategy that would direct development and ensure protection where it was warranted (Chudleigh, 2000). After agreeing that these coastal areas were important, the next step for the Ontario government was to implement the strategy for balancing protection and development in the GLHC. A GLHC project office was created within the Ontario Ministry of Natural Resources and charged with implementing the strategy. Tenders were called and a consortium of consultants was selected to provide information about the area under the GLHC designation and direction for how it might be used or protected.

In a workshop in Thunder Bay in September 2002, the consortium of consultants set out its planning process. Recognizing that the entire GLHC, at approximately 3000 kilometres in length, was too large to be considered as one area, the consortium, somewhat arbitrarily, divided it into three parts: the Lake Superior shore, the Lake Huron shore and the shore of Georgian Bay. Members of the consortium then examined the three areas for valuable ecological areas requiring protection. Another group in the consortium began working with local people in the three areas to identify tourism development projects. Those discussions led the consultants to identify settlements ('nodes') where tourism developments should be directed.

To suggest that local people along the Lake Superior shore were bemused by the GLHC would be an understatement. Certainly, they recognized the names of people selected to be 'champions' of the heritage coast – for example, Bobby Orr, Robert Bateman and Fred Gilbert – but their understanding of what the GLHC was meant to achieve was clouded. Some applauded the Ontario government for a belated entry into coastal zone management; others appreciated the focus on tourism, but wondered how it would play out in their local communities.

The consortium's process certainly raises questions. One in particular stands out: the decision to break the GLHC into three areas for planning purposes. While the three areas chosen may make some limited sense because they focus on different bodies of water, they are inadequate to deal with local perceptions of community. People on the north shore of Lake Superior have little in common, in economic or social terms, with people at the eastern end of the lake. More importantly, people on the north shore have a clear sense of both themselves and the area in which they live as distinct and separate from other areas in the Lake Superior basin. The consortium's decision to include them with the rest of the people and area of the Lake Superior shore zone ignores their feelings of community.

Another question concerns the decision to employ environmental consultants to determine, with no assistance from local people, areas of high environmental quality along the coast. This part of the strategy runs contrary to north shore residents' feelings of stewardship of the environment along their section of Lake Superior and, indeed, belittles their extensive knowledge of that environment. The consortium's process here, too, might have been organized to be both more sensitive to local concerns and more respectful of local knowledge. These omissions must have created a sense of déjà vu for people living in the Rossport area. Many there had keenly participated in an earlier effort to chart the course of the archipelago of islands off Rossport (Rossport Islands Management Board, 1994), only to have the Ontario Ministry of Natural Resources ignore their recommendations completely.

The issue of local control over development that was mentioned earlier has not yet arisen on the north shore. Elsewhere, however, that issue has been the focus of disagreements between local people and the Ministry of Natural Resources and its consultants. One area of the GLHC, on lower Georgian Bay, has a long tradition of both community and community activism. In that area, the Georgian Bay Association, and its associated Georgian Bay Land Trust, is working to develop a biosphere reserve along the shoreline. In doing so, the association feels that its interests in protecting the area and in managing tourism will be better served than they will through the GLHC. Here local people have not only sound knowledge of the local environment, but also the organizational capability to challenge the direction of the GLHC. On Lake Superior's shore, the consortium's decision to treat the entire shore as one homogeneous area runs counter to north shore people's stated desire to retain control of decision-making in their region.

Conclusion

As in many other hinterlands, the long-term prospects for the role of ecotourism as a tool in regional development will reflect the existing economic, social and natural frameworks. Logistical constraints aside, the realistic view of this potential must accept the overriding interest of local people in the kind of development taking place in Northwestern Ontario. There is tremendous potential for further development of nature-based tourism, and specifically ecotourism. Local people along the north shore of Lake Superior have indicated a degree of interest in tourism development, but are very cautious about a wholehearted endorsement of tourism as the key to regional economic development. They are interested in tourism that they themselves deem appropriate. Their concerns must be heeded if the National Marine Conservation Area and the Great Lakes Heritage Coast are to be successful as management frameworks for ecotourism. Economic transformations of the type being experienced in this peripheral region of Ontario encourage consideration of the potential for tourism to fill the gap left by industrial decline. Like any other industry, tourism, and specifically ecotourism, must mesh with the desires of local people.

References

Beckley, T. (1995) Community stability and the relationship between economic and social well-being in forest-dependent communities. *Society and Natural Resources* 8 (3), 261–266.

Bradbury, J. and St Martin, I. (1983) Winding down in a Quebec mining town: Case study of Schefferville. *The Canadian Geographer* 27 (2), 128–144.

Chudleigh, T. (2000) *The Great Lakes Heritage Coast: A Part of Ontario's Living Legacy*. Toronto: Ontario Ministry of Natural Resources.

Dawson, C.P. (2001) Ecotourism and nature-based tourism: One end of the Tourism Opportunity Spectrum? In McCool, S.F. and Moisey, R.N. (eds) *Tourism, Recreation and Sustainability: Linking Culture and Environment* (pp. 41–53). New York: CABI Publishing.

Economic Solutions Inc. (2002) *Ontario Resource-based Tourism Diversification Opportunities Report*. Toronto: Ontario Ministry of Northern Development and Mines.

Environmental Assessment Board, Ontario (1994) *Class Environmental Assessment by the Ministry of Natural Resources for Timber Management on Crown Lands in Ontario. Reasons for Decision and Decision*. Report No. EA-87-02. Toronto: Environmental Assessment Board.

Gill, A. (1994) Resource towns in British Columbia: The development of Tumbler Ridge. In Johnston, M.E. (ed.) *Geographical Perspectives on the Provincial Norths* (pp. 134–150). Toronto: Copp Clark Longman and Lakehead University Centre for Northern Studies.

Johnston, M.E. and Lorch, B.J. (1996) Community distinctiveness and company closure in a Northern Ontario mining town. *The Great Lakes Geographer* 3 (1), 39–52.

Lucas, R. (1971) *Minetown, Milltown, Railtown: Life in Canadian Communities of Single Industry*. Toronto: University of Toronto Press.

McBride, S., McKay, S. and Hill, M. (1993) Unemployment in a northern hinterland: The social impact of neglect. In Southcott, C. (ed.) *Provincial Hinterland: Social Inequality in Northwestern Ontario*. Halifax: Fernwood.

McKercher, B. (1992) Tourism as a conflicting land use. *Annals of Tourism Research* 19 (3), 467–481.

Ministry of Natural Resources, Ontario (2001) *Management Guidelines for Forestry and Resource Based Tourism.* Toronto: Queen's Printer.

Ministry of Tourism, Ontario (1998) *An Economic Profile of Resource-based Tourism in Northern Ontario 1996.* Toronto: Queen's Printer.

Muirhead, B., McBride, S. and Lundmark, K. (1992) *Politics Versus Markets: Employment Strategies in Peripheral Regions.* Research Report No. 27. Thunder Bay: Lakehead University Centre for Northern Studies.

National Round Table on the Environment and the Economy, Canada (2003) *Conservation Case Studies: Lands for Life Process (Ontario).* Available at: http://www.nrtee-trnee.ca/eng/programs/Current_Programs/Nature/Case-Studies/Lands-for-Life-Case-Study-Complete_e.htm.

Parks Canada (1995) *Sea to Sea to Sea: Canada's National Marine Conservation Areas System Plan.* Ottawa: Ministry of Supply and Service.

Parks Canada (1999) *Frequently Asked Questions about A National Marine Conservation Area Proposal for Lake Superior.* Available at: http://parkscanada.pch.gc.ca/progs/amnc-nmca/proposals/faq/LS-faq_e.asp.

Parks Canada (2001) *Recommendations for a Lake Superior National Marine Conservation Area.* Available at: http://parkscanada.pch.gc.ca/progs/amnc-nmca/proposals/recom/index_e.asp.

Parks Canada (2003) *National Marine Conservation Areas.* Available at: http://www.parkscanada.pch.gc.ca/progs/amnc-nmca/system/system1_E.asp.

Payne, R.J., Johnston, M.E. and Twynam, G.D. (2001) Tourism, sustainability and the social milieu in Lake Superior's north shore and islands. In McCool. S.F. and Moisey, R.N. (eds) *Tourism, Recreation and Sustainability: Linking Culture and Environment,* (pp. 315–342). New York: CABI Publishing.

Randall, J. and Ironside, R.G. (1996) Communities on the edge: An economic geography of resource-dependent communities in Canada. *The Canadian Geographer* 40 (1), 17–35.

Reid, D. and Holland, K. (1997) The land by the lakes: Nearshore terrestrial ecosystems. Background paper. State of the Lakes Ecosystem Conference, 1996.

Rossport Islands Management Board (1994) *Strategic Plan and Land Use Guidelines 1994.* Rossport: Rossport Islands Management Board.

Saarinen, O. (1986) Single sector communities in Northern Ontario: Historical perspectives. In Shelter, G. and Artibise, A. (eds) *Power and Place.* Vancouver: UBC Press.

Southcott, C. (2000) *Single Industry Towns in a Post-industrial Era: Northwestern Ontario as a Case Study.* Research Report No. 42. Thunder Bay: Lakehead University Centre for Northern Studies.

Chapter 3

Tourism in the Northern Wildernesses: Wilderness Discourses and the Development of Nature-based Tourism in Northern Finland

JARKKO SAARINEN

Introduction

In recent years, the Northern wilderness areas have been increasingly in the economic, social and political focus. In the European context, the North as a region has become prominent when defining EU politics, the use of natural and energy resources, environmental issues, regionally uneven development, internal changes in Russia, and the position of the indigenous people. One of the new factors influencing the Northern wilderness areas has been the tourism industry and its new forms of utilising and changing wildernesses, their meanings and uses.

Wilderness as a concept is a contested idea. It is a culturally loaded landscape. From a constructionist perspective it can be argued there are no natural landscapes of wilderness. Even the most 'natural' spaces are invested with cultural meanings through representations of them (see Winchester *et al.*, 2003). Not only tourism, but also the 'traditional' economies and uses of the wilderness, including modern conservation, are based on a certain kind of representations of wilderness and their value. These modern wilderness representations, uses and values are increasingly defined in distant global scale processes.

In societal processes wilderness accommodates new meanings and values, and some of the previous ones may become relics, traces of the past with thinning connotations for modern people. The tourism industry has an effective mechanism to influence the meanings of the wilderness through marketing: place promotion and commodification. In addition, compared to many other uses of wilderness environments, tourism often represents the only economy in peripheries that has a realistic development potential in global markets.

On an analytical level, we can understand the conceptual transformation and the changing meanings of wilderness as discourses. This chapter discusses present, central and often competitive ideas of wilderness – *wilderness discourses* – and the underlying social processes and value systems constructing them in a Northern Finnish context. Developing tourism as the 'latest' significant transformation factor of the Northern environment is at the centre of this discussion.

Tourism and the Competing Ideas of Wilderness

Wilderness as discourse

The Northern wilderness areas, their meanings, management and use are not historically unquestionable by nature. The different ideas of wilderness, wilderness discourses, are ways of thinking that are constructed historically in social practices and they, at the same time, construct and change the present social reality. Through the practices linked to discourses, they also affect the physical environment: discourses are not only words and meanings, but they are also made concrete in actions and the use of power (see Hall, 1997).

Obviously, power relations between discourses change. This process of change is about a struggle for power: a hegemonic struggle where some meanings, images and ways of using the wilderness succeed in the social process of denoting meanings better than the others. This is a political debate that takes place not only between different actors but also on and between different regional levels. Therefore, wilderness, its value and possible uses are often perceived in different ways on local, national and global scales. Thus, wilderness is characteristically a deeply political but also geographical concept. Wilderness is situated in a place, but it is also defined from a space that is socially and culturally constructed.

Despite the numerous, often competitive and contradictory concepts of wilderness, there exists a discourse that is, at a certain period of time, a more dominant way of speech and thought than others. At the moment, tourism has challenged the 'traditional' ideas of wilderness, whether those ideas are linked to the local uses of the natural environment by indigenous people or other such populations or to the Western notion of wilderness as untouched and 'human-free' nature. Globally, it can be argued that tourism has become significant as one of the main values attached to wilderness environments. According to Hall and Page (1999) the growing demand for tourists to experience the wilderness and other wild lands has been based on the changed and more positive attitudes towards the environment in general. In addition, better access to natural areas has integrated peripheral areas more closely to global and national tourism markets.

In particular, specific forms of nature-based tourism, such as eco-tourism and adventure tourism, are capitalising on the increasing need to experience nature and peripheries by Western people. However, the development of nature-based tourism in wilderness environments has not only an effect on the range of tourist products and experiences among Western customers, it also has impacts on the resources and people in peripheries. For a long time nature-based tourism has been a useful tool to introduce new use patterns and ideas of nature to peripheries. For example tourism was integrated with nature conservation from the very early stage of the national park movement (see Butler & Boyd, 2000). In Finland, for example, the aesthetic values of nature for tourism and recreation were deeply involved with the establishing process of the first national parks in the 1930s. In the last highly contested conservation debate on old virgin forests in the mid-1990s, nature-based tourism was also introduced as an alternative activity to compensate for the declining economic effects of forestry due to additional conservation of forests in Northern Finland (Saarinen, 2001).

Historically, the relation between tourism and nature conservation has been a synergistic one, but as nature-based tourism has grown, this positive relationship has turned into one of conflict in many places. From the perspective of 'traditional' branches of the local economy, nature-based tourism development can represent a competing and conflicting land-use activity and idea of nature. Global competition over resources in land use and the global tourism industry are increasingly affecting wilderness environments and the ideas their uses are based on. By analysing the different discourses related to the wilderness, it is possible to make the contradictions related to the use of wilderness areas, and the current change in the future of the use and meanings of wilderness more understandable. These are discussed in the context of the Northern Finnish wildernesses.

Finnish Wilderness?

Traditional wilderness

In Finland the value of the Northern wilderness areas has for a long time been defined in relation to the South, its culture and nature. Historically, wilderness (*erämaa*) has signified a region outside permanent settlement that has economic importance in terms of hunting and fishing (Lehtinen, 1991; Hallikainen, 1998). In the medieval system of the hunting economy, the wilderness is considered to have been an integral part of the structure of society at that time. In the system, the hunting areas and especially their taxation were often organised according to families and communities.

By using Raymond Williams' (1988: 140–141) cultural theory and its terms, *traditional wilderness*, reflecting the historical ground of the wilderness idea, refers to a relic cultural element and its characteristics. The relic cultural element has a current impact and it is under constant revision, but its content is in many ways formed in the past. Traditional wilderness is primarily an economic resource and subject to usage. Thus, the values connected to traditional wilderness are mainly related to the utilistic attitudes towards nature and the local meanings of wilderness.

Regardless of its relic nature, the traditional wilderness concept has for a reasonably long time formed the hegemonic Finnish wilderness discourse and it still represents it in some contexts. The traditional wilderness concept is manifested, among others, in the current *Finnish Wilderness Act* (1991), according to which designated wilderness areas are founded for: (1) maintaining the wilderness character of the areas; (2) securing Sami culture and traditional livelihoods; and (3) developing the versatile use of nature and possibilities for the different (economic) uses. Apart from the first somewhat vague and open definition, the goals of the Act are notably similar to the concept of wilderness of hunting culture. The traditional wilderness described in the Act is a resource inside culture and economy, and it is defined mainly through its local use and economic value.

Conserved wilderness

The Finnish wilderness concept, however, cannot be solely understood by the practices of the fishing and hunting economy. Another ground and perspective was formed at the end of the 19th century as the sense of 'Finnishness' nationhood was constructed. It was closely related to the *Karelianism* movement whose background reflected pan-European ideological thinking (Lehtinen, 1991). Then, the national identity – separating 'us' from others – was actively searched for from North East Finland, Karelia, the land of almost untouched nature and wilderness, and later, Northern Finland. The *Karelianistic* wilderness did not, however, appear as a mainly economic and operational part of the society and the dominant culture, as was the case in the period of hunting and fishing economy, but it caused the idealisation of wilderness and estranged it from people, and as such, wilderness become a positively loaded landscape outside the dominant culture (see Varnedoe, 1988).

The need for legislative protection of the wilderness became more prominent in public only in the mid-1980s. Then, *conserved wilderness* challenged the traditional concept of wilderness. This was made concrete in the process and conflicts related to the *Wilderness Act*, through which 'protection' in accordance with a rather traditional concept of wilderness resulted along with the 12 designated wilderness areas (see Lehtinen, 1991).

Conserved wilderness is, in many parts, based on the Western concept of wilderness and the corresponding history of using the wilderness. Historically, wilderness and wilderness nature with its primitive inhabitants were seen as opposite to, even as a hindrance to, civilisation and development in the Western countries, especially Anglo-Saxon and Anglo-American societies. The Western concept of nature is thus mainly formed through conquering wilderness, transformation and through the juxtaposition of nature and culture – not through living in and from the wilderness (Short, 1991). As Roderick Nash (1982: xiii) writes in his book *Wilderness and the American Mind*: 'Civilisation created wilderness'. Saying this, he refers to the construction of the juxtaposition of nature and culture in the North American societies, and to the clear line drawn between wilderness and organised society.

In North America, the increasing disappearing, 'civilisation', of wilderness finally resulted in the need to protect the remaining areas of wilderness. As a consequence, the first *Wilderness Act* was prescribed in the United States in 1964. It was preceded by social and political debate over conserving areas that lasted more than 100 years (see Nash, 1982; Hall, 1998). According to the *Wilderness Act* of the United States (Public Law, 1964), wilderness is placed outside society and culture:

> A wilderness, in contrast with those areas where man and his own works dominate the landscape, is hereby recognized as an area where the earth and its community of life are untrammelled by man, where man himself is a visitor who doesn't remain [. . .].

The idea of the Act – 'man himself is a visitor who doesn't remain' – is somewhat opposite to the basis of the *Finnish Wilderness Act* and the content of the traditional wilderness discourse.

The *Karelianistic* concept of wilderness outside culture was based on the same juxtaposition of nature and culture as the Western idea. In Finland, this formed, for its part, a romanticised image of conserved wilderness. In this sense, the rise of nationalism and the industrialisation in the late 19th century represents the 'civilisation process' of the Finnish society in the very meaning described by Roderick Nash (1982) in the North American context. The romantisation of wilderness also formed a fruitful basis for the needs of modern tourists and the tourism industry to evolve in wildernesses areas.

Touristic wilderness

In spite of their placement outside culture or strong local connections, wilderness areas are increasingly an integral part of modern societies and their institutional and economic relations in the globalised world. One central international phenomenon created by modernisation and, for its part, using, producing and reproducing the ideas of wilderness, is tourism. The impacts of tourism on wilderness and the surrounding regional structures are not simply directly physical, economic or affecting the local employment. Tourism, and especially the related advertising and media (travel programmes and literature), constructs images of distant places, destinations and cultures on the basis of our own culture and way of life. Thus, images of the remote Northern wildernesses, its use and value can be constructed without people having direct personal contacts to this region. The created images, however, may affect the practices related to distant wilderness, for example, through nature politics and touristic demands.

The *touristic wilderness* constructed through direct and indirect tourism development is based on consumption, marketing, visualising natural environments and staging wilderness settings for touristic purposes. In advertising, positive images, such as freedom, naturalness and authenticity, are connected to the product to be marketed, and eventually as a part of the identity of the consumer, namely, the tourist.

Touristic wilderness is a commercialised space. It is a commodity: a resource and product that can be produced, replicated and consumed. In the touristic wilderness, the boundary between nature and culture is often unclear. Thus, travel advertising may combine the possibilities and rights of consuming and way of life created by the modern society, and the images of freedom, adventure and experiences in the wild, 'past' and exotic. Similarly, the built environments of tourist attractions are often designed so that they would refer to wilderness and the connected cultural characteristics.

The basis of touristic wilderness represents the process of change affecting wilderness that is both global, perceived through the eyes of outsiders, and partly local. In tourism, wilderness is a 'glocal' unit. As an idea, it combines local economic benefits and uses with global values attached to the wilderness. Wilderness emerges as a resource inside the local and a wider economic system and culture. Touristic wilderness is a place where the consumer is a visitor who doesn't remain. It is based on the active production, reproduction and recycling of the representation of wild, free, harsh and rugged nature, and their combination in relation to the modern cultures of consumerism.

Box 3.1 summarises the various wilderness discourses. The discourses should not be considered all-inclusive nor do the discursive structures exhaustively define all the possible interpretations, understandings and discourses of wilderness. Rather they are presented as 'meta' ideas forming the current conceptualisations of wilderness, and it is possible and fruitful to construct other more detailed discursive structures in a specific case context than the ones listed here.

Box 3.1 The main current wilderness discourses constructing and defining wilderness environments and their meanings, values and uses in Northern Finland

Traditional wilderness

Based on:	Historical and cultural tradition of usage (usufructuary area)
Image:	An internal resource of the culture and (local) economic activity
Constructed:	By traditional use
Perspective:	Mainly local

Conserved wilderness

Based on:	Western and Anglo-American concept of wilderness
Image:	Area outside the main culture, a place where man is only a visitor who doesn't remain
Constructed:	By conquering and through the civilisation process of the society
Perspective:	Global and Western

Touristic wilderness

Based on:	Modernisation and consumption
Image:	A commodity that can be produced and consumed, an inside resource of economic operations and a place where the consumer is a visitor who doesn't remain
Constructed:	By producing and reproducing in marketing and by consuming the 'commodity'
Perspective:	*'Glocal'*

Tourism and Northern Wilderness Areas

The development of nature-based tourism in Northern Finland

Tourism is perhaps the latest significant form of economy and consumption using the Northern wilderness areas. Internationally, tourism is considered highly important and a form of economy that greatly uses the wilderness environments in its operations (see Butler *et al.*, 1998; Hall & Page, 1999). This is an essential perspective for the future of the Northern wilderness areas, because nature-based tourism and ecotourism in general are considered as one of the fastest growing sectors of international tourism.

In the recent years, tourism has intensively developed in Northern Finland. In 2001, tourism statistics indicated a total of over 3.3 million overnight visits in Northern Finland, and over 1.5 million person/nights spent in tourist accommodation in Lapland, where most of the remaining wilderness areas are located. Unfortunately, there is no clear knowledge of the scale of tourism in the designated wilderness areas. It can be assumed that the development of tourism in the national parks in Northern Finland corresponds to the development of the use of wilderness areas, at least relatively to some extent. The national parks can be considered to be wilderness-like in nature, and it can be assumed that the tourism in the national parks also more widely reflects the development of nature-based tourism in Northern Finland in different kinds of areas with different degrees of access.

Table 3.1 shows the development of the visits in those national parks in Northern Finland that have uniform follow-up statistics for the period of several years. The total average sum of visitors has more than doubled in the 1990s in the selected national parks (NP). The development, however, is not equally distributed among different parks. The development of nature-based tourism has not been as strong in the parks that are far from the main tourist attractions and routes, e.g. in Lemmenjoki NP. Riisitunturi NP and especially Oulanka NP are located near the Ruka tourist destination with approximately 15,000 bed places. Rokua NP is along a main road near the urbanised Oulu region, with almost 200,000 inhabitants.

The conclusion can be drawn that the use of designated and other wilderness areas in Northern Finland that are, on average, slightly more difficult to access by tourism transportation than the national parks will not follow the most optimistic development estimations of nature-based tourism, at least in the near future. According to the estimations, the annual growth of nature-based tourism in Finland would be as high as 8–10% (see Ympäristöministeriö, 2002). However, even lower direct growth of touristic use of wilderness areas and the new forms of tourism activities can significantly influence the use and character of these areas, and the relationships between different forms of use (see Hall & Johnston, 1995).

'New tourism' and Northern wildernesses

Structural changes related to tourism have been visibly present in the development of tourism during the last two decades. In particular, the strong growth of nature-based tourism and the decrease in the relative importance of mass tourism have been highlighted in academic literature (see Poon, 1993; Fennell, 1999). On a more general level, these changes are related to wider shifts in consumption and economic

Table 3.1 The visitor numbers of selected national parks in Northern Finland in 1992–2000

National park	1992	1993	1994	1995	1996	1997	1998	1999	2000
Lemmenjoki	8000	8000	10,000	10,000	10,000	10,000	10,000	10,000	10,000
Oulanka	60,000	65,000	80,000	100,000	100,000	100,000	145,000	150,000	145,000
Riisitunturi	2000	2000	2000	2000	2500	2000	5000	6000	10,000
Rokua	4000	6000	5000	5000	5000	15,000	15,000	20,000	30,000
Total	74,000	81,000	97,000	117,000	117,500	127,000	175,000	186,000	195,000
Average	18,500	20,250	24,250	29,250	29,250	31,750	43,750	46,500	48,750

Source: Forest and Park Service

production that are often described as moving from Fordist production towards post-Fordist production and the related new ways of consuming (see Urry, 1990).

In terms of the tourism industry and marketing, this would mean 'moving' from mass tourism towards individual travelling and products that effectively segment consumers (see Mowforth & Munt, 1998). The move does not, however, mean the end of mass tourism but rather challenging it and the appearance of new forms of tourism and tourists in the markets. Therefore, the new tourism represents rather a new nature of tourism production with increasing flexibility, individuality, hybridity and activity (see Poon, 1993), than a specific form or activity of tourism.

In this respect, nature-based tourism can be regarded here as an integrated part of the tourism industry, which needs partly, and usually mainly, the same infrastructure as 'average tourism' and which uses the same transportation systems in order to get people to the peripheries where the natural resources for tourism to utilise are usually located. Therefore, the economic impacts of nature-based tourism, for example, separate from that of other types of tourism are rather difficult to estimate at a regional level.

The Northern wilderness areas have traditionally offered touristic opportunities for recreation activities based on nature. In the summer, these have especially been backpacking, hiking, fishing and hunting, and skiing in the winter (see Saastamoinen, 1982; Kauppi, 1996). In addition, canoeing and boating have gained more prominence than previously among the forms of tourism in the wilderness areas. During the last decade, the use of the Northern wilderness areas for tourism has experienced both quantitative and qualitative changes. Snowmobile trekking has become one of the most central and the most visible form of the new nature-based tourism activities. Traditional Nordic skiing is, however, still economically the most important form of nature-based tourism activities that directly use nature in Northern Finland. It has been estimated that in Lapland alone Nordic skiing brought direct tourist income in total of about 40 million euros in 1998 (Table 3.2) (There are no equivalent statistics available for all Northern Finland (Kainuu and North Ostrobothnia).). The direct income from snowmobile trekking was about 19 million euros, sledge dog and reindeer safaris almost 10 million euros. The part of foreign demand has been significant especially in sledge dog and reindeer safaris, as well as snowmobile trekking. Generally, the degree of internationalisation of the tourist structure and the tourism using wilderness environments in Northern Finland has risen in recent years (see Saarinen, 2003).

The many characteristics of these nature-based tourism activities connect them to the rise of the new tourism in wilderness environments. Especially snowmobile trekking, sledge dog safaris, mountain biking and

Table 3.2 The estimated direct income (million euros) of nature-based
tourism activities using wilderness nature in Lapland in 1998

Nature-based tourism activity	Domestic demand	International demand	Total
Nordic skiing	30.3	9.4	39.7
Snowmobile trekking	11.6	7.1	18.7
Sledge dog and reindeer safaris	2.7	6.9	9.6
Fishing	6.9	1.4	8.3
Hiking and backpacking	4.7	1.4	6.1
Mountain biking	0.7	0.7	1.4
Canoeing and kayaking	0.8	0.7	1.5
Total (million euros)	57.7	27.6	85.3

Source: Lapin Matkailumarkkinointi (1999)

canoeing/kayaking are carried out through recreation service enterprises.
They benefit from the use of wilderness and the related images, and
often tailor their products to meet the demands and needs of different
customer groups.

Northern Wilderness Areas: Local Past, Touristic Future?

The juxtaposition of nature and culture has for a long time influenced
the discussion on Northern wilderness areas and their use: the aim has
either been a clearer division or to bridge the gap. This will affect the
public discussion on wilderness areas and their use in Northern Finland
in the future. Alongside this, there are other more extensive trends that
will emphasise the importance of touristic wilderness and tourism in the
use of the Northern wildernesses. In this context some of the most
important and visible changes are:

(1) Tourism, especially nature-based tourism and its new forms will
    increase in wilderness areas. Also, the structure of the tourism
    industry in Northern Finland will become more international which,
    for its part, supports the development of tourism and recreation
    service activities based on wilderness environments.
(2) The importance of the traditional Northern livelihoods, such as rein-
    deer husbandry and forestry, will decrease and, in the future, they
    cannot be used as tools for developing the local economy in the
    same way as tourism in the peripheral areas of Northern Finland.
    For example, in Lapland, tourism already employs more than any

other industry that directly uses natural resources. This will also locally decrease the importance of the idea of traditional wilderness.

(3) Regardless of some evolving contradictions, there is still synergy and symbiosis between tourism and the nature conservation – especially in their relation to the traditional wilderness and the questions on how *not* to use the wilderness. The increasing internationalisation of tourism in the region encourages the adoption of the Western idea of wilderness with its commodification element of 'the wild'.

(4) The wilderness areas in Northern Finland are managed by the state and the Finnish Forest and Park Service. From the perspective of the land management organisation, nature-based tourism and the operations of tourism enterprises that are subject to licences are easier forms of usage to control and manage than the forms of traditional local economy and indigenous or other local people ancient 'over generational rights' to use wilderness.

Despite the trends of change listed above, there are still many institutional structures supporting the idea of traditional wilderness, the strongest of which is probably the *Wilderness Act*. In addition, the traditional use of wilderness is supported by the international pressure to acknowledge the rights of the indigenous people (i.e. Sami) to land in Finnish Lapland. There is an ongoing ethnic debate over questions of management discourses and practices related to the use of land, including tourism, and the power to define meanings concerning the wilderness areas in Northern Lapland. From the point of view of the struggle for hegemony, the essential question related to the meaning of wilderness is whose wilderness the traditional and new concepts are really about. In a hunting culture, especially in the Middle Ages as the fishing and hunting commercialised, separate wilderness areas provided wealth to the areas of permanent settlement and commercial operators (see Jutikkala & Pirinen, 1962). This kind of financial profit distribution system replaced and later forced the indigenous Sami people to move further North. It also acculturated the Sami more closely with the dominant culture, its livelihoods and ways of living.

Partly due to this historical development, some Sami researchers perceive the whole concept of wilderness as a colonial one. Also the new grounds of the concept are sometimes evaluated as post-colonialattempts to take Northern natural resources under more severe national, non-local and political control. For example, Aikio and Aikio (1993: 104–105), the present president of the Sami Parliament, states about the concept of wilderness and its use: 'I do not say in the wilderness because in the areas of the old Lappish villages of the Sami people wilderness as deserted, uninhabited and unused, as defined by wilderness enthusiasts, has never existed.' Stating this, he also refers to the idea that the Northern wilderness is not open to external management, harsh environmental protection measures dictated from the South, or touristic use.

Obviously, tourism will not completely replace the traditional or conserved meaning structures and values of wilderness. However, nature-based tourism has bought a new and very influential addition to the layers of the cultural and economic meanings and uses of the Northern wilderness. More than the direct use of wilderness, tourism constructs people's ideas of wilderness through the indirect touristic use, such as marketing and the related images of wilderness as a 'product'. At the same time, it affects people's opinions concerning the suitable uses of wilderness areas. In future, these processes and related discourses localised in the peripheries will most probably change the wilderness landscapes more permanently than the present scale of nature-based tourism could directly ever do.

Growing and increasingly international nature-based tourism along with conservation effects in Northern Finland represent the ideas from the core in the geographical system of core–periphery, while the traditional uses of local environment are valued lower in the priorities of development discourses. The challenge for the peripheries lies in the relationship between nature-based tourism development and regional development. Nature-based tourism and tourism in general are potentially good tools for regional development and the production of well-being, sustainable use of environment and resources in peripheral areas. However, tourism is primarily an industry that often has its own goals, which may also be contradictory to the regional and even national development objectives in specific places. Wilderness environments and the peripheral communities relying on the local uses and meanings of wilderness are in a critical position in this respect. Without integration to the communities, other economies, uses and ideas of destination regions and an active purpose to create mutual benefits with the localities, the global tourism industry may create uneven regional development in the peripheries. The identification of the different discourses related to the use of specific wilderness areas may create the possibilities to discover mutual benefits but also a basis for more sustainable use of the last remaining wildernesses.

References

Aikio, M. and Aikio, P. (1993) Saamelaiskulttuuri ja matkailu. In Huopainen, R. (ed.) *Selviytyjät* (pp. 80–103). Lapin maakuntamuseon julkaisuja 7.

Butler, R.W. and Boyd, S.W. (eds) (2000) *Tourism and National Parks: Issues and Implications*. Chichester: Wiley.

Butler, R.W., Hall, C.M. and Jenkins, J.M. (eds) (1998) *Tourism and Recreation in Rural Areas*. Chichester: John Wiley.

Fennell, D. (1999) *Ecotourism: An Introduction*. London and New York: Routledge.

Hall, C.M. (1998) Historical antecedents of sustainable development and ecotourism: New labels on old bottles? In Hall, C.M. and Lew, A.A. (eds) *Sustainable Tourism: Geographical Perspectives* (pp. 13–24). New York: Longman.

Hall, C.M. and Johnston, M.E. (1995) Introduction: Pole to pole: Tourism issues, impacts and the search for a management regime in polar regions. In Hall, C.M. and Johnston, M.E. (eds) *Polar Tourism: Tourism in the Arctic and Antarctic Regions* (pp. 1–26). Chichester: John Wiley & Sons.

Hall, C.M. and Page, S.J. (1999) *The Geography of Tourism: Environment, Place and Space* (1st edn). London and New York: Routledge.

Hall, S. (1997) The spectacle of the 'other'. In Hall, S. (ed.) *Representation: Cultural Representations and Signifying Practices* (pp. 223–279). London: The Open University/Sage.

Hallikainen, V. (1998) The Finnish wilderness experience. *Metsäntutkimuslaitoksen tiedonantoja* 711.

Jutikkala, E. and Pirinen, K. (1962) *A History of Finland*. London: Thames and Hudson.

Kauppi, M. (1996) Suomen luonto kansainvälisenä matkailutuotteena. *Suomen Matkailun Kehitys Oy julkaisuja* A 70.

Lapin Matkailumarkkinointi (1999) Lapin matkailu 1998. Rovaniemi: Lapin matkailumarkkinointi Oy.

Lehtinen, A. (1991) Northern natures: A study of the forest question emerging within the timber-line conflict in Finland. *Fennia* 169, 57–169.

Mowforth, M. and Munt, I. (1998) *Tourism and Sustainability: A New Tourism in the Third World*. London and New York: Routledge.

Nash, R. (1982) *Wilderness and the American Mind* (3rd edn). London: Yale University Press.

Poon, A. (1993) *Tourism, Technology and Competitive Strategies*. Wallingford: CAB International.

Public Law (1964) Public law 88–577. 88th Congress. S. 4, 3 September 1964.

Saarinen, J. (2001) The transformation of a tourist destination. *Nordia Geographical Publications* 30 (1).

Saarinen, J. (2003) The regional economics of tourism in Northern Finland: The socio-economic implications of recent tourism development and future possibilities for regional development. *Scandinavian Journal of Tourism and Hospitality* 3 (2) (in press).

Saastamoinen, O. (1982) Economics of the multiple-use forestry in the Saariselkä fell area. *Communicationes Instituti Forestalis Fenniae* 104.

Short, J.R. (1991) *Imagined Country: Society, Culture and Environment*. London: Routledge.

Urry, J. (1990) *The Tourist Gaze*. London: Sage.

Varnedoe, K. (1988) *Northern Light: Nordic Art at the Turn of the Century*. New Haven: New Haven University Press.

Williams, R. (1988) *Marxismi, kulttuuri ja kirjallisuus*. Jyväskylä: Vastapaino.

Winchester, H.P.M., Kong, L. and Dunn, K. (2003) *Landscapes: Ways of Imagining the World*. Harlow: Prentice Hall.

Ympäristöministeriö (2002) Ohjelma luonnon virkistyskäytön ja luontomatkailun kehittämiseksi. *Suomen ympäristö* 535.

Chapter 4

Mountain Scenic Flights: A Low Risk, Low Impact Ecotourism Experience within South Island, New Zealand

NICHOLAS J. WESTWOOD AND STEPHEN BOYD

Introduction

This chapter presents research from a recent flightseeing industry study that argues scenic flights in general across New Zealand have been understated as an important component of this country's ecotourism activity base. The chapter is in two parts: first, a description is offered on the flightseeing industry across New Zealand to give the study scope, as there has been very little research undertaken in this area. From a survey carried out in 2001 the extent of the industry, including numbers of operators, planes used, jobs created, and financial information is presented. Those operators that specifically operate within a mountain environment in the South Island are then compared to the findings from the national survey to assess the extent of their importance to the industry as a whole. The second part of this paper argues that the scenic flight operators in the mountains of New Zealand share qualities in accordance with ecotourism. This position is further supported by a case study of the Milford Sound region, where flightseeing activity is compared with tramping. The results of this case study reveal that while flight operators can offer large numbers of visitors the opportunity to observe flora and fauna with limited ecological impact (distant sighting of aircraft, low residual noise, minimal air pollution, minimal disturbance of wildlife), tramping activity on the Milford Track with a set number of users (12,500) costs the New Zealand government substantial dollars (over NZ$170,000 per year) in maintenance alone, and that the popularity of some tracks may result in the displacement of some users to other less known tracks or to avoiding tramping altogether. Flightseeing warrants more attention and the chapter concludes that as a component of the New Zealand tourism industry it has value as a profitable ecotourism activity.

Flight Seeing as Ecotourism Activity

Ecotourism has become a well-established form of tourism that is offered in a wide range of places. It has often been closely linked with other types of tourism such as adventure tourism on the basis that opportunities to engage in thrill-like activities are often set in exotic natural settings (Fennell, 1999). A major difference between thrill seekers and ecotourists is that while both seek out natural settings, the former have a very passive relationship with the setting in that they value it in terms of being the backdrop against which they can engage in thrill/adventure activities. Flightseeing may be viewed as an activity that overlaps between ecotourism and adventure tourism. From an ecotourism perspective, the opportunity that flightseeing offers differs little from the description of how Ceballos-Lascurain (as cited in Boo, 1990) defined ecotourism. The original definition stated the following '. . . travelling to relatively undisturbed or uncontaminated natural areas with the specific objective of studying, admiring and enjoying the scenery and its wild plants and animals, as well as any existing cultural manifestations found in these areas'. One may argue that flightseeing accomplishes this with the one difference being that it involves travelling 'over' untouched nature or wilderness as opposed to travelling per se 'to' areas. There has been much discussion of what are key elements of ecotourism, and Boyd and Butler (1999: 128) have summarised these to be:

- environmentally and socially responsible;
- focused on elements of the natural environment;
- managed in such a way as to have minimal environmental and social impacts;
- non-consumptive in character;
- capable of providing desired economic benefits to local residents;
- appropriate in scale for conditions and environment.

Flightseeing adheres to many of the above elements. It is responsible in that it offers tourists an experience of untouched nature or wilderness, while at the same time educating them about the areas they fly over via in-flight commentary. It focuses on elements of the natural environment, as it is these elements that are the primary reason to undertake a flightseeing trip. Impacts are minimised as there is limited physical contact with the setting, other than some landings, but many of these are hardened locations. Also, scenic flights are environmentally friendly as they discharge low levels of pollution, and create low levels of noise pollution for wildlife and other tourists. Furthermore, impacts are mitigated through the risk minimisation procedures that are followed by operators (following safety procedures in the air, and flying at an appropriate altitude given the setting and weather conditions). Flightseeing is a non-consumptive activity, taking nothing out of the environment other than perhaps photographs of the environment they came to experience. Perhaps one aspect where flightseeing differs from the expectations of ecotourism is with regard to the benefits it generates for local areas. While revenue may not feed back into conserving settings, benefits do accrue in the form of investment in local transportation networks as well as creating jobs for interpretators and guides on flights as well as management of clients at bases.

In terms of adventure tourism, flightseeing could be classed as an example of passive adventure. Reasoning for this includes the nature of adventure involved, the low level of skill required, the low level of perceived risk involved and the well-developed safety procedures (in-flight briefings and instruction regarding the safety of clients) that are in place to minimise danger. Those taking a scenic flight do so to experience and see nature close to hand; they do not choose the activity because they wish to engage in risk taking. On saying that they accept the level of risk involved understanding that it remains a risky activity as it often has to contend with changing climatic elements, all of which are outside the control of those offering this type of tourist experience.

Methodology

The primary data collected has been drawn from two surveys undertaken in 2001 that examined risk communication in the flightseeing industry across New Zealand. The first survey was nationwide, and was sent to all operators of scenic flights; the second survey was an on-site participant survey within select flightseeing bases within the South Island. The nationwide survey was used to gain an overview of the entire industry in New Zealand, its size, growth, and in particular how operators brief tourists. A postal survey was carried out in November and December in 2001 of all 156 possible operators in New Zealand. Further inquiries by phone identified that only 116 operators in New Zealand offer flightseeing activities. Of these operators, 58 responses were received, representing half of the actual industry.

The on-site survey was focused on those that engaged in flightseeing as a tourist activity. A self administered survey was carried out at four commercially operated flightseeing companies during the summer months of February, March, and early April 2002 in the lower South Island, particularly companies associated with the Southern Alps region. By defining their operational terrain as mountainous, they were taken as offering a mountain focused ecotourism experience. Between the four operators, 256 participants completed surveys. The survey was administered immediately after a flight and was designed to collect information on motivation, demographics as well as visitor views on safety information given both prior to flying and during the flight. The surveys were initially administered by the flightseeing company staff, however two-thirds of the sample was administered on site in early April after a poor number of responses was collected. Of the 256 questionnaires filled out, all were useable, offering a comparable data set to that of the nationwide survey. As only one case study is to be presented in this paper, namely the Milford Sound region, only the responses of clients who undertook a scenic flight within this region will be examined. Of the 256 responses, 65 were collected from bases operating within the Milford Sound region. Prior to describing the findings of this sample population, results from the nationwide survey of operators are presented in order to establish information about the size of the flightseeing industry within New Zealand.

Results of the Nationwide Flightseeing Industry Survey

The following section details the characteristics of the New Zealand flightseeing industry in order to provide an idea of its scope, size, value and capacity.

Nature of business

When asked what their main business was, the majority (55%) stated this to be flightseeing. Another 14% saw flightseeing as a secondary activity. What this meant is that based on responses to the survey, 32 full-time operators are involved in flightseeing industry in New Zealand.

Fleet demographics

Based on survey responses, the number of aircraft currently in the flightseeing industry is 187 and 97 of these are helicopters. The average capacity for both types of aircraft is 5.3 passengers per trip, with total capacity of both being quite similar. Of the helicopters, the most popular models were the Aerospatiale AS350 six-seater (20), and Hughes 500D four-seater (14), with the Cessna 172 four-seater (22), and Cessna 206 six-seater (15) clearly the most popular of the fixed wing aircraft. The most popular makes of aircraft were the Cessna (61) fixed wing, and the Aerospatiale helicopter (28) aircraft ranges. Typically these aircraft are not new, with an average age of 17 years for helicopters, and 25 years for fixed wing aircraft. On average, helicopter companies can make 46 flights a day in peak season, with the fixed wing operations only able to make 27 trips daily due to longer duration of flights. The number of flights available in the off-season decreases dramatically by approximately 25% per operation for both types of aircraft. Also, while the use of the capacity provided by these aircraft flights has no doubt increased (155,416 people were carried last year), the efficiency or use of aircraft is still quite low with only 6% of the total available capacity actually being used.

Geographic spread, change and growth

As Table 4.1 indicates, in terms of geographic location, flightseeing companies are currently concentrated mainly in the lower South Island (40% of the total). There is also a large concentration around the large tourist centres of Queenstown and Rotorua, with most of these companies operating out of Queenstown and Rotorua but with many also based in Te Anau and Bay of Plenty (BoP).

Through looking at the age of the companies that responded to the nationwide survey it was found that the industry is steadily growing, with two new companies joining every year since 1980. Table 4.1 shows that of these 44 companies, the areas with the largest growth were Queenstown/Te Anau (nine companies) and Rotorua/BoP (six companies). It is important to note that this growth correlates well with the

Table 4.1 Regional growth by company, numbers since 1980

Region	*1980*	*2001*	*Inc.*	*% Inc.*
Greater Auckland	0	4	4	n/a
Rotorua/BoP	1	7	6	600
Taupo/Tongariro	1	5	4	400
East Coast	0	3	3	n/a
Other North Island	3	3	0	0
North Island total	5	22	17	340
Westland NP	2	6	4	200
Mt Cook NP	3	3	0	0
Wanaka	1	4	3	300
Queenstown/Te Anau	1	10	9	900
Kaikoura	0	2	2	n/a
Nelson	0	4	4	n/a
Other South Island	2	7	5	250
South Island total	9	36	27	300
Nationwide increase	14	58	44	314

Source: Westwood (2002: 81)

rapid increase of tourism in these areas. The median age of the companies who responded to the nationwide survey was 15 years, however this ranged from less than 2 years in operation to over 70 years. The average age of 18.3 years is one by which most companies would be relatively well set up, and it belies the aforementioned growth trend. However when this is further examined, much of this skewed age of companies results from those set up prior to 1980.

The location of operations has also changed nationwide with a shift in activity of over 10% towards the North Island by comparison to 1993 statistics. However, the three major areas of Queenstown/Te Anau, Mt Cook National Park, and Westland National Park in 1993 (Ministry of Tourism, 1993), have maintained their 60% market share, despite a North Island increase driven by Rotorua's 9% growth of market share.

Location and seasonality factors

The survey asked what type of terrain companies flew over. The majority of operators (30) stated they flew over mountainous terrain. Of these, 23 operate around the Southern Alps of the South Island. The coastal operations equal approximately 25% of all operations in New Zealand, however they are scattered geographically and the volume of passengers carried is much less per company with an average of 2098, which is under half that of the industry (4200).

Flightseeing companies operate over two clear seasons, peak and off-peak. This seasonality has lessened slightly over the last nine years. A 1993 Ministry of Tourism survey stated the peak season to be between November and March, whereas the survey carried out in 2001 indicated the peak season extended to April. The slight decrease of seasonality is likely to be due to the stabilising of rapid growth as the seasonality trend is most marked in the turnover of companies who operate in areas that have grown most rapidly, (Queenstown/Te Anau and Rotorua/ BoP), and least apparent in the oldest area of Aoraki/Mt Cook.

Human resources

From a population of 58 operations, the total number of employees was 365 with an average of 6.3. However with 116 confirmed flightseeing operations, the number of people employed industry wide will be much larger. Within each operation the typical break down of full-time equivalent (FTE) staff is 3.4 pilots, 1.4 front-line staff, 0.9 management staff, and 0.6 'other' staff such as drivers. Since the 1993 Ministry of Tourism report, the number of employees per company has changed, with more people employed over the whole industry, but fewer very large companies (50 plus staff), as opposed to more mid-sized companies (6–15 staff).

Financial considerations

Some 65% of companies had a yearly turnover of less than NZ$600,000, and only ten companies exceeded a turnover of NZ$1.2m. Yet on average the small companies had a lower than average growth over the last five years (24%), compared to the total average of 27.6%. Those companies who posted the largest average increase (44.4%) had a turnover of between NZ$2.4m and NZ$3m. It is not surprising to find these companies operating within New Zealand's largest tourist flightseeing areas.

Overall, this industry is steadily growing in both the number of companies, and their economic value. The majority of New Zealand companies are small operations that employ less than six people and have less than NZ$600,000 in turnover per annum. However, the most profitable companies have proven to be those in the rapidly expanding and seasonal areas of Queenstown/Te Anau and Rotorua. Interestingly, though yet profitable, the industry is operating at well below its current capacity and its potential for a larger economic value is substantial and as yet unrealised. The next section of the chapter addresses flightseeing as an activity within the mountain regions of the South Island, commencing with the research that has been undertaken on the effects of flightseeing to other activities.

Mountain Flightseeing Industry Characteristics

To date, little research has been undertaken on the effects of scenic flights in the South Island. The main geographical areas that research has been carried out on are Aoraki/Mt Cook, and Westland National Park, with a study that looked at trampers in the Fiordland National Park by the Department of Conservation that asked one question regarding flightseeing activity. Some work on the effects of aircraft on recreation has been undertaken. For example Booth *et al.* stated 'the primary effects of aircraft over-flights on recreation users are related to aircraft noise' (1999: 33). Thus, the primary focus of aircraft research has been on the effects of aircraft on Department of Conservation land users, and how aircraft noise or annoyance caused by aircraft has affected ground users. Apart from a proposed study on the effects of a heliport that was to be built near an ecologically important estuary in Auckland, very little is known about the effects of aircraft on flora and fauna in New Zealand's national parks. Studies that have been carried out in the areas of Fox and Franz Josef Glaciers in Westland National Park focused on social impacts such as carrying capacities, inferred through annoyance levels (Oliver, 1995; Sutton, 1998; Corbett, 2001). These studies found there to be low overall levels of annoyance generally at aircraft in the glacier region. Similar research done in the Aoraki/Mt Cook region looked at the overall effects of aircraft in an ongoing study at the sites of Blue lakes (2000), Muller Hut, and lower

Hooker Valley (2001). It was found that over the three sites the numbers of visitors annoyed was never more than 25%, and that up to 15% actually enjoyed aircraft presence (Horn, 2001).

The remainder of this section examines those operations (52% of surveys received) that operate in mountain regions in the South Island, comparing them to the industry overall in order to give a comparative view of the size and value of mountain flightseeing operations.

Nature of business

The main business of companies that operate in the mountains was again flightseeing with 76% of companies nominating this as their primary activity, followed by 23% who stated transport, and 20% hunting, as their secondary activity. Seven companies said the 'camera work' was their third business, illustrating that a relationship exists between flightseeing and 'eco' activities.

Some 90% of the mountain flightseeing companies are concentrated in the South Island, with the largest clusters of operators around the Queenstown/Te Anau region (nine) and the Fox and Franz Joseph Glaciers (six). All these operations are based around the tourist destinations of Milford Sound and the West Coast glaciers/Mt Cook, with five companies operating out of Queenstown, four from Te Anau, four from the Franz Joseph Glacier, and two from Fox Glacier. Also important to note is the small cluster of three well-established operations in Mt Cook region, which are geographically close to the glaciers and operate flights over these. These companies contribute a large amount (per company) to the overall flightseeing numbers carried, namely 23%, compared to the six glacier companies that contribute 20% of overall flightseeing carriage.

The age of the companies involved in mountain flightseeing range from just over one year to 46 years. In terms of growth, this sector of the industry is also steadily growing; a factor noted earlier concerning the industry as a whole. Median age is slightly younger than the industry total at 15.8 years, yet interestingly there were only six companies who began before 1980, indicating a relatively younger set of companies overall. The areas with the largest growth in numbers (over the last 20 years) were Queenstown/Te Anau (nine companies) and the West Coast glaciers (four companies).

Human resources

From the 30 operations the total number of employees was 213 with an average of 7.3 staff, which is larger than the industry average. Within each operation the typical breakdown of FTE staff was almost exactly the same, however there are more front-line staff, as mountain operations employed 0.8 more FTE staff.

Fleet demographics

As stated above, the number of aircraft currently in the flightseeing industry is 187. Some 60% of these are in mountain operations, with an average of 3.8 aircraft per operation, compared to 2.6 for the rest of the industry. The aircraft split for this cartage is 66 helicopters to 47 fixed wing, with a potential cartage ratio of 52:48, yet there are only 11 fixed wing companies, which indicates the small number of aircraft owned by most helicopter companies.

On average, mountain scenic flight companies can make 32 flights per day, however this decreases dramatically to 24 per day in the off-season. The use of the capacity provided by these aircraft flights is currently higher than that of the rest of the industry as there were 100,477 passengers carried by these companies (65% of the total carried from 113 aircraft). However, the efficiency or use of aircraft is still quite low.

Financial considerations

Of all mountain-related flightseeing companies, 43% had less than NZ$600,000 in turnover for the 2000–2001 financial year, and unlike the whole industry, 20% of companies had turnover over NZ$2.4m, an increase of 7%. On average the small companies had higher than average growth in turnover in the last five years (51%) compared to the total average of 29.3% of mountain flightseeing companies, which is a complete reversal of the trend industry trend (27.6%).

Case Study of the Milford Region

This case study begins by looking at the effects of the interaction between tramping activity on the Great Walks and flightseeing. It is based on research carried out by the Department of Conservation (DoC). While the survey is rather dated now (undertaken in 1993), it nevertheless provides us with some indication as to how activities on the ground are affected by overhead flightseeing activity. In the summer of 1993–1994 the Department of Conservation conducted surveys on visitor satisfaction, impact perceptions and attitudes toward management options on the Milford, Routeburn and Kepler multi-day walking tracks known as the 'Great Walks'. A total sample of 982 was obtained over the period of collection that was conducted through surveys filled out at huts. Contained within this survey was a single question that asked about overhead flights, and in particular whether they noticed any aircraft and to what extent it bothered them. Respondents had four options to choose: (1) did not notice; (2) noticed but were not bothered; (3) bothered a little; and (4) bothered a lot.

The findings are interesting. For instance, among the Kepler Track sample (n = 454), 46% noticed aircraft, however less than half of these (19%) noted any level of annoyance at this activity. Much of the aircraft activity in the Milford area is between Queenstown and Milford Sound, flying over the Routeburn and Milford Tracks. It is therefore not surprising that 63% of the Routeburn sample (n = 144) acknowledged aircraft activity, but yet less than half of these were 'bothered' to any degree, despite what is likely to be a much higher level of aircraft activity than would be experienced on the Kepler Track. The Milford Track had the highest level of annoyance of all three tracks with a 'very high aware-ness and negative perception of aircraft noise among all types of visitors' (Cessford, 1998a: 7), with 41% 'bothered a lot' by the aircraft activity. A smaller proportion of just under one-third did not notice (9%), or were not bothered (21%) by aircraft activity. Still, however, a high overall proportion (69%) of people on the Milford Track found the aircraft activity to be disturbing, even though the number of flights would not have been that dissimilar to those flying over the Routeburn Track. What this data reveals is that it is not only the presence of aircraft, but also where they are seen and the nature of the wilderness experience sought by ground users which effect annoyance levels of clients towards aircraft activity. Most importantly and as an overall point to make, none of the surveys found that aircraft activity whether flightseeing or not (as this was not specified, but implied) effected the clients satisfaction levels. The Department of Conservation ranked aircraft activity according to an impact perception scale, and although the Milford Track was ranked first, the Routeburn Track ranked third and the Kepler Track ranked ninth, the DoC concluded that overall levels of dissatisfaction were negli-gible, and very few visitors considered the experience to be below their expectations (Cessford, 1997, 1998a, 1998b). Thus the research conducted to date has failed to produce evidence that the presence of aircraft in the Milford region is in fact significantly affecting client satisfaction.

Based on the 2001 survey, data were collected on 9 of the 21 opera-tors that fly into the Milford Sound region (broadly defined as Fiordland National Park). Combined the 9 companies operate 39 aircraft, where clients can experience the fiords by both helicopter and fixed wing aircraft, offering on average 34.6 trips per day throughout the year. Capacity is influenced by the breakdown in aircraft characteristics in this region. Of the companies that responded, four were airplane and five helicopter operations with an average of 4.6 and 4.0 aircraft per opera-tion, making the area's aircraft operations much larger on average than that of total industry (3.3 and 3.0). Also the number of employees was much larger with 63 full-time equivalent employees (average of 7.1).

By using percentage of turnover as an activity indicator, it is possible to estimate that the companies do 67.2% of their business in the peak season (November to March), and 32.8% in the off-season (April to October). This activity equates to an estimated 376 flights that are possible in each fully operational day in the peak season. When looked at by operation type this works out at 52 per day by each helicopter operation (due to the typically shorter duration of flights), and 29 per fixed wing operation. In sum, this equates to 56,776 flights over 151-day period, and a peak season maximum capacity of 1574 clients per day, and a total of 237,614 passengers. In the off-season the number of flights possible drops to 44 per day for helicopter operations and 20 for fixed wing operations due to the weather and light conditions of the winter. The lower number of flights per day (300) means that 304,512 passengers can be flown in the off-season.

Thus the total available capacity for the nine companies that responded is 542,126 for the whole year, however this is assuming that the companies are operational 365 days a year. This is unlikely as Air Milford (2002) noted that fluctuating weather conditions on the Fiordland coast often dictates that Milford is accessible by air for approximately only 225 days per year. The above capacity figure should therefore only be taken as a guide given such unforeseen variables.

Data is very sparse on the actual number of clients taken on flights in the Milford area. Only five companies offered this information out of the potential nine that responded to the questionnaire. The reasons given for the non-completion of this question were based around commercial sensitivity as well as some citing a general difficulty in finding this type of information. As such, the total number of passengers that respondent companies carried was 26,379 over the entire year with 17,730 carried in the peak season and 8667 in the off-season. Although according to Air Fiordland's Captain Russell Baker (who has considerable experience and standing within the flightseeing industry) this is more likely to be around 80,000 passengers per year in reality (in 2001). When this is broken down into the type of operation, the helicopter operators had an average of 2284 clients in the peak season, compared to the much larger average of 3862 by operators using fixed wing aircraft. In the off-season this difference is similar with 1116 helicopter clients carried compared to 1888 fixed wing, but overall the fixed wing operations carried most of the clients (59%). This can be explained in part through the larger average aircraft size of the fixed wing operations (5.6 passengers), which is half a passenger larger than the helicopter average, and also through a lower cost per hour – therefore lower 'flag fall' fixed wing aircraft are cheaper to take for a flight as both types were found to be economically viable at 2.4 passengers per flight (at current costing).

The remainder of this section assesses the responses from clients (65) who participated in a flightseeing trip that originated from the Milford Sound region. Their demographic profile is compared to New Zealand population based on the 2001 census and the population breakdown of those partaking in tramping, in particular the Milford Track, based on the research by Cessford (1998a, 1998b).

Typically the flightseeing market is much older than the New Zealand population (2001 census), with the only similarities being the 15% of respondents in the 15–24 and 34–44 age categories, otherwise the sample has large differences at each end of the age scale with 14% less 0–14 year olds, and 11% more 55–64 year olds. When this is compared to trampers on the Milford Track (where 70% were between 20–40 years old), there are some similarities in that 50% of the sample was below 44 years old. Also the main nationalities were similar in both samples, with the domestic market (32% fly, 40% walk), the United Kingdom (38% fly, 15% walk), the United States (14% fly, 8% walk) and Australia (9% fly, 7% walk), the largest in the sample. However in the Milford Track sample the German market figured much higher at 14% compared to the flightseeing sample of 2% (Cessford, 1998a: 10).

The flightseeing visitors stayed between two and three weeks (33%) or four weeks plus (31%), in what were typically a FIT (free and independent traveller) (71%) or a VFR (visit friends and relatives) (15%) type holiday. The yearly household income of those surveyed was also much higher than that of the New Zealand average with 15% of the sample earning over US$105,000 per annum, clearly showing the wealth of this niche market. Although education levels were not included in the data collection, the occupation was, and through this it is possible to report, that 57% of the sample were employed in professional positions, with 30% of the sample employed in secondary industries and 13% in the primary industries. This finding is in keeping with their household incomes, and therefore due to the nature of the positions that they hold, a full secondary type education and possible tertiary education may be inferred.

To many, based on motivation, ecotourism may be seen as soft adventure tourism. This is borne out in the responses flightseeing clients gave to why they choose to undertake this activity with 75% regarding 'being close to the scenery' as 'very important', and with another 14% regarding this as 'important', meaning that less than 11% actually took the flight for its own means. When asked what importance clients placed on a sense of adventure, two-thirds ranked this as 'important', and 40% stated this was 'very important' in their decision to take a scenic flight, suggesting that flightseeing is both 'adventure' and 'scenery' related. Conversely, clients did not consider experiencing 'a sense of risk' to be an important motivator for participating. Some 60% stated this as 'not important', and, within that, 44% went further to rank this as 'not very important', showing a clear dislike of any association with forms of psychological or physical risk. This is further backed up 85% of respondents ranking 'a feeling of safety' as 'important', and within that 57% stating this to be 'very important'. What may be concluded from these findings is that while adventure is indeed sought, it is not the kind that is by any means risky or that makes the client feel in any way unsafe. These are characteristics of an activity that is quite arguably soft adventure and low risk. As the primary attraction for clients is viewing the scenery, and because the impact on settings is minimal, flightseeing should be regarded as a form of ecotourism.

An interesting point on which to conclude this section is the fact that tramping activity costs the New Zealand government over NZ$170,000 per annum to maintain the Milford Track alone, this is a considerable sum given that the number of walkers approximate 12,500 per year according to a Department of Conservation estimate in 2002). This scenario equates with tramping as having high impact for relatively low numbers, compared to flightseeing where impact is perceived to be low with large numbers involved. So on the basis of individual users, it could be argued that flight seeing is more environmentally friendly.

Conclusion

Flightseeing has received limited attention in the tourism literature. This is unfortunate as it is a sector within tourism related to transport that has the potential to expand. It is also an important market sector where clients on average have higher socio-economic status resulting in them spending more money on holidays. This chapter provides a brief glimpse into this industry in New Zealand. It updates the survey undertaken by the Ministry of Tourism in 1993, showing the extent of growth both nationally and within regions. Operators within the South Island, particularly areas of the lower South and the Southern Alps, dominate the industry. Findings here would suggest though that the industry is operating well below capacity.

Apart from providing statistics on the industry, the authors put forward the argument that the characteristics of flightseeing have much in common with the labels we apply to ecotourism, as well as fitting into the passive end of the adventure tourism spectrum. Responses of clients within a case study of the Milford Sound region would infer that appreciation of scenery overrides adventure and that risk is not at all regarded as a main motivator for taking a scenic flight. Based on data of users on the ground, there does not appear to be much evidence that flightseeing is a disruptive activity that impacts on satisfaction levels. Given the experience offered, the low number of actual flights taking place compared to what is possible, the evidence that impacts on the physical and social environment are minimal, perhaps it is time to consider the opportunities flightseeing can offer as part of the wider ecotourism industry. With much of New Zealand's ecotourism industry based on observation of nature, and travel within the Conservation Estate Lands, scenic flights open up new areas for ecotourists to enjoy soft adventure.

References

Air Milford (2002) *Conditions of Service.* Available at: www.airmilford.co.nz/ conditions-of-service.html (accessed 18 July 2002).

Boo, E. (1990) *Ecotourism: The Potentials and Pitfalls.* Washington, DC: World Wildlife Fund.

Booth, K.L., Jones, N.C. and Devlin, P.J. (1999) *Measuring the Effects of Aircraft Overflights on Recreationalists in Natural Settings.* Wellington: Department of Conservation Technical Series.

Boyd, S.W. and Butler, R.W. (1999) Definitely not monkeys or parrots, probably deer and possibly moose: Opportunities and realities of ecotourism in Northern Ontario. *Current Issues in Tourism* 2 (3/4), 123–137.

Cessford, G.R. (1997) *Visitor Satisfactions, Impact Perceptions, and Attitudes Toward Management Options on the Kepler Track.* Science for Conservation 70, Wellington: Department of Conservation.

Cessford, G.R. (1998a) *Visitor Satisfactions, Impact Perceptions, and Attitudes Toward Management Options on the Milford Track.* Science for Conservation 87, Wellington: Department of Conservation.

Cessford, G.R. (1998b) *Visitor Satisfactions, Impact Perceptions, and Attitudes Toward Management Options on the Routeburn Track.* Science for Conservation 92, Wellington: Department of Conservation.

Corbett, R. (2001) *Social Impact Issues Among Visitors to Franz Josef Glacier, Westland National Park.* Wellington: Department of Conservation Science & Research Internal Reports.

Fennell, D.A. (1999) *Ecotourism: An Introduction.* London: Routledge.

Horn, C. (2001) *Monitoring the Effects of Aircraft on Recreationists in Aoraki/Mt Cook National Park, 2001.* Wellington: Department of Conservation Technical Series.

Oliver, G. (1995) *Social Impacts of Visitors and Aircraft in the Vicinity of the Fox and Franz Josef Glaciers: Assessing the Carrying Capacities.* Unpublished M.Sc. Thesis, Aberystwyth University, Wales.

Ministry of Tourism (1993) *Review of Tourist Scenic Flying Safety.* Wellington: Ministry of Tourism.

Sutton, S. (1998) *Visitor Perceptions of Aircraft Activity and Crowding at Franz Josef and Fox Glaciers.* Science for Conservation 94. Wellington: Department of Conservation.

Westwood, N.J. (2002) The New Zealand flightseeing industry: Magnitude, growth, and risk communication. Unpublished Masters of Tourism thesis, University of Otago, Dunedin, New Zealand.

Chapter 5

Regional Contrasts in Ecotourism in Australian Rainforests: A Comparative Study of Queensland and Victoria

WARWICK FROST

Introduction

Opened in 2003, the Fly rainforest canopy walkway is promoted by its operators as the tallest of its kind in the world. Built at a cost of AUS$5 million, its all steel walkway extends for over 600 metres, reaching a height of 25 metres above the rainforest floor. In addition it has a 50 metre high viewing tower. Its private operators forecast that it will attract 500,000 visitors per year (Tinkler, 2002; Barrett, 2003).

Such a mass tourism venture, we might imagine, would be placed is a destination renowned for its rainforests, such as Queensland, Costa Rica, Malaysia or Brazil. Instead, it is located in Victoria, an Australian state not usually associated with rainforests. Indeed, while the Fly is in a popular tourism region – the Great Ocean Road region – this is a destination much more well known for its beaches, surf and coastal scenery.

The opening of the Fly canopy walk is indicative of two major trends in tourism in Australia's rainforests. First, there is a growing 'rainforest canopy race'. Ecotourism in Australian rainforests has primarily been dominated by Queensland's tropical and sub-tropical rainforests. However, in recent years, Australia's southern states have attempted to out compete each other in infrastructure-based development projects in order to gain a greater share of this market. Such capital-intensive projects are aimed at mass markets rather than ecotourists, providing a short experience with little emphasis on interpretation (Frost, 1999, 2001). Second, ecotourism in forests in the southern states is increasingly being seen as a means to combat rural economic decline, especially in logging areas. Such a view is not just confined to rainforests, for example in 2002 the Victorian government announced plans (and AUS$20 million expenditure) for four new National Parks in the Box-Ironbark eucalyptus forests.

Such developments have rarely been explored in the tourism literature. Generally studies of tourism in Australian rainforests have focused on the established and successful operations in tropical and subtropical rainforests, particularly around Cairns in far north Queensland (Valentine, 1991; Pearce & Moscardo, 1994; Chapman, 1996; Moscardo, 1996, 1998; Moscardo *et al.* 1996; Getz, 1999) and to a lesser extent in southern Queensland (Weaver & Lawton, 2002) and New South Wales (NSW) (Parsonson *et al.*, 1989; Staiff *et al.*, 2002). Valuable as these studies are, there is a need for a broader comparative approach, a balance between macrostudies and microstudies. If we are to fully understand the growth of ecotourism in Queensland (or indeed in other popular rainforest destinations, such as Costa Rica), we need to examine peripheral instances where it has failed to develop to the same extent.

The approach of this study is to consider ecotourism in rainforests across Australia, contrasting and comparing trends in the various states (Frost, 1999, 2001, 2002a, 2002b). In this chapter it is the aim to continue this approach in examining the regional variations that occur in Australia. In particular, to consider Queensland as a destination where rainforests are at the core of its tourism marketing and experience and contrast this with Victoria, where rainforests are peripheral to the established tourism attractions. In examining these contrasts, this chapter is divided into three sections. The first two examine the current situation in Queensland and Victoria. The concluding section analyses recent strategies in Victoria through comparison with patterns and experiences in Queensland.

Queensland

Ecotourism in rainforests in Queensland has a mature quality. Its rainforests are a widely recognised and promoted destination attribute. International and domestic marketing has consistently focused on the state as having a 'reef and rainforest' and being where the 'rainforest meets the sea'. The state combines tropical climate, rainforests and beaches for 1000 kilometres from Cape Tribulation in the north to the Gold Coast in the south. It is in this long narrow strip that most of the state's tourism industry is to be found, including a large number of accommodation, tour and other service operators who promote themselves as connected to rainforests. Only Costa Rica is comparable to Queensland in successfully integrating rainforests into such a well-developed tourism industry.

Intriguingly, we do not know how many tourists visit rainforests in Queensland (or any other state in Australia). Data for domestic tourists are particularly weak, despite evidence that over half the visitors to rainforests are locals (Parsonson *et al.*, 1989; Valentine, 1991). A potentially ideal source is the National Visitor Survey conducted by the Bureau of

Tourism Research. This is a large-scale nationwide survey of domestic tourists, which asks questions about activities. However, it combines bushwalking and rainforest walks as one activity, so that it is not possible to distinguish which ecosystem tourists are walking in.

In contrast, the International Visitor Survey does collect data more specific to rainforests. For Queensland it asks international visitors whether they visited certain rainforest locations. The 1999 International Visitor Survey found that:

- The Tropical North Queensland tourist region, which is centred on Cairns and contains the rainforests of the Wet Tropics World Heritage Area, was the fourth largest region for international visitors in Australia.
- 20% of all international visitors to Queensland (nearly 400,000) visited Kuranda, the 'Village in the Rainforest' in the tableland above Cairns.
- 18% of internationals (360,000) visited the 'Gold Coast Rainforests/ Mountains/ Hinterlands' in southern Queensland.
- 8% of internationals (160,000) visited rainforested Fraser Island in central Queensland. (BTR, 2000: 37, 49)

Despite this lack of statistical information it is possible to make some general observations about the structures and patterns of ecotourism in Queensland's rainforests. Four main features are identifiable.

First, a major tendency of tourists in Queensland is to stay in major centres and make short trips (perhaps only day trips) to rainforests. Cairns is a major example of this (Moscardo, 1996; Getz, 1999). With its international airport, railway terminal and port facilities capable of handling cruise liners, Cairns is the main gateway to far north Queensland. It boasts a wide variety of accommodation, cafes, shops, bars and nightclubs. However, the tourist attractions of the region are not in Cairns. Instead these attractions, including the Great Barrier Reef, the Daintree Rainforest, the Atherton Tableland and Kuranda, are one to three hours' travel from Cairns. Such a pattern is repeated down the coast as far as Byron Bay in northern NSW.

This is a common pattern in ecotourism and tourism in general. The tourism expenditure (and resulting economic benefits and employment) occurs not so much at the site of the attractions, but rather at centres (often based on transport hubs) some distance away. In the case of Queensland, tourists to rainforests spend their money on accommodation, food and shopping in the cities of Cairns and the Gold Coast. Unfortunately, such a pattern may result in the misleading conclusion that there is little economic benefit from ecotourism in rainforests.

Second, there is a tendency for clustering. Tourist attractions and service providers often find that they are more successful if they are located close to others, either in a centre or along a tourist route. The advantages of concentration and co-operation outweigh any disadvantages of competition. Variety in attractions adds to the appeal of the mix. The most significant of these clusters is based on Cairns. Others include:

- Kuranda near Cairns. The town may be reached by rail or cable car, both of which are attractions in their own rights rather than mere modes of transport. In the town are shops, markets, cafes and tours.
- Fraser Island and Hervey Bay, combine rainforests with beaches and whale watching.
- The hinterlands of the popular coastal resorts of the Gold Coast and Noosa.

Tourists to Queensland value the diversity of experiences that clustering brings. Rainforests generally fit in as a secondary experience, perhaps even a background or ambient one. Much of the tourist flow to rainforests is drawn from the nearby coastal resorts. Holidaymakers value a break from the beach or the reef, with a venture into the mountain rainforests. A good example of this linkage is provided by P&O Australian Resorts. They operate five island resorts in Queensland and one rainforest resort – Silky Oaks Lodge in the Daintree Rainforest. In marketing their operations they encourage potential tourists to vary their holidays by moving between the different resorts. While there are some accommodation operators who have developed as rainforest ecotourism specialists (Moscardo *et al.*, 1996; Weaver & Lawton, 2002), in turn there are hundreds of accommodation operators who utilise rainforests as background.

Many rainforest tours are packaged as a diverse range of experiences in order to broaden their appeal. This is illustrated by the example of a day bus tour from Cairns to the Daintree that mainly caters for young backpackers. It contains guided walks through the rainforest that have a strong educational focus. However, these are broken up with more general activities including: a boat cruise along the Daintree River (looking for crocodiles), a visit to a wildlife centre, a swim in a waterfall pool and lunch at an 'authentic' Aussie pub.

This association of rainforests with other activities and attractions provides great benefits for ecotourism operators. They do not have to rely on a narrow market. By appealing to a broader market, development has tended to be stable. Indeed, it is interesting that the tendency has been towards a large number of small- to medium-sized operators, rather than a handful attempting to dominate the market with iconic attractions.

The third important feature is that Queensland has a long history of National Parks, especially rainforested ones. This may seem a surprising statement, for Queensland also has a long history of resource exploitation by 'development at any cost' governments. Without much of a manufacturing base, Queensland governments have tended to look towards grandiose development schemes involving primary industries. This has tended to disguise an effective conservation movement, which was able to have extensive rainforest National Parks declared before the Second World War.

In 1908, Queensland's first National Park was declared: 324 acres of rainforest at Mount Tamborine in the south of the state. Much has been made of a comment by the then Director of Forests that the land was 'unfit for any other purpose'. The common interpretation of this has been that the National Park was *only* approved because it had no value (see for example Hall, 1992: 98). On the contrary, the rainforest was under threat, the Tamborine Shire Council had petitioned for the National Park, 'owing to the way land in the vicinity is being cleared' (Groom, 1949: 66). The Director of Forests' comment has to be seen against the context of ongoing battles between forestry and agricultural interests for access to rainforested lands, rather than as an objective assessment.

The instance of the Lamington Plateau in southern Queensland illustrates the contested nature of these declarations (Frost, 2004). In 1896 Queensland MP Robert Collins called for its development for *both* agriculture and tourism. In 1908 the Queensland Government announced that parts would be set aside as a National Park. However, a change of government led to a rejection of the National Park concept. Instead the Lamington Plateau was opened for settlement. 1n 1911 eight O'Reilly brothers and cousins followed the track cut by the proponents of the National Park and began clearing the rainforest. The ensuing outcry and further changes in government led to a final decision to create a National Park in 1915. Even then the government vacillated for over a decade as to whether to buy out the O'Reillys or not. As the O'Reillys struggled to clear the rainforest and establish their dairy farms, they found themselves with a steady stream of visitors. Despite the lack of a road up the steep plateau, the rainforest was a magnet for tourists. The O'Reillys gained valuable income (and status) through providing food, accommodation and guiding to these early ecotourists. By 1926 they could see that they would always struggle as farmers and believing their future lay in tourism, they opened a guesthouse (Groom, 1949: 64–89; Frost, 2002a: 11–13).

While the story of the O'Reillys was extraordinary (indeed in 1949 it was made into a feature film – *The Sons of Matthew*), it was not unique. Tourism preceded the creation of National Parks (for an account of an early tourist party (self-styled naturalists, surely the forebears of today's ecotourists) into the rainforests near Lamington before it was declared a National Park, see Barrett, 1919: 182–199). As National Parks were established tourism boomed. A group of enthusiasts established a co-operative guesthouse – Binna Burra – on the next ridge to the O'Reillys. In the north, guesthouses modelled on those of the Indian hill resorts were established near the volcanic lakes of the Atherton Tableland. The publication of E.J. Banfield's *The Confessions of a Beachcomber* (1908) encouraged tourists to visit offshore rainforested islands.

The final feature of Queensland is that the experiences offered to tourists are wide-ranging. They include walking and driving tours, cable cars, novelty transport (for example amphibious ducks), wildlife viewing, adventure activities, accommodation in rainforest settings and canopy walks. The rainforest itself varies from tropical to temperate, from coastal to mountain. Much of the rainforest is natural, but some experiences take place in manufactured settings. Some operators place a heavy emphasis on providing educational experiences, others provide little.

Victoria

Victoria has extensive rainforests in the Great Dividing Range and to a lesser extent in the coastal mountain ranges of the Otways and South Gippsland. Most are contained in National Parks and State Forests, including areas of water catchment that are closed to tourists (other areas of rainforest closed to visitors in Australia include the recently discovered stand of Wollemi Pine – the 'Dinosaur Tree' – at a secret location near the Blue Mountains in NSW and the ecologically sensitive Thornton's Peak in Queensland's Daintree Rainforest).

There has been a long history of tourist interest in Victoria's rainforests (Ritchie, 1989: 133–151). In the 19th century a widespread public fascination with rainforests arose from a combination of the English craze for ferns (*pteridomania*) and the value placed on coolness, shade and moisture in the hot and dry Australian climate (Frost, 2002a). The public display of Eugene von Guerard's painting *Ferntree Gully in the Dandenong Ranges* (1857) attracted large numbers of tourists to the site it depicted (Bonyhady, 2000: 105–107). In 1881 the gully was reserved for recreational purposes and was often referred to as a National Park, though it was not officially classified as such until 1928. The surrounding Dandenong Ranges became a popular tourism destination, as did Healesville (which opened its native wildlife sanctuary as a tourist attraction in the 1920s), Marysville and Lorne (which in the Queensland style combined a beach with its rainforests). For many early tourists, the strongest attraction was the opportunity to see very tall trees (Bonyhady, 2000).

In an isolated corner of South Gippsland, the local farming community successfully lobbied for the establishment of National Parks at two small rainforest gullies – Bulga (1904) and Tarra Valley (1909). In 1938 the local shire council that managed the National Parks (at this time there was no centralised National Parks agency) brought in a second-hand bridge to span the gully at Bulga. The idea was to provide tourists with an elevated scenic view of the rainforest. Whether their choice of a suspension bridge was deliberate or not is unknown, however it captured the public's imagination. This was probably the first purpose-built rainforest canopy walk in the world (Frost, 2002b).

While Victoria shares with Queensland a long history of tourism in rainforests, in the last 50 years or so it has developed along a different path. In Victoria there is little in the way of rainforest-specific tourism operators. There are very few tours, for example no operator advertises tours at Bulga. There are few accommodation providers in rainforest settings and no large guesthouses similar to O'Reilly's.

However, there are tourists in the rainforests. Statistics are fragmented, but do indicate a presence. The 1999 International Visitor Survey indicates that the Great Ocean Road (which passes through the rainforests of the Otway Ranges) was the most popular regional attraction for overseas tourists, attracting 31% or nearly 35,000. The Dandenong Ranges attracted 17% of internationals, nearly 25,000 (BTR, 2000: 48). As noted above, statistics for domestic tourists are limited. However, the 2001 National Visitor Survey estimates that in the Yarra Valley and Dandenongs Region, 149,000 overnight visitors and 186,000 day trippers engaged in bushwalking and rainforest walks. For the Great Ocean Road region, 200,000 overnight visitors and 105,000 day trippers engaged in bushwalking and rainforest walks (Tourism Victoria, 2003). Given the nature of the forests in both regions, it is reasonable to assume most of these visitors are in rainforests.

What tourists appear to be doing in Victoria's rainforests is sightseeing by car, walking and picnicking in National Parks and shopping and eating in nearby towns. As in Queensland, the tourist expenditure is not in the rainforest (most of Victoria's National Parks do not have admission charges). Rather it is in nearby centres, particularly towns such as Healesville, Marysville and Lorne, which have a long history of servicing rainforest visitors. As in Queensland, the rainforests are often secondary or background attractions. However, few accommodation and tour operators link themselves with rainforests.

In recent years, Victoria has seen a number of attempts to provide rainforest-specific attractions. In particular, Victoria has become increasingly involved in building more elaborate rainforest canopy walks. In the late 1990s Parks Victoria constructed two rainforest boardwalks on the Great Ocean Road (at Melba Gully and Mait's Rest), built a new visitors centre at Tarra-Bulga National Park and opened a rainforest canopy walk (the Rainforest Gallery) in the Yarra Ranges National Park. The latter was the first major rainforest canopy walk to be built within 100 kilometres of an Australian capital city. However, results have been mixed. While Melba Gully and Mait's Rest have been popular, the visitor centre at Tarra-Bulga is only open irregularly and the Rainforest Gallery has attracted little visitation, probably due to insufficient publicity.

The development of this infrastructure can best be understood in terms of a race between various states to capture the rainforest canopy walk market. The race was triggered by the Tree Top Walk at the Valley of the Giants in the Walpole-Nornalup National Park Western Australia (Hughes & Morrison-Saunders, 2002), although it should be noted that the forest it is located in is not a rainforest. This has been regarded as a great success, attracting around 200,000 paying visitors a year and achieving, especially through extensive television coverage, an iconic status. It is a success which Victorian tourism authorities have been keen to replicate.

Evidence of this competition is seen in the publicity surrounding the announcement of the Fly venture. When the proposal was first announced, it was promoted as 'the world's longest and highest treetop walkway', 600 metres long and with a tower peaking at 45 metres above the rainforest floor. In contrast, 'the Tasmanian walkway [Tahune, opened recently in southern Tasmania] was 525m long, about 20m above ground, with a 37m high peak, while the Otway project's other rival, in Perth's [sic] Walpole National Park, was also less than 600m, with a 40m peak' (Tinkler, 2002). Though not mentioned, the Rainforest Gallery, at 40 metres, would also be just smaller. However, upon opening, such claims were modified. The Fly was then promoted as 'the longest and highest canopy walkway *of its kind in the world* (Barrett, 2003, emphasis added).

Underlying this focus on mass-tourism walkways is a public policy concern regarding regional economic decline. There is a growing realisation that Victorian forestry has been at unsustainable levels, that woodchips are a low value export with the processing taking place overseas, that the loss in water generation is far greater than any timber revenue and that forestry employment has been falling for over 30 years (Frost, 1998). As timber towns die, there has been a tendency to turn to tourism as their saviour.

This trend is best seen in East Gippsland, a remote area 400 kilometres east of Melbourne. In the last ten years the state government has declared two National Parks and developed short rainforest walks, ironically at locations it recently strenuously denied should be classified as rainforests. There is currently a proposal to use government funding promised to help declining timber towns to construct a 300 kilometres wilderness walk. Linking the Snowy River, coast and mountain rainforests, it will include serviced accommodation en route. Its models are the Milford Track in New Zealand and Cradle Mountain Walks in Tasmania. Its supporters include green groups and some former timberworkers (Miller, 2002). While the proposal has its critics, it is difficult to see any other likely project that would have as large an impact on employment in this declining area.

A Comparative Analysis

In comparing ecotourism in rainforests in Queensland with Victoria, a number of similarities are apparent:

- Both have extensive areas of rainforests.
- These rainforests are relatively close to major centres and coastal resorts, providing very large pools of potential tourists.
- There are large areas of rainforests protected in National Parks. In both cases protection of rainforests in National Parks began in the first decade of the 20th century.
- Rainforests are not the primary tourist attraction, rather they form a background for related tourist activities.

In contrast there are also differences:

- Ecotourism in rainforests is at a mature phase in Queensland, whereas it is still relatively undeveloped in Victoria.
- In Queensland a wide range of operators make use of the rainforests. In contrast, in Victoria, operations such as guided tours and rainforest accommodation are virtually absent.
- In Queensland, successful ecotourism operations in rainforests are clustered near to complementary tourist attractions and hubs.
- In Victoria there has been a strong emphasis on rainforest canopy walks. These do not occur to the same extent or scale in Queensland. Where they do occur in Queensland they are often incorporated into commercial accommodation operations.
- Recent developments in Victoria are driven by public policy objectives of boosting tourism and economic development in areas where the timber industry is in decline.

The key question for tourism planners in Victoria is what can be learnt from the Queensland experience. Currently, there are efforts to stimulate ecotourism in rainforests in the southern state. However, the strategies developed in Victoria seem at odds to successful practices in Queensland.

Victoria has become heavily committed to rainforest canopy walks. These have the potential to give Victoria's rainforests a strong and distinctive profile. However, they may also be seen as high-risk ventures. Highly capital-intensive, they require high volume of visitors to justify their cost. While they have been successful in Western Australia, this does not guarantee success in Victoria. There is as yet no evidence of tourists being serial rainforest canopy walkers. A tourist who has experienced a canopy walk in Western Australia or Tasmania may now be completely satisfied and have no reason to wish to visit one in Victoria. Furthermore, why will a tourist pay to visit Fly when they can visit nearby Mait's Rest or Melba Gully for free? Will tourists differentiate between a private venture and nearby National Parks? This is speculation, but the point being made here is there has been no independent research into visitation of these rainforest canopy walks. That visitor numbers to the Rainforest Gallery are low and that no operator has developed complementary ecotours at Tarra-Bulga are worrying indicators. Estimates from the Bureau of Tourism Research (2000) are that 35,000 international tourists visit the Great Ocean Road and that about 300,000 domestic tourists engage in bushwalking and rainforest walks in the area. Is that a sufficient base for forecasts of 500,000 visitors per year to the Fly? The spectacular failure of the public–private Seal Rocks Sea Life Centre on Victoria's coast cost the Victorian Government $80 million. One of the main reasons for its failure was the false assumption that nearly all nature-based tourists to the area would visit it (Frost, 2003).

In contrast the emphasis in Queensland has been on clustering, linking rainforest experiences with nearby attractions. This may be approached in two directions. First, emphasising rainforests as a secondary attractions in general destination marketing (Queensland's alliterative 'reef and rainforest'). Second, encouraging tourism operators to include rainforest elements in their services, for example accommodation in a rainforest setting or tours incorporating visits to existing rainforest sites. Such a strategy might be far more effective for Victorian tourism planners in the long run.

References

Banfield, E.J. [1908] *The Confessions of a Beachcomer*. Sydney: Sydney University Press, SUP edn, 2002.

Barrett, C. (1919) *In Australian Wilds: The Gleanings of a Naturalist*. Melbourne: Melbourne Publishing Company.

Barrett, P. (2003) Come Fly with me, up among the tall timbers. *The Age*, 8 September 2003, p. 3.

Bonyhady, T. (2000) *The Colonial Earth*. Melbourne: Miegunyah.

BTR (Bureau of Tourism Research) (2000) *International Visitors in Australia 1999*. Canberra: BTR.

Chapman, K. (1996) Skyrail: Rainforest cableway. In Charters, T., Gabriel, M. and S. Prasser, S. (eds) *National Parks: Private Sector's Role* (pp. 134–139). Toowoomba: University of Southern Queensland Press.

Frost, W. (1998) Timber industry. In Davison, G., Hirst, J. and MacIntyre, S. (eds) *The Oxford Companion to Australian History* (pp. 640–641). Melbourne: Oxford University Press.

Frost, W. (1999) Straight lines in nature: Rainforest tourism and forest viewing constructions. In *Proceedings of the Tourism, Policy and Planning Conference, Oamaru New Zealand* (pp. 163–173). Dunedin: University of Otago.

Frost, W. (2001) Rainforests. In Weaver, D.B. (ed.) *Encyclopedia of Ecotourism* (pp. 193–204). Oxford: CABI.

Frost, W. (2002a) Did they really hate trees? Attitudes of farmers, tourists and naturalists towards nature in the rainforests of eastern Australia. *Environment and History* 8 (1), 3–19.

Frost, W. (2002b) Recent trends in ecotourism in Australia's rainforests. *Journal of Tourism* 5 (1), 5–19.

Frost, W. (2003) The financial viability of heritage tourism attractions: Three cases from rural Australia. *Tourism Review International* 7 (1), 13–22.

Frost, W. (2004) Tourism, rainforests and worthless lands: The origins of National Parks in Queensland. Paper presented at Council of Australian Universities Tourism and Hospitality Educators Conference, Brisbane.

Getz, D. (1999) Resort-centered tours and the development of the rural hinterland: The case of Cairns and the Atherton Tableland. *Journal of Tourism Studies* 10 (2), 23–36.

Groom, A. (1949) *One Mountain After Another*. Sydney: Angus and Robertson.

Hall, C.M. (1992) *Wasteland to World Heritage: Preserving Australia's Wilderness*. Carlton: Melbourne University Press.

Hughes, M. and Morrison-Saunders, A. (2002) Repeat and first time visitation in an experience: The Valley of the Giants Tree Top Walk. *Journal of Tourism Studies* 13 (1), 20–25.

Miller, C. (2002) The river runs through it. *The Age*, 11 June 2002, p. 11.

Moscardo, G. (1996) An activities based segmentation of visitors to Far North Queensland. In Prosser, G. (ed.) *Tourism and Hospitality Research, Australian and International Perspectives: Proceedings from the Australian Tourism and Hospitality Research Conference 1996* (pp. 379–396). Canberra: Bureau of Tourism Research.

Moscardo, G. (1998) Interpretation and sustainable tourism: Functions, examples and principles. *Journal of Tourism Studies* 9 (1), 2–13.

Moscardo, G., Morrison, A.M. and Pearce, P.L. (1996) Specialist accommodation and ecologically-sustainable tourism. *Journal of Sustainable Tourism* 4 (1), 29–52.

Parsonson, R., Wearing, S., Anderson, K., Robertson, B. and Veal, T. (1989) *New England-Dorrigo Tourism Rainforest Study*. Sydney: Kuring-Gai College.

Pearce, P.L. and Moscardo, G. (1994) *Understanding Visitor Travel Plans for, Visitor Expectations of, and Visitor Reactions to, the Wet Tropics World Heritage Area*. Cairns: Report to the Wet Tropics Management Authority.

Staiff, R., Bushell, R. and Kennedy, P. (2002) Interpretation in National Parks: Some critical questions. *Journal of Sustainable Tourism* 10 (2), 97–113.

Tinkler, C. (2002) Otway view to be tops in the world. *Herald Sun*, 9 June 2002, p. 27.

Tourism Victoria (2003) *Domestic visitors to Victoria's Regions*. Available at: www.tourismvictoria.com.au/pdf/regional_summary_2001.pdf (accessed 8 September 2003).

Valentine, P.S. (1991) Rainforest recreation: A review of experience in tropical Australia. In Werren, G. and Kershaw, P. (eds.) *The Rainforest Legacy: Australian National Rainforest Study Vol. 3*. Canberra: Australian Heritage Commission, 1st pub. 1984.

Weaver, D.B. and Lawton, L.J. (2002) Overnight ecotourist market segmentation in the Gold Coast Hinterland of Australia. *Journal of Travel Research* 40 (3), 270–280.

Chapter 6

Mountain Resorts in Summer: Defining the Image

ROSLYN RUSSELL, PHILIPPA THOMAS AND ELIZABETH FREDLINE

Introduction

Mountains are a unique and valuable environmental, cultural and social resource. The global significance of mountains was officially recognised in 2002 as the International Year of the Mountains. The aim is to ensure preservation of the ecological systems, culture and inhabitants of mountains by raising awareness of these precious resources worldwide. This recognition provides a valuable opportunity to focus on the unique aspects of mountains and their value to tourism. Australia was probably not foremost in the minds of the United Nations members when they decided the world should focus on the preservation of mountains and their communities. However, Australian mountains, in particular the 'Australian Alps', are a significant national economic and environmental resource.

The region commonly known as the Australian Alps are the highest mountainous areas that are situated in south-east of Australia including the Brindabella Range near Canberra, the Snowy Mountains in New South Wales, the 'alpine' area north-east of Melbourne and highland areas in south eastern Tasmania. Most of these areas that are often referred to as 'alpine' areas are not truly alpine and in global comparison can hardly be thought of as mountains. Mt Kosciusko in NSW is the highest peak reaching not much more than 2000 metres. Even so, these regions are very beautiful, are high enough to have fostered a significant snow-based tourism industry (albeit unpredictable) and have the beginnings of a growing summertime tourist market. In the past, the snow-based activities have contributed AUS$410 million every year to the national economy (Konig, 1998) and there has been significant infrastructure invested to support tourism in these regions.

Mountain regions globally are extremely sensitive to climate change (Messerli & Winiger, 1992; Parish & Funnell, 1999), placing snow-based tourism in an increasingly vulnerable position. The winter ski season in

Australia is becoming more unpredictable, shorter in duration and is consequently facing greater competition with other winter destinations relatively close by such as New Zealand. The market is becoming more reluctant each year to book accommodation in advance and most tend to 'wait and see' before deciding on a snow-based holiday. The stakeholders and surrounding communities in these mountain regions are becoming concerned about the increase in the number of months in the year that the facilities are laying dormant. There is a slow realisation that attention needs to be given to increasing tourism in the summer months if these seasonal alpine destinations are to survive. While mountain holidays in the summer have always been popular in other parts of the world, especially in Europe, in Australia the mountain resorts do not have an image as a summer holiday destination.

This chapter portrays the perceptions of visitors and non-visitors to alpine mountain regions in considering these traditional winter destinations as possible summer destinations. What is the 'destination image' that is portrayed? What are the perceptions of visitors and non-visitors of the mountains in the summer? And, what perceptions prevent non-visitors from choosing the mountains as a summer holiday destination? The geographical region of this study is the Victorian 'alpine' mountains. This region includes: Mt Hotham, Dinner Plain, Mt Buller, Mt Stirling, Mt Buffalo, Falls Creek, Mt Baw Baw and Lake Mountain. In determining the image of Victorian 'alpine' mountains in summer, this study adopted a broad approach and did not focus on any individual mountain.

Over the last ten years there has been a growing body of tourism research on mountain destinations (Gill & Williams, 1994; McKercher, 1997; Williams & Todd, 1997; Konig, 1998; Digance & Norris, 1999; McIntyre, 1999; Buckley *et al.*, 2000; Flagestad & Hope, 2000). However, most have focused on snow-based activities, winter markets or environmental issues. The impact of climate change is causing concern at national and state government level with the Victorian government releasing a discussion paper: *Alpine Resorts 2020* (DNRE, 2002). This discussion paper is the first stage of a government strategy to ensure the sustainability of regional economies, recognising the value of the natural environment that provides the main attraction for tourists while considering the importance of the economic vitality of regions closest to these alpine resorts. A suitable 'starting point' in developing a strategic direction in the development of sustainable year-round mountain resorts is to assess the potential market's perception of summer tourism in the mountain regions.

Destination Image

Successful management of any destination, especially fragile environments, depends on comprehensive awareness of the impacts or potential impacts that may inhibit sustainability. Tourism has created a range of impacts on mountain environments – some positive and some negative. The type of visitors, the activities they undertake, how long they stay and how often they visit will dictate management strategies and operations. Taking the process back one step, it is useful to first understand how visitors and potential visitors *perceive* the destination. Strategies, particularly marketing plans can then be better directed and focused towards a select type of visitor. Significant differences are found when the market is created from responsible strategic marketing rather than from uncontrolled market demand. 'Mountains are not like chocolate bars: they are a complex arrangement of communities and ecosystems and marketing needs to reflect this as a product. More segmentation, niche approaches and sensitivity are required' (Bryden, 1998). The importance of understanding a destination's image has been well established in the tourism literature over the last 30 years (Hunt, 1975; Mayo, 1975; Goodrich, 1978; Crompton, 1979; Chon, 1990; Echtner & Ritchie, 1991; Driscoll *et al.*, 1994; Baloglu & Brinberg, 1997; Walmsley & Young, 1998; Baloglu & McCleary, 1999; Jenkins, 1999) with the general conclusion being that tourist behaviour can be better predicted if the destination image is known (Embacher & Buttle, 1989).

However, destination image is a complex phenomenon and difficult to measure. Exacerbating the problem is the variety of meanings that have emerged from a range of disciplines that are attached to the term 'image'. In psychology 'image' implies a visual component whereas to behavioural geographers it encompasses a range of concepts including overall impressions, knowledge, emotions and values (Jenkins, 1999). Most research papers on destination image have used Crompton's (1979: 18) definition 'the sum of beliefs, ideas and impressions that a person has of a destination'.

In the past, efforts have been made to measure the destination images of countries such as Mexico (Crompton, 1979); Finland (Haati & Yavas, 1983); India (Kale & Weir, 1986); USA and Canada (Richardson & Crompton, 1988). Others have investigated the image of different states in the USA – Montana, Utah, Colorado and Wyoming (Hunt, 1975; Gartner, 1989); Montana (Reilly, 1990); Texas (Crompton & Duray, 1985); Utah (Gartner & Hunt, 1987).

However, as the tourism market is continually being sliced into smaller pieces, with niche products becoming more significant, it means that it is also necessary to become aware of the image of destinations within destinations. To adequately serve these niche markets, tourism bodies are now challenged to produce separate marketing strategies for the same region highlighting different features and aimed at different markets (Bryden, 1998). For example, through Tourism Victoria's successful marketing initiatives, Victoria, Australia has been promoted in a jigsaw segmentation campaign, where each region of this geographically small state has been broken into even smaller marketable pieces each with their own unique characteristics and image. A few researchers have assessed the destination image of regions: Walmsley and Jenkins (1993) and Young (1995) have studied the north coast of New South Wales and Ross (1991, 1993) measured the perceptions of backpackers in the wet tropics of north Queensland.

Before attempting to define a destination's image, we must be aware of the components that make up the destination image. A destination is comprised of both tangible and intangible elements – which means that some are easier to measure than others. The elements of the destination image that are largely intangible, fuzzy variables – individual beliefs, ideas and impressions, are attributes that are difficult to assess in a structured, quantitative manner. However, the majority of studies attempting to measure the image of a particular destination have employed quantitative techniques and have therefore focused predominantly on measurable items – the more tangible attributes of a destination such as price, infrastructure and available services have not been able to successfully capture the intangible elements of the image. These intangible elements can sometimes be the most important in terms of attraction and perception and by not using the most appropriate measuring techniques these significant variables are missed.

Gallarza *et al.* (2002) have undertaken a recent review and taxonomy of all destination image studies conducted over the last 30 years so their efforts will not be repeated here. All recent destination image studies agree that Echtner and Ritchie (1991, 1993) have presented the most comprehensive framework for measuring destination image. Echtner and Ritchie devised a multi-dimensional framework that included intangible psychological elements, holistic impressions and takes account of unique attributes as well as the common, functional characteristics of a tourist destination. They also advocate the inclusion of qualitative techniques to better identify the intangible elements.

In determining the image of the Victorian 'alpine' region as a summer destination, this study utilised Echtner and Ritchie's (1991) conceptual framework and found it to be a valuable tool, bringing to light a number of unique attributes that may have otherwise been missed.

The Destination Image Framework

Echtner and Ritchie (1991, 1993) sought to overcome the shortcomings of previous studies by including holistic and psychological components in their destination image framework. They suggest that every destination image can be divided into two major components: attribute-based and holistic, with both of these containing functional (tangible) and psychological (intangible) characteristics (1993: 3). In addition, images can also contain common as well as unique functional and psychological characteristics. Figure 6.1 represents the conceptual framework diagrammatically, although the print medium does not allow full appreciation of its three dimensional form as intended by Echtner and Ritchie.

As depicted in the diagram, there are three continuums:

- attribute–holistic (horizontal);
- functional–psychological (vertical);
- common–unique (diagonal).

Echtner and Ritchie have drawn from the disciplines of psychology and consumer behaviour to suggest that any tourism product can evoke images of individual features or attributes (infrastructure, climate, local people etc.) in addition to the creation of more general feelings or holistic images about the destination or product – feelings that are hard to explain and cannot be pinpointed to any specific feature. Using these two major components, Echtner and Ritchie further distinguish the features of the destination by separating the functional or physical characteristics from the psychological or intangible elements of the destination. For example, the imagery that is produced by the physical scenery would be seen as functional/holistic while the mood or atmosphere would be psychological/holistic. More specific attributes such as the climate, prices, services provided would be functional attributes while the friendliness of the local people or staff would be seen as a psychological attribute.

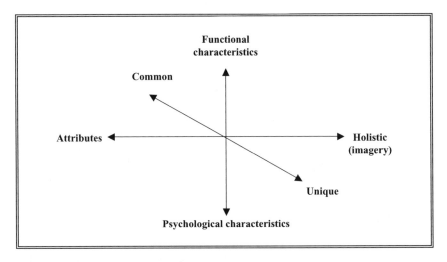

Figure 6.1 The components of destination image

Source: Echtner and Ritchie (1991)

Impact of time, market and unpredictability on destination image

In conjunction with the framework and methodology advocated by Echtner and Ritchie, other factors have been found to be significant in the formation of destination image. Temporal considerations need to be taken into account as destination image has been found to change over time, even within short periods (Gartner, 1986). Also, different market segments can have different perceptions of the destination. Hence, the destination image must be seen through the eyes of the desired market. Sociodemographic factors influence how the destination attributes are perceived (Baloglu & McCleary, 1999). While peace and isolation may be attractors for some, the same attributes represent boredom to others.

Most importantly, destination image must be seen as dynamic – being affected by time, market changes, social trends and unpredictable events. The recent addition of Chaos and Complexity theories to the tourism discipline (Faulkner & Russell, 1997; McKercher, 1999; Russell & Faulkner, 1999) can also provide valuable insight into the theoretical underpinnings of destination image. These perspectives highlight among other things the value of holistic viewpoints and the significance of unpredictability. One cannot help but notice the immediate impact the events of September 11 had on the image of the USA, Afghanistan and the Middle East as potential tourist destination choices. More relevant to this particular study is the impact of a disaster such as the landslide in Thredbo, New South Wales in 1997 when the fragile nature of the environment became the focus of attention following 18 deaths and lodge destruction in a very popular ski resort. Even more recently, the image of Australian 'alpine' mountains has been negatively affected by the devastating bushfires throughout the national parks in New South Wales and Victoria during the summer of 2002/2003. While it is not suggested that these images are always permanent, unpredictable events do have or should have significant implications for strategic marketing efforts.

This study has utilised the framework of Echtner and Ritchie to bring to light the valuable intangible elements of destination image, but is also working from the perspective of the destination and its image being an organic phenomenon and affected by constant change, time, unpredictability and therefore adapting accordingly. Stakeholders will also need to take these factors into account in their planning and management.

Methodology

This study utilised qualitative and quantitative methods. The first stage consisted of focus groups to determine the components that comprise the image of the Victorian 'alpine' mountains as a summer holiday destination. A total of eight focus groups (four of previous visitors; four of non-visitors) were conducted, consisting of approximately 70 participants in total. The second stage consisted of a survey to gauge the perceptions of the general public regarding the ski resorts as potential summer holiday destinations. The survey was administered randomly to 260 respondents in the Melbourne CBD. Face-to-face interviews were conducted and a 100% response rate was achieved.

Determining the Image Components

The aim of conducting the focus groups was to determine the components (as indicated by Echtner and Ritchie's framework) of the destination image of the ski resorts in summer as determined by visitors and non-visitors. The focus groups were especially valuable in identifying the intangible elements of the image – the holistic and psychological components.

The images of the mountain resorts were categorised using the conceptual framework of Echtner and Ritchie (1991). As it is difficult to portray the three-dimensional view on paper, three diagrams, Figures 6.2, 6.3 and 6.4 will illustrate the various image components revealed in the study. A brief discussion follows on the elements that are the most significant.

Holistic images

There were no marked differences between the images held by visitors and non-visitors of the mountain resorts in the summer. It was evident by the responses that many of the image elements were intangible and confirmed the findings of Echtner and Ritchie's study (1993). Indeed, if the study had focused only on the measurable qualities, many of the unique aspects of the destination image would have been overlooked. A significant part of the 'magic' of mountain destinations comes from the holistic characteristics or overall imagery. For example, focus group participants talked of simultaneous but contradictory images – feeling insignificant when faced with the vastness but also a sense of power and achievement from being 'on top of the world'. The spectacular 'views' from the mountains were a prominent positive image that is unique to mountain destinations. It is the 'views' that evoke the psychological elements of the image.

The 'Man from Snowy River' legend provides a strong association with the image of the mountains in the summer. Participants also envisaged empty chalets and cottages, non-crowded and 'ghost town' type of images. Visitors did mention that many of the facilities like restaurants and cafes were not open all the time during summer and while this was not a concern to some of the participants it could have been a detractor for others.

Psychological/unique attributes

Most respondents revealed that visiting the mountains in the summer would be relaxing and stress-free. When asked how these psychological benefits would differ from taking holidays in other places, i.e. what would be *unique* about a summer mountain holiday, the most common responses from visitors were 'invigorating' and 'feeling healthy'. Some visitors felt they always experienced a sense of 'self-discovery' while they were in the mountains and learning was an important part of the holiday experience. It is these images that are of most value to stakeholders and the most difficult to measure.

Functional characteristics/attributes

Visitors and non-visitors found it easier to describe the functional attributes of mountain destinations with 'fresh air', 'wild-flowers', and 'water-falls' being the most common images revealed. Those who had visited the mountains previously found the cooler temperatures a relief during the often harsh Australian summers.

The findings revealed that even though the respondents described mostly positive images of the mountains in the summer, only older non-visitors and visitors said they would like to holiday in the mountains during the summer for more than two days. Most of the younger participants thought that it would be boring to spend extended lengths of time in the mountains without snow-based activities. The lack of nightlife and isolation was not appealing to younger visitors or non-visitors, most preferring the atmosphere of active beach resort destinations. This confirmed the findings from the Baloglu and McCleary (1999) study regarding the importance of market sociodemographic factors in the perception of destination image.

Visitors also commented on the lack of services and limited facilities available on the mountains in the summer. Many noted the outdated lodges, expensive tariffs for accommodation and high priced services and food. Camping was the favoured mode of accommodation and was often the only alternative for families. Visitors who had frequented the mountains in summer when their children were young, found that as the children reached teenage years they changed holiday destination as they felt that the teenage/youth market was not well catered for in the mountains. Often, parents returned to the mountains in the summer when their children left home and no longer holidayed with them.

Common characteristics/attributes

Many visitors holidayed in the mountains with family and friends, enjoying picnics and time spent together without the usual distractions

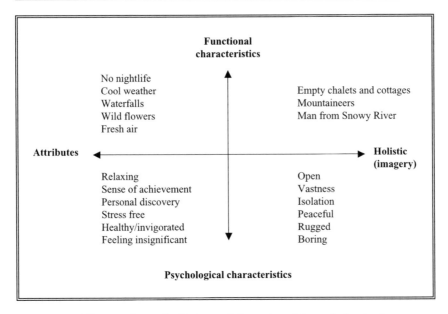

Figure 6.2 The attribute/holistic and functional/psychological
components of the destination image of Victorian
mountain resorts in the summer

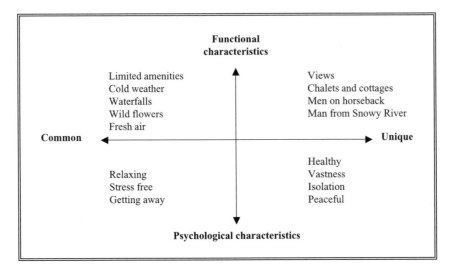

Figure 6.3 The common/unique and functional/psychological
components of the destination image of Victorian
mountain resorts in the summer

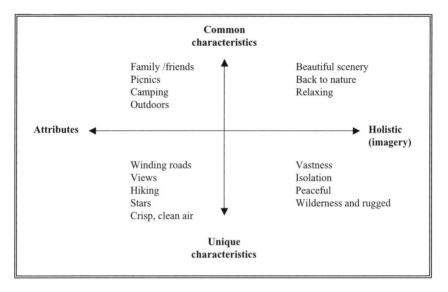

Figure 6.4 The attribute/holistic and common/unique components of
the destination image of Victorian mountain resorts in the
summer

of television and everyday life. The participants also mentioned the
'outdoors' element, and although this is not unique to mountains, it is
one of the attributes that is represented by a mountain holiday. Activities
such as hiking, camping and fishing are also not unique to these regions
but are associated with the mountain destinations.

Desired Attributes of Summer Holiday Destinations

In order to explore further the image of the ski resorts as a possible
summer holiday destination, it was important to find out what the
respondents desired and looked for in a destination. What were the attributes that were significant in the decision-making process? Table 6.1
provides a snapshot of elements that were preferred when choosing a destination. There were no significant differences between the preferences of
those who had previously visited alpine mountains and those who had
not. Most preferred the beach, a warm climate, peaceful atmosphere and
expected to learn something while on holidays.

The focus groups were also a valuable means for exploring the viability
of the alpine mountain resorts becoming part of the possibilities of
choice for a summer holiday. The answer was quite clear. To Australians,
summer holidays are equated with the beach. Both visitors and non-
visitors immediately related the image of summer with the beach and

Table 6.1 Desired holistic attributes of summer holiday destinations

		Visitors	*Non-visitors*	*Overall*
Climate	Cool	29.9%	27.0%	27.8%
	Warm	70.1%	73.0%	72.2%
Arousal level	Peaceful	81.8%	81.0%	81.2%
	Busy	18.2%	19.0%	18.8%
Destination	Beach	68.4%	65.7%	66.5%
	Mountain	31.6%	34.3%	33.5%
Learning expectation	Yes	65.0%	60.6%	61.9%
	No	35.0%	39.4%	38.1%

beach activities like surfing and swimming. It is apparent that the beach and coastal destinations are ingrained in the Australian psyche – history will prove to be a challenging opponent in attempting to introduce alternative summer destinations. Mountains were only mentioned by a few who regularly visit the mountain areas in the summer. Activities like camping and hiking were mentioned more frequently, which alludes to more inland destinations. However, the most popular Australian destinations that hold a more prominent summer image to the participants are places like: Byron Bay in northern New South Wales; Gold Coast, Queensland; Wilson's Promontory, Victoria; Great Ocean Road, Victoria.

In addition to the broader, holistic attributes of a destination there are more specific functional attributes that come into play when choosing a holiday. Pricing and accommodation are usually of primary importance; other facilities like nightlife, activities, restaurants and shopping can also be critical to the image of the destination. Respondents were asked to rate, in terms of importance, a number of destination attributes they considered important or desirable in choosing a summer holiday destination. The scale ranged from 1 (least important) to 7 (most important). Table 6.2 shows the overall mean scores for each attribute along with a comparison for previous visitors and non-visitors to alpine resorts. These mean differences were examined using independent t-tests, and three significant differences were observed. Non-visitors rate night entertainment venues, scheduled events and organised tours or activities as being significantly more important than do visitors.

A useful method of discovering negative perceptions about a destination is to identify reasons why people would *not* visit there. What are the perceptions that inhibit the choice of mountains for summer holidays? The respondents to the survey were asked what would prevent them from taking a summer mountain holiday. Table 6.3 shows that cost

Table 6.2 Importance ratings of functional holiday destination attributes

	Overall	*Visitors*	*Non-visitors*	*Difference*
Pricing of accommodation	5.40	5.01	5.57	
Luxury of accommodation	4.09	3.90	4.18	
Night entertainment venues	4.27	3.84	4.47	$t = -2.7, p < 0.05$
Scheduled events	3.98	3.63	4.13	$t = -2.3, p < 0.05$
Organized tours or activities	3.92	3.05	4.31	$t = -4.9, p < 0.05$
Wide variety of restaurants	4.34	4.16	4.42	
Views and scenery	6.13	6.16	6.11	
Shopping	3.66	3.49	3.74	

Table 6.3 Reasons preventing respondents from taking a summer mountain holiday

	Visitors		*Non-visitors*	
	f	*% of respondents*	*f*	*% of respondents*
Too expensive/money	21	26.25	60	33.33
Friends/family don't want to go	6	7.5	22	12.22
Lack of activities/poor variety/boring	4	5	32	17.78
Climate/temperatures/weather (i.e. cool warm, etc.)	10	12.5	54	30.00
Time/work/school	23	28.75	34	18.89
Injury/health problems	10	12.5	12	6.67
Distance/accessibility/transportation	14	17.5	35	19.44
Other more appealing options (beach)	6	7.5	30	16.66
Lack of information/promotions (i.e. don't know about it, etc.)	2	2.5	15	8.33

was a significant factor for non-visitors and visitors alike. Other significant perceptions among non-visitors were the lack of activities (fear of being bored); difficulty in access, transportation; and climate (either too hot or too cold).

Implications

These results indicate that currently in Victoria Australia, traditional ski resorts portray a mixed image as summer holiday destinations. Several implications were identified from the findings.

The Victorian mountains do not hold a strong image as a summer destination. Most of the non-visitor respondents admitted that they had not visited the mountains in the summer because it had never occurred to them to do so. The lack of awareness coupled with the strong beach culture in Australia creates a non-image effect for the mountains in the summer. This presents severe challenges to stakeholders in the resorts and those wishing to extend the winter season to summer.

There is a need also to overcome perceptions of remoteness, cost and unpleasant weather. The threat of bushfires has in recent times become a major negative component of the mountains' image in summer. Although in most cases the effects of unpredictable natural disasters are temporary, they need to be addressed so that the perception of danger is removed from the potential visitor's mind. Further research needs to investigate more specifically the effect of unpredictable events on a destination's image, how long they last and the most effective strategies in overcoming negative perceptions.

The most positive attribute of the image of the mountains in the summer is the 'uniqueness'. There is enormous potential for resort managers to capitalise on the psychological and holistic attributes. In order to compete with the usual beach holiday, there needs to be emphasis given to the feelings that are experienced when visiting the mountains in summer that are not so easily found at crowded beach resorts. The 'self-discovery', feelings of 'vitality', 'tranquillity' and 'health' are very much in demand by holiday seekers – especially those wanting a nature-based or mountain adventure experience. In particular, this market is usually from higher socioeconomic sectors and is more likely to be appreciative and protective of the fragile environment (Whelan, 1991; Wight, 1996; Triandos & Russell, 2001; Beedie & Hudson, 2003).

Conclusion

The Victorian 'alpine' mountain resorts have traditionally been snow-based holiday destinations and are now becoming popular in the summer. However, while the mountains portray a clear and positive

image in relation to their physical and natural features, there are somewhat negative images associated with infrastructure and available
services.

In terms of Butler's (1980) Tourism Area Life Cycle model, some of
the Victorian resorts are at the point of either rejuvenation or decline as
possible year-round resorts. Many of the lodges were constructed in the
1970s when the ski industry was booming and are now at the stage
where they are looking tired and run-down. Outdated infrastructure can
be extremely detrimental to the image of any destination (Warnken *et
al.*, 2003) and long-term strategies need to be implemented to prevent
this. In the summer particularly, without the forgiving snow cover, the
infrastructure is more visibly exposed and can detract from the natural
beauty of the destination. Some of the resorts, however, have begun to
implement strategies to gain a competitive advantage over other mountain resorts. For example, Mt Buller has had an active rejuvenation
programme over the last few years where many of the old lodges have
been replaced by architect designed self-contained apartment blocks.

Echtner and Ritchie's (1991, 1993) conceptual framework provides a
valuable tool for assessing the destination image of the mountains in the
summer. This chapter also recommends that the determination of a
destination image also needs to take into account factors such as time,
the market and unpredictability. The qualitative techniques advocated
by the framework brought to light many intangible elements of the destination image, including holistic and psychological characteristics. These
elements will be of particular benefit to resort managers wishing to
promote the unique characteristics of the mountains to a select market.
In essence, this increasingly competitive environment requires destinations to create an image that highlights the unique aspects rather than
the common to attract the desired market. In addition, heightening the
awareness of the unique attributes of destinations with fragile environments will hopefully ensure better directed efforts in protecting that
which is valuable.

References

Baloglu, S. and Brinberg, D. (1997) Affective images of tourism destinations.
    Journal of Travel Research Spring, 11–15
Baloglu, S. and McCleary, K.W. (1999) A model of destination image formation.
    Annals of Tourism Research 26 (4), 868–897.
Beedie, P. and Hudson, S. (2003) Emergence of mountain-based adventure
    tourism. *Annals of Tourism Research* 30 (3), 625–643.
Bryden, D. (1998) CBMT: The balance – whose balance? In Mountain Forum
    (1999) *Community-based Mountain Tourism: Practices for Linking Conservation with
    Enterprise: Synthesis of an Electronic Conference of the Mountain Forum/The
    Mountain Institute.* Franklin: Mountain Forum Global Information Server Node.

Buckley, R., Pickering, C.M. and Warnken, J. (2000) Environmental management for alpine tourism and resorts in Australia. In Godde, P., Price, M. and Zimmerman, F. (eds) *Tourism and Development in Mountain Regions* (pp. 27–45). London: CABI.

Butler, R.W. (1980) The concept of a tourist area cycle of evolution: Implications for management of resources. *Canadian Geographer* 24 (1), 5–12.

Chon, K.S. (1990) The role of destination image in tourism: A review and discussion. *The Tourist Review* 2, 2–9.

Crompton, J.L. (1979) An assessment of the image of Mexico as a vacation destination and the influence of geographical location upon that image. *Journal of Travel Research* 17 (4), 18–23.

Crompton, J.L. and Duray, N.A. (1985) An investigation of the relative efficacy of four different approaches to importance-performance analysis. *Journal of the Academy of Marketing Science* 13 (Fall), 69–80.

Digance, J. and Norris, R.H (1999) Environmental impacts of tourism in the Australian Alps: The Thredbo River Valley. *Pacific Tourism Review* 3, 37–48.

DNRE (Department of Natural Resources and Environment) (2002) *Alpine Resorts 2020 Discussion Paper*. Melbourne: DNRE.

Driscoll, A., Lawson, R. and Niven, B. (1994) Measuring tourists' destination perceptions. *Annals of Tourism Research* 21, 499–511.

Echtner, C.M. and Ritchie, J.R.B. (1991) The meaning and measurement of destination image. *Journal of Tourism Studies* 2 (2), 2–12.

Echtner, C.M. and Ritchie, J.R.B. (1993) The measurement of destination image: An empirical assessment. *Journal of Travel Research* Spring, 3–13.

Embacher, J. and Buttle, F. (1989) A repertory grid analysis of Austria's image as a summer vacation destination. *Journal of Travel Research* Winter, 3–7.

Faulkner, B. and Russell, R. (1997) Chaos and complexity in tourism: In search of a new perspective. *Pacific Tourism Review* 1 (2), 93–102.

Flagestad, A. and Hope, C.A. (2001) Strategic success in winter sports destinations: A sustainable value creation perspective. *Tourism Management* 22, 445–461.

Gallarza, M.G., Saura, I.G. and Garcia, H.G. (2002) Destination image: Towards a conceptual framework. *Annals of Tourism Research* 29 (1), 56–78.

Gartner, W.C. (1986) Temporal influences on image change. *Annals of Tourism Research* 13, 635–644.

Gartner, W.C. (1989) Tourism image: Attribute measurement of state tourism products using multi-dimensional scaling techniques. *Journal of Travel Research* 28 (Fall), 16–20.

Gartner, W.C. and Hunt, J.C. (1987) An analysis of state image change over a twelve-year period (1971–1983). *Journal of Travel Research* 16 (Fall), 15–19.

Gill, A. and Williams, P. (1994) Managing growth in mountain tourism communities. *Tourism Management* 15 (3), 212–220.

Goodrich, J.N. (1978) The relationship between preferences for and perceptions of vacation destinations: Application of a choice model. *Journal of Travel Research* 17 (Fall), 8–13.

Haati, A. and Yavas, U. (1983) Tourists' perception of Finland and selected European countries as travel destinations. *European Journal of Marketing* 12 (2), 34–42.

Hunt, J.D. (1975) Image as a factor in tourism development. *Journal of Travel Research* 13 (Winter), 1–7.

Jenkins, O.H. (1999) Understanding and measuring tourist destination images. *International Journal of Tourism Research* 1 (1), 1–15.

Kale, S.H. and Weir, K.M. (1986) Marketing third world countries to the western traveller: The case of India. *Journal of Travel Research* 25 (Fall), 2–7.

Konig, U. (1998) Climate change and tourism: Investigation into the decision-making process of skiers in Australian ski fields. *Pacific Tourism Review* 2, 83–90.

McIntyre, N. (1999) Towards best practice in visitor use monitoring processes: A case study of Australian protected areas. *Australian Parks and Leisure* 2 (1), 24–29.

McKercher, B. (1997) Developing a strategic approach to skiing in Victoria. In Brown, B.G. (ed.) *Global Directions: New Strategies for Hospitality and Tourism* (pp. 333–356). London: Cassell.

McKercher, B. (1999) A chaos approach to tourism. *Tourism Management* 20, 425–434.

Mayo, E. (1975) Tourism and the national parks: A psychographic and attitudinal study. *Journal of Travel Research* 14, 14–18.

Messerli, B. and Winiger, M. (1992) Climate, environmental change and resources of the African Mountains from the Mediterranean to the equator. *Mountain Research and Development* 12 (4), 315–336.

Parish, R. and Funnell, D.C. (1999) Climate change in mountain regions: Some possible consequences in the Moroccan High Atlas. *Global Environmental Change* 9, 45–58.

Reilly, M.D. (1990) Free elicitation of descriptive adjectives for tourism image assessment. *Journal of Travel Research* 28 (Spring), 21–26.

Richardson, S.L. and Crompton, J. (1988) Cultural variations in perceptions of vacation attributes. *Tourism Management* 9 (June), 128–136.

Ross, F.G. (1991) Tourist destination images of the wet tropical rainforest of North Queensland. *Australian Psychologist* 26 (3), 153–157.

Ross, F.G. (1993) Ideal and actual images of backpacker visitors to Northern Australia. *Journal of Travel Research* 32 (2), 54–57.

Russell, R. and Faulkner, B. (1999) Movers and shakers: Chaos makers in tourism development. *Tourism Management* 20, 411–423.

Triandos, P. and Russell, R. (2001) Mountain tourism in the summer: A case study of Mt Buffalo, Victoria. In Pforr, C. and Janeczko, B. (eds) *Capitalising on Research, Proceedings of the 11th Australian Tourism and Hospitality Research Conference*. Canberra, 7–10 February 2001. Canberra: University of Canberra.

Walmsley, D.J. and Jenkins, J.M. (1993) Appraisive images of tourist areas: Application of personal constructs. *Australian Geographer* 24 (2), 1–13.

Walmsley, D.J. and Young, M. (1998) Evaluative images and tourism: The use of personal constructs to describe the structure of destination images. *Journal of Travel Research*, 36 (Winter), 65–69.

Warnken, J., Russell, R. and Faulkner, B. (2003) Condominium developments in mature destinations: Potentials and problems of long-term sustainability. *Tourism Management* 24, 155–168.

Whelan, T. (1991) Ecotourism and its role in sustainable development. In *Nature Tourism: Managing for the Environment* (pp. 3–9). Washington, DC: Island Press.

Wight, P. (1996) Ecotourism: North American ecotourists: Market profile and trip characteristics. *Journal of Travel Research* 34 (4), 2–10.

Williams, P. and Todd, S. (1997) Towards an environmental management system for ski areas. *Mountain Research and Development* 17 (1), 75–90.

Young, M. (1995) Evaluative constructs of domestic tourist places. *Australian Geographical Studies* 33 (2), 272–286.

Chapter 7

Time–Space Use Among Cross-country Skiers in Abisko (Sweden) and Vercors (France)

LUDOVIC DUPUIS AND DIETER K. MÜLLER

Introduction: Emerging Pleasure Peripheries

Recently, pleasure peripheries have experienced an increasing popularity among tourists as place for leisure activities. Globalisation and economic restructuring have also embraced peripheral areas and destroyed employment in the local communities. This development can be seen as a blueprint of the emergence of new global patterns of production and consumption, putting peripheral rural areas at disadvantage. Tourism is more and more promoted as a solution to the resulting poor socio-economic situation (Townsend, 1997; Hall & Jenkins, 1998; Jenkins *et al.*, 1998). Hence, local planners and entrepreneurs have adopted Christaller's (1963) idea that areas in the periphery would develop into main tourist destinations as their common vision. Depressed areas are supposed to be transformed into pleasure peripheries and into a global playground catering for tourists' requirements (Pedersen & Viken, 1996).

Many mountain areas are part of this periphery due to physical conditions and socio-economic structures. Thus, tourism development is usually welcomed. Indeed, since the 19th century, mountains and other peripheries have been appreciated by tourists (Hall, 1992; Godde *et al.*, 2000; Nilsson, 2001). Moreover, mountain areas are often pinpointed as tourist attractions because of their national park or national reserve status (Butler & Boyd, 2000). New tourism trends such as ecotourism acknowledging these fragile environments, imply an increased demand for these areas and consecutively, a need for management and planning (Boyd, 2000; Sowman & Pearce, 2000). This mirrors the integration of peripheral areas into international tourism circuits leading a growing number of tourists into formerly unreachable and wild areas.

During the winter season most of these areas remain a wilderness to a large part of society. However, even then a growth of tourism is recorded pushing tourism beyond recent limits and causing conflicts regarding land use and the preservation of apparent pristine environments (Sandell, 1995; Abrahamsson, 1998; Lindberg *et al.*, 2001). This chapter focuses on cross-country skiing activity in two peripheral areas in Europe, which experienced a growing tourist interest even during winter: Abisko National Park in Sweden, and the Reserve naturelle des Hauts-Plateaux du Vercors in France.

Abisko National Park is the oldest park in Sweden established in the early 20th century. It is located north of the polar circle (latitude 70th) and features a sub-Arctic environment; nearby is the village of Abisko (with 300 inhabitants). The 7700 hectares of protected area are far away from significant population centres. Inside the park some infrastructures are available such as few fireplaces, bridges, guarded refuges belonging to a private company (Swedish Touring Club), and track information. The local economy is mainly based on tourism but also on traditional Sami (Lappish) reindeer herding.

The nature reserve of Hauts-Plateaux du Vercors is located between the French Alps and the Rhone river valley, at one or two hours driving distance from the main cities of Grenoble and Lyon. The reserve is the only dedicated area for protection in the Regional Natural Park (RNP) of Vercors. The RNP is a union between 68 communities since 1970, based on an agreement to promote the local economy, mainly for tourism purposes, and at the same time enforce the patrimonial value, particularly on landscape and nature's protection. The 16,200ha of the reserve are mainly composed of a high plateau (average of 1600m high) and a steep mountain range. Inside the park infrastructure is sparse and has no population with the exception of some shepherds during the summer transhumance.

A patchwork of forests and open fields composes the vegetation cover of both places. In France it is a *subalpin* or *alpin* floor (coniferous forests, shrubbery, glades and grasslands), whereas in Sweden it is defined as a *taïga* (birch forest, wetland and mire). An essential difference between the parks and their policies of management is that the ambition of Vercors is to let landscape redesign itself as an isolated reserve, meanwhile the idea followed in Abisko is to provide access to wilderness for inexperienced people.

During winter cross-country skiers, people with snowshoes or just walkers (depending on the snow condition) are the main consumers of both areas. These individuals comprise two groups: the hikers and the strollers. The strollers require 'normal' overnight accommodation, whereas the hikers will use their own equipment or some basic facilities that are offered by the owner or manager of the land such as refuges or huts.

The increase of winter tourism in both areas forms new challenges for park management. The commodification of outdoor activities entails that park visits are no longer associated with purely passive consumption of the scenery, but also with activities such as snowmobile driving and dog sledge tours. Also guided cross-country skiing tours increase the pressure on the protected areas. However, the main consequence is the more dispersed flow of tourists through the park and the subsequent dispersion of tourist impact to remote and maybe more sensitive parts of the parks.

Visitor behaviour inside parks is mostly unknown, which presents major management issues as it's also the place of conflicts and impacts. Park officers are rarely able to provide a clear answer about what happened inside the park, and hence, it is also one of their interests. Thus, the purpose of this chapter is to map the differences in space–time use among different groups of visitors in protected areas.

Tourism in Protected Areas

The social construction of nature as a place of relaxation and enjoyment is well known from the emergence of modern tourism (Hall, 1992; Boyd & Butler, 2000; Hall & Page, 2002). Behind the idea of preserving a last piece of wilderness and its biodiversity and endangered species, there was also another purpose of the protection: to save places for the pure enjoyment of nature and for the experience of qualities not available in urban life.

The park status forms an important touristic marker. Hence, protected areas serve as effective merchandising tool for tourism marketing (Goodwin, 2000). To the local community they usually provide an attractive product with a label of quality assigned by the natural reserve or park status. The labels suggest an area of pristine nature, at least concerning the usual perception by tourists. A problem in this context is to preserve this image and at the same time to manage visitation. For instance, the park management of Hauts-Plateaux du Vercors decided to stop all investment inside the reserve carrying in mind the idea to create a truly wild place. Hence, their action forms an example for a policy of 'demarketing' (Groff, 1998) to attract people with the image of the *real wilderness*. Consequently, parks promise an authentic experience of nature and wilderness, and their status identifies them as worth seeing.

Although parks form important destinations, large parts of the parks are seldom visited. It has been shown for areas close to Paris that individuals tend to avoid penetrating far into nature, and instead they prefer the security and facilities close to the entrance (Kaloara, 1993). Usually more than 80% of the visitors stay within 1km distance from the car park (Lazzarotti, 1995). The remaining 20% of the visitors penetrate further inside the park and really consume the space. Similarly it was shown for Abisko National Park that the majority of tourists never leave the immediate neighbourhood of the car park and the tourist station (Bäck, 1993).

The composition of winter tourism to nature areas is different. Notwithstanding that the mass visitors of the vicinities are still concentrated within a short distance from the car park, on the ski slopes (Abisko) or on the prepared cross-country tracks (Vercors) nearby the protected areas, it seems the winter consumption of nature areas requires more space than the summer one. The winter conditions erode barriers and tracks visible during summer and allow tourists to enter an area with less signposts and markers. The diffusion of tourists can hence be expected to be more random.

Time–Space Consumption in Winter Destinations

Consumption can be defined as 'the utilization of goods in the satisfaction of wants resulting chiefly in their destruction, deterioration, or transformation'. Consumption of space can be formulated as the degradation of the ground by pedestrian erosion, but there are other ways to conceptualise it. The consumption of space includes not only two or three dimensions, but also time. Hence, consumption of space implies also that a *moment of space* is used. This notion is important, last but not least, regarding crowding of visitors in certain moments of space.

With this approach, it is assumed that concentration includes proximity of visitors to each other both in space and time. The analysis of concentration in this time–space context enables not only to determine the impact of tourism on the physical space, but also the competition and friction emerging from different activities.

The main problem emerging from space consumption particularly regarding nature areas is related to the carrying capacity of the area, which could be interpreted as an indicator of successful planning. Moreover, crowding is increasingly experienced as a threat to visitor satisfaction of a locality (Chardonnel, 1999; Kearsley & Coughlan, 1999). In fact, crowding adds the dimension of time to the carrying capacity concept. Glyptis (1991) observed for a recreational site in Great Britain that visitors were usually rather concentrated in space during the entire day. The vicinity of the car park was an important factor influencing the visitors' behaviour. Enclosure to a certain woodland area and an 'edge effect' attracting visitors to the edges of woodlands were other factors obviously influencing the distribution of the visitors in the park. Patmore (1983) conceptualises the visitor dispersion at a recreational site in a simple descriptive model. Accordingly, the first visitors establish themselves in a few favourite spots within the site. The majority of visitors arriving in the early afternoon (the 'invasion') reinforces and extends the initial patterns. Then, a consolidation of visitor dispersion occurs, sometimes also intensification due to late arriving visitors. After that, patterns are more dispersed again.

The main activities of winter visitors in the mountain areas are sports and promenades on skies. New fashions occur all the time, such as snowboarding and snowmobiling, that are often not well tolerated by other not so fashionable tourists and hence, some tensions appear. However, sports are not the main purpose for holidays in the mountains. A significant number of tourists visit mountain areas and do not practice skiing at all, but only enjoy the scenery. Moreover, resorts often offer a lot of other activities such as fishing or shopping.

Differences in how space and time are used can be also seen between the local community and the tourists. The knowledge of the local area enables the members of the local population to use the parks and at the same time avoid crowded and beaten tracks. However, by occupying certain places, visitors force the locals to avoid these places at certain times of the day, or simply to accept that they have to be shared with numerous visitors. Outside the limits of the winter resorts, land use pressure usually decreases quickly and after few kilometres only lonesome trekkers or strollers can be found.

Methodology

This chapter is based on the results of two questionnaires conducted during fieldwork in winter 2001/2. The surveys were not aiming at a comprehensive coverage of tourists or local consumers in these peripheries. Instead, the main intent was to elaborate behavioural rules that can be used for modelling impacts of planning activities on consumption patterns in the protected areas. The sites for collecting data were the state reserve of Hauts-Plateaux du Vercors in southern part of France and the Swedish national park Abisko in the northern county of Norrbotten. The interviews were personal and hence, also information about equipment and behaviour could be observed and noted. The questions addressed two main issues:

- Activities: Where have the individuals been and how long did they spend for their activities?
- Perception of the environment: How was the environment perceived, and what knowledge was available regarding this environment?

Field observations have been added to the interviews, such as tracks left in the snow and behaviours of individuals met or just seen. This source of information helps to analyse the situations and find out 'normal' reactions to the environment. Places and times of consumption as well as behaviour in space are the results of the analyses.

The collected information was not analysed quantitatively and hence, results are not presented in figures. This is partly because the sample is rather small, and not accurate enough to be representative (97 routes representing the journey of 293 individuals: 51 routes (162 individuals) in France; 46 routes (131 individuals in Sweden), and partly because the surveys were conducted as an interview of the journey, and then the reactions and answers were so different that a traditional quantitative analysis probably would not contribute to the understanding of the visitors' behaviour.

The aim of the research induced a rather small sample size. As stated above, people generally stay at the gates of the parks particularly during the winter season. Studying cross-country skiers implies, however, that focus was on those few visitors entering the inner areas of the park. Moreover, a lack of snow in both places during the data collection period served to limit the sample size. Furthermore, the research was conducted in two countries allowing for estimating the influence of two different outdoor cultures. It is assumed that Swedes are closer to nature; meanwhile in France city dwellers' wilderness experience is rather limited.

Time–Space Use in Abisko and Vercors

The visitors

According to Decoupigny (2000), there is a clear distinction between hikers (who are going to spend at least a night in the natural area) and strollers (who promenade) regarding their abilities of movement and their wishes concerning nature experience. Table 7.1 offers a typology of the park users indicating differences between hikers and strollers and local and incoming visitors, respectively. The responses included visitors of almost all age groups and both genders. Males between 20 and 35 years old are represented more among the hiker category, where women are less represented, or alternatively teenagers accompanying adults. In general, visitors arrive in groups containing a variety of backgrounds and gender. Families often with children (even with young ones) predominantly use the parks. For many of them it is the first experience of wilderness and thus, they are taught in cross-country skiing or building igloos. The parks offer a rather safe arena for acquiring these skills. Therefore, the parks seem to become a kind of school to promote outdoor life experience including right behaviour and respect for the environment.

An important observation underlines that people tend to do only one activity, which is based on the mean of transportation, for instance: 'we came to ski, we came to practice snowshoes'. Actually few people had a second activity such as photography or scientific interest as other motives for visiting the parks. Hence, one can separate visitors who came for sporting reasons (ski or sport) and focus especially on training, and visitors who came for the pleasure to being in the peripheral location

Table 7.1 Main characteristics of the groups of hikers, strollers, tourists and locals

	Hiker	*Stroller*
Local	Short distance Weekend consumers Leave track easily	Long distance per day Early start Lonely person Second activity
Tourist	Long total distance Several days Group of friends Dependant on public transportation Trip schedule fixed Stay on tracks	Short distance per day Afternoon consumers Family Stay on tracks

(nature and relaxation) and focus especially on landscape and silence. Members of the local community came because they live in the area or because they have a cottage in the area.

Constraints on accessibility

The major spatial factor influencing the diffusion of visitors is distance. In fact the main difference between hikers and strollers is distance travelled during the entire itinerary. Strollers ski an average of 15km while hikers do an average trip around 25km. However, the median distances skied by ski-hikers and ski-strollers are almost the same, i.e. around 15km. Hence, a lot of hikers do not ski a longer total distance than strollers but usually reach a more remote point to spend a night and then return the day after. A huge difference appears when hikers spent more than one night in the field; then distances can be four or five times longer (40km to 100km). The distance by day is often shorter for the hikers (i.e. generally 10km) than the strollers, mainly because of the backpack carried.

Distance consumption is also dependant on cultural habits. In Sweden people ski longer, up to 150km, compared to France (rarely > 35km). The averages of distance consumption are significant (i.e. Vercors = 16,6km, Abisko = 24km). In France 37 journeys were done within a circle with a 4km radius centred at the car park (73% of the visitors). This limitation does not appear in Sweden. Swedish families with small children (from three years) manage journeys of 8km. In France similar trips are made with teenagers. Level of equipment may explain these differences, especially the *'pulka'* (sledge) commonly used in Sweden, which allows more people or equipment to be carried. Obviously, the differences derive from the long tradition in Sweden of spending time in natural areas during wintertime that is absent in France.

Topology and the physical constitution of the hikers form important constraints influencing the route choice. Throughout winter, climatic conditions allow people to go almost anywhere, as opposed to summertime when vegetation can form obstacles limiting access. During winter many borders disappear as lakes, rivers and vegetation are covered in ice or snow, but the quantity of snow builds new borders as much as it erases them ('we go everywhere, because there is so little snow'), or the modification of snow into ice strongly limits the recreational diffusion process ('we stayed on track because it was too icy').

Besides these physical constraints even emotional constraints play an important role. Partly, visitors long for adventurous situations and hence take detours, partly they stick to the tracks to avoid risks or perceived creepy situations. Beaten tracks appear to be attractive for strollers or less experienced hikers who do not feel confident about where they are going. A feeling of security is extremely important particularly in Sweden and among occasional strollers. Consequently, seeing other people will look appealing to a Swedish walker for security reasons while the French will deliberately try to escape from it.

If space plays an important role, time is obviously even more important for the route choice. Time is related to speed and hence, the accessibility of certain areas varies with the skills of the individual skier. The speed is a constraint to the possibility to reach a certain place or not. The speed depends on individual physical abilities and the weight of equipment carried. Hence visitors usually have some kind of time-budget identifyied start and end of the journey.

The continuity of everyday habits influences visitor groups in different ways. Strollers follow the normal time schedule, while hikers are more flexible. However, sleeping time forces the latter to reach a suitable place to be able to have a comfortable night. That is why they usually have a goal in their mind, and have to plan the trek in advance. Also within the parks certain rush hours occur. At the entrance visitors crowded between 10 and 11 a.m. for departure and between 4 and 5 p.m. for return. The rest areas become a point of crowding at lunchtime, causing complaints that other people are there, too. At the refuges the arrival time is usually around 5 p.m., even if some more experienced hikers can afford to arrive later.

Important stations

Some places have special effects on the behaviour of the visitors. They are important factors influencing the decision-making process of visitors. Several of these places can be identified (see Figure 7.1).

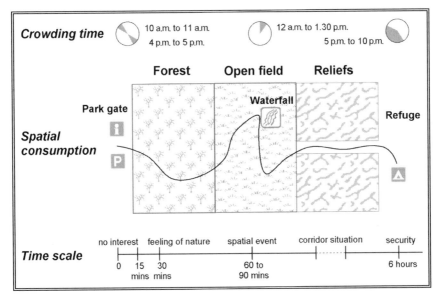

Figure 7.1 Typology of space and its influence on visitor behaviour

The gate: at the entrance the most significant impact can be spotted. Cars and noise disturbance are significant features. However, visitor number decreases with increasing distance from the entrance point.

The beginning of the track is usually a *space of non-interest*. From the non-mass-tourism entrance, within a distance of 500m almost no signs of dispersion can be seen, the tracks are narrow and well laid out. Visitors are not concerned too much with this type of surrounding because they are in a hurry to reach nature and leave civilisation behind. After a distance of 15 minutes walking, individuals experience the *feeling of real nature*: 'we came to experience the wilderness'.

The first major rest area is the first important *spatial event* people will encounter. A spatial event is a break in the continuity or pseudo-homogeneity of the space, i.e. a waterfall, lookout point, buildings or distinct landscape such as grassland, glade, and lakes. Sunny open fields in a middle of a forest allow for enjoying the scenery and make great places for a break. Usually people have their lunch, at around 12 o'clock. Hikers leave their backpacks there, and strollers decide to go back after the break.

Some zones influence heavily the behaviours of visitors; the shape of the milieu creates a *corridor situation*. Canyons and cliffs are the typical situation where it is possible to see a corridor. The path usually seems hazardous, and may be a heavy obstacle. Here people utter their feeling about wilderness.

An equipped area will provide the best place for the night, because of security and comfort on offer. Refuges or fireplaces always attract several parties and even self-equipped hikers find these more convenient to spend the night in these areas.

Routes

As a result altogether, four types of routes can be identified, each of them integrating some points of interest.

Tour and retour routes are typical for Sunday strolls and are the main choice in both countries. It is the main strategy for visitors who are not so interested by nature or landscape, but rather enjoy skiing or just to be out. The availability of a particular sight is extremely important. There the decision to return is made often rather spontaneously.

Circular routes are mainly used by strollers, and the start and finish are at the same point, usually at the car parks close to the gates of the park. Visitors interested in enjoying the nature and landscape usually employ this strategy, as access to a particular sight is extremely important. However, the sight does not form the extreme point of penetration. Designed circular tracks tend to link sights along the entire track.

Traverse routes, leaving from one point and arriving to another, are used by hikers only. In general such trips are well planned in advance, and follow a strict time schedule. The route can be off-piste, hikers use a map and compass or the area is well known to them. For security reasons hikers will never follow other tracks deliberately because 'you never know if the person who did the trail knew where he went'. The logistical problems are solved by using public transportation or by ordering a taxi, asking another person to come to pick them up or leaving a car close to the exit gate few days before. Such behaviour is observed in France.

Visitors who cannot take a traverse route for practical reasons and have to leave by the same gate typically use *randomised routes*. These are composed of several day trips in different directions.

Steps of colonisation

One main observation can be made regarding the diffusion of the visitors in space. Five steps in the diffusion process have been observed (see Figure 7.2).

(1) Pioneer: After an important snowfall, first marks are fine, and narrow and randomised. It is the opening of the wilderness. Often done by local people 'I did the first track of the season, and I will obviously do the last', the first track will follow the usual path, but it is difficult to distinguish the part of the habits, and the influence of the milieu.

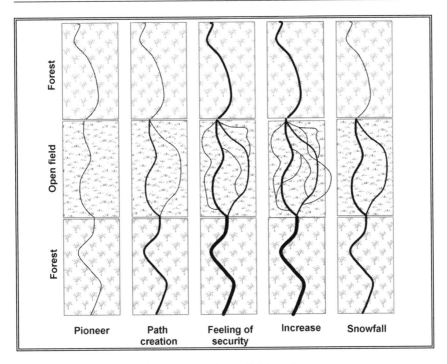

Figure 7.2 Steps of colonisation of a wild location

Nevertheless the first tracks will be an important factor for the diffusion of further visitors.

(2) Creation of paths: Day after day people continue to follow the pioneers' tracks. The repetitive pressure designs a strong path of approximately 30cm wide (ski tracks). In open or secure fields the main track gives birth to several new tracks more randomised and lighter. Those new tracks rejoin the main path since the open field is ending. The main track is often on the lowest part of the field or on the riverside, and the colonisation takes place time after time on slopes and riverbeds.

(3) Feeling of security: While the sun is shining, in open fields some of those free ways become deeper drawn into the landscape. It is quickly possible (generally no more than three days) to see several paths (narrower than the one before: 20cm wide), each of them giving birth to new lighter tracks and so on.

(4) Increase: Day after day, the sprawling of tracks colonises all the area and is becoming more and more adventurous. People begin to penetrate into the wood, go behind rocks, and use the riverbed. Starting generally by a short circular path, these new tracks become

increasingly randomised. Finally, these short-distance exploratory behaviours will be stopped with the next snowfall.

(5) Snowfall: After a new snowfall, only the main tracks remain visible. Over the next days, the consumption will be re-concentrated on it. The main paths are quickly reaching 70cm to 1m wide (especially within a forest setting). Then a new cycle begins influenced by the precedent impacts. The main paths are now designed and will stay for the entire season.

The main difference between strollers and hikers is that hikers almost always have precise ideas about where they want to go, while strollers just come to have a promenade. Strollers improvise in relation to the milieu. The decision on the way to go is taken step by step. But the milieu constraints are stronger on stroller behaviour. This is obviously dependent on the knowledge of the area but also on the available equipment. People with limited knowledge are more or less tied to existing tracks and do not try to leave them, although episodic *exploratory* detours can be observed. On the other hand, hikers avoid following tracks when they are in the deep zone. During the first part they use the classical track to enter into *nature* faster. Then the diffusion becomes completely randomised and dispersed (especially in France), with one track for each group. In Sweden the main track is followed for longer because of distribution of refuges designing a corridor and probably due to the relative natural dangers from the environment. When there is a choice between two tracks, visitors usually take the wider one, because it looks more interesting, safe or logical. If there are two trails and one of them bends, people generally follow the straighter one.

Climate appears to be most important for all visitors: on sunny days there are higher peaks of visitation. But weather does not look like a strong limiting factor. Having put aside local people who are able to choose the best conditions for their consumption, the observations indicate visitors come in any climatic situation. However, strollers adapt the time of consumption in relation to what the weather looks like, and a sudden change of the weather conditions brings about an effect on the decision to return earlier than expected. Hikers are prepared for any conditions and long-distance hikers do not care at all about weather conditions.

Conclusions

The consumption of a fragile environment tends to become a new fashion supported by the development of the democratisation of long distance transportation facilities. The peripheral areas are becoming accessible and tend to be rather attractive.

Wilderness is mainly consumed for enjoyment and nature experiences. In the protected areas, the essential activities are actually composed by different types of walking, and the impacts they have on the surrounding are rather similar and apparently inexistent. The diffusion of visitors depends on their goals and their capacities to respond to environmental characteristics. At a first examination, the behaviours related to *what people do* and *where people go* seem to be randomised. But it has been found that space, time and social constraints seem to be rather common among the visitors: special areas concentrate people and visitors follow certain patterns. Even if the consumers' behaviour had not been categorised, the categories would have emerged during the analysis. Following two axes based on activity (hikers or strollers) and origin (local or tourist) of individuals, the behaviours observed in the field have been divided into various categories.

The similarities between French and Swedes are numerous, but some differences clearly appear regarding the distance of consumption and the knowledge of natural areas. It is important to take into consideration that those dissimilarities may be a result of the remoteness of Abisko compared to Vercors, which is located in the middle of a dense urban system. Visitors coming to Abisko are generally more experienced regarding wilderness.

Park management offices have to consider the activities practiced within the inner area in order to conciliate nature protection and tourism. The opening of the area to diverse consumptions tends to create problems of duality between activities. The role of the management offices is to bring in solutions to avoid the problems. Using forecasts for such work can be a relevant support to their management and decision-making.

References

Abrahamsson, K.-V. (1998) Sounds of silence? The dispute over snowmobiling in the Swedish mountains. In Sandberg, L.A. and Sörlin, S. (eds) *Sustainability: The Challenge – People, Power and the Environment* (pp. 130–8). Montreal: Black Rose.

Bäck, L. (1993) Torneträskområdet. In Aldskogius, H. (ed.) *Kulturliv, rekreation och turism*. National Atlas of Sweden (pp. 106–7). Stockholm: SNA.

Boyd, S.W. (2000) Tourism, national parks and sustainability. In Butler, R.W. and Boyd, S.W. (eds) *Tourism and National Parks* (pp. 161–86). Chichester: Wiley.

Boyd, S.W. and Butler, R.W. (2000) Tourism and national parks: The origin of the concept. In Butler, R.W. and Boyd, S.W. (eds) *Tourism and National Parks* (pp. 13–27). Chichester: Wiley.

Butler, R.W. and Boyd, S.W. (2000) Tourism and parks – a long but uneasy relationship. In Butler, R.W. and Boyd, S.W. (eds) *Tourism and National Parks* (pp. 3–11). Chichester: Wiley.

Chardonnel, S. (1999) *Emplois du temps et de l'espace: Pratiques des populations dans une station touristique de montagne*. Ph.D. thesis. Grenoble: IGA.

Christaller, W. (1963) Some considerations of tourism in Europe: The peripheral regions – underdeveloped countries – recreation areas. *Regional Science Association Papers* 12, 95–105.

Decoupigny, F. (2000) *Accès et diffusion des visiteurs sur les espaces naturels: Modélisation et simulations prospectives.* Ph.D. thesis. Tours: CESA.

Glyptis, S. (1991) *Countryside Recreation.* Harlow: Longman.

Godde, P.M., Price, M.F. and Zimmermann, F.M. (2000) Tourism and development in mountain regions: Moving forward into the new millennium. In Godde, P.M., Price, M.F. and Zimmermann, F.M. (eds) *Tourism and Development in Mountain Regions* (pp. 1–25). Wallingford: CABI.

Goodwin, H. (2000) Tourism, national parks and partnerships. In Butler, R.W. and Boyd, S.W. (eds) *Tourism and National Parks* (pp. 245–62). Chichester: Wiley.

Groff, C. (1998) Demarketing in park and recreation management, *Managing Leisure* 3, 128–35.

Hall, C.M. (1992) *Wasteland to World Heritage: Preserving Australia's Wilderness.* Melbourne: Melbourne University Press.

Hall, C.M. and Jenkins, J.M. (1998) The policy dimension of rural tourism and recreation. In Butler, R., Hall, C.M. and Jenkins, J. (eds) *Tourism and Recreation in Rural Areas* (pp. 19–42). Chichester: Wiley.

Hall, C.M. and Page, S.J. (2002) *The Geography of Tourism and Recreation: Environment, Place and Space* (2nd edn). London: Routledge.

Jenkins, J.M., Hall, C.M. and Troughton, M. (1998) The restructuring of rural economies: Rural tourism and recreation as government response. In Butler, R., Hall, C.M. and Jenkins, J. (eds) *Tourism and Recreation in Rural Areas* (pp. 43–68). Chichester: Wiley.

Kaloara, B. (1993) *Le musée vert: Radiographie du loisir en foret.* Paris: L'Harmattan.

Kearsley, G. and Coughlan, D. (1999) Coping with crowding: Tourist displacement in the New Zealand backcountry. *Current Issues in Tourism* 2, 174–96.

Lazzarotti, O. (1995) *Les loisirs à la conquête des espace périurbains.* Paris: L'Harmattan.

Lindberg, K., Denstadli, J.M., Fredman, P., Heldt, T. and Vuorio, T. (2001) Skiers and snowmobilers in södra Jämtlandsfjällen: Are there recreation conflicts? *ETOUR Working Paper* 2001: 12. Östersund: Etour.

Nilsson, P.Å. (2001) Tourist destination development: The Åre valley. *Scandinavian Journal of Hospitality and Tourism* 1, 54–67.

Patmore, J.A. (1983) *Recreation and Resources.* Oxford: Blackwell.

Pedersen, K. and Viken, A. (1996) From Sami nomadism to global tourism. In Price, M.F. (ed.) *People and Tourism in Fragile Environments* (pp. 69–88). Chichester: Wiley.

Sandell, K. (1995) Access to the 'North': But to what and for whom? Public access in the Swedish countryside and the case of a proposed national park in the Kiruna mountains. In Hall, C.M. and Johnston, M.E. (eds) *Polar Tourism: Tourism in the Arctic and Antarctic Regions* (pp. 131–45). Chichester: Wiley.

Sowman, P. and Pearce, D. (2000) Tourism, national parks and visitor management. In Butler, R.W. and Boyd, S.W. (eds) *Tourism and National Parks* (pp. 223–43). Chichester: Wiley.

Townsend, A.R. (1997) *Making a Living in Europe: Human Geographies of Economic Change.* London: Routledge.

Chapter 8

The Importance of Health as a Factor in Achieving Sustainability in a High Altitude Destination of a Less Developed Country: A Case Study of Sagarmatha National Park, Nepal

GHAZALI MUSA

Introduction

Nepal is renowned as one of the most important adventure, cultural and ecotourism (ACE) destinations in the world. Its main attractions are the highest mountain range in the world, the Himalayas, which include the world's highest mountain, Sagarmatha. Trekking and mountaineering activities contribute most to the country's economy in terms of longer stay and spending distribution. Many have regarded trekking tourism in Nepal as one of the foremost examples of ecotourism operation (e.g. Gurung & DeCoursey, 1994). This is mainly due to its being nature-based and involving the local population. However, the ACE tourism product is fragile and requires proper management to ensure its sustainability. One of the main components of sustainable tourism is mitigating the impact of the tourism. Impact does not just harm the destination alone, it also affects tourist satisfaction. This chapter examines several of these issues in reference to Sagarmatha National Park (SNP), particularly with respect to health.

The chapter begins with a review of trekking tourism in Nepal, tourism and its impact in SNP and health issues in high altitude destinations. Research justification is given in view of the apparent neglect among tourism researchers of incorporating health issues and sustainable tourism management in their research on many peripheral areas, which are often poorly serviced in health infrastructure. This is followed by a brief description of methodology. Finally the results, conclusions and recommendations are given and discussed.

Trekking tourism in Nepal

Nepal is blessed with many cultural and natural attractions. However, overarching all the attractions are the mountains that make the country outstanding for most people and that generate high levels of international tourist demand. Eight of the 14 mountains in the world over 8000 metres are in Nepal including the world's highest, Sagarmatha (Mount Everest).

Since the opening of the country to foreigners in 1953 (Belk, 1993), Nepal has gradually replaced its image as a hippy destination in the 1960s with its present image of a mountain and adventure tourism destination, which began to emerge in the mid-1970s (Simmons & Koirala, 2000). Even though the majority of tourists visit Nepal for holiday and pleasure, trekkers and mountaineers who account for 23% of all the visitors, are regarded as the most important market in economic terms (Cockerell, 1997). Zurick (1992) claims that 80% of tourists could have engaged in some form of ecotourism activity in which on most occasions trekking is involved. Trekkers also stayed longer, on average 25.8 nights, compared with 9.3 nights by other tourists in 1990 (Parker, 1993). Even though they spent only US$24.72/day compared with other tourists (US$47.69/day), their longer duration of stay accumulates higher total spending. Their spending not only occurs in Kathmandu valley but also in the rural areas and improves the economy of the relatively deprived mountain people.

Since National Parks in Nepal are inhabited, in order to ensure sustainable tourism development the involvement of local people in managing the Park is crucial (Gurung & DeCoursey, 1994). Gurung and DeCoursey (1994) and Barracharya (1998) stress that the involvement of local people in decision-making has brought great success in the Annapurna region, which has set a prime example of ecotourism management throughout the world.

Among trekkers, 58.2% visited the Annapurna Conservation Area, while SNP and Langtang were visited by 17.5% and 10.6% respectively (Simmons & Koirala, 2000). SNP however, is the most important area in the promotion of Nepal as a tourist destination, and this may be attributable to the internationally promoted image of Sagarmatha itself. A great many researchers, travel writers and journalists from every corner of the globe flock into the Park to discover and experience the high mountain ranges and the culture of the people living in it. However, the area has been widely reported as suffering serious impacts from tourism development such as deforestation, pollution and cultural degradation as discussed below.

Tourism in SNP

SNP was established in 1976 with the help of the New Zealand government and was inscribed as a World Heritage Site in 1979 for its outstanding natural and cultural attributes (Rogers, 1997). The area covers 1148 square kilometres extending north to the Tibetan border. The altitude of the area varies from 2805 metres at the entrance of the Park to 8848 metres at the peak of Mount Sagarmatha.

The Park is inhabited by approximately 3000 Sherpas who migrated from eastern Tibet in the 16th century (Brower, 1991; Rogers, 1997). In the centuries since, they had been relying on subsistence farming, livestock grazing and trading with Tibet. When China closed its trading border in 1959, trekking and mountaineering gradually became the mainstay of the Khumbu economy (Furer-Haimendorf, 1984; Stevens, 1993; Brower 1991; Rogers, 1997). The growth of tourism activities was spurred by the opening of Lukla airstrip in the region (Robinson, 1992), and the opening of the area to visitors other than mountaineers (Stevens, 1993).

According to the secondary data taken from the registration book at the entrance of SNP tourist arrivals to the region have increased at the rate of 13% yearly (Musa, 2002). The total number of tourists visiting

Table 8.1 Tourist arrivals to SNP by nationality, 1999

Nationality	Percentage (n = 2456)
USA	18.2%
UK	14.7%
Japan	11.7%
Germany	9.7%
Australia	8.4%
France	6.0%
Canada	5.3%
Holland	3.0%
Switzerland	3.0%
Austria	2.2%
Italy	2.1%
New Zealand	2.0%
Belgium	1.5%
Sweden	1.4%
Spain	1.2%
Czech Republic	1.2%
Israel	1.1%
Denmark	1.1%
Others	6.2%

SNP in 1999 amounted to 24,651 (Musa, 2002). The number has far exceeded the carrying capacity suggested by Gurung (1991) of 15,000.

The most numerous tourist arrivals to SNP by nationality were USA, UK, Japan, Germany and Australia (Table 8.1). Males constitute 63.3% of tourists while females 36.7%. The average stay in the Park was calculated to be 12.7 days. The main age group of tourists to SNP was 30–39.

Tourism Impact in SNP

SNP is the subject of many studies and reports in literature. Most are based on qualitative research in the forms of observations, interviews, literature-based reviews and personal experiences. Anthropology is the most widely discussed subject in the SNP literature (Sherpa, 1982; Bjoness, 1983; Pawson *et al.*, 1984; Draper, 1988; Fisher, 1990; Brower, 1991; Adams, 1992; Stevens, 1993). The discussion surrounds the origin of Sherpas, their religion and culture and their adaptation to the introduction of tourism development in the region. The cultural impact of tourism is also reported extensively in the literature. Tourism is reported as having had a negative impact upon traditional customs and ways of life (Jefferies, 1982; Pandey, 1994); upon community and agro-pastoral systems (Bjoness, 1983; Draper, 1988; Brower, 1991; Stevens & Sherpa, 1992); and upon monastic activities (Bjoness, 1983; Furer-Haimendorf, 1984). However, Adams (1992), Fisher (1990) and Robinson (1997) argue that the local inhabitants have adapted remarkably well to tourism development with no significant loss of culture. The current changes in Sherpa culture are therefore likely to be caused more by ongoing processes of modernization, of which tourism is only one element.

Deforestation in SNP is another major issue that is constantly being referred to in the literature. Hinrichson *et al.* (1983), Bjoness (1983) and Jefferies (1982) express their concern that tourism development has caused serious deforestation in SNP. However, later research by Houston (1987), Stevens (1993), Baker (1993) and Ledgard (1994) argue that previous writers often exaggerate deforestation within the Park and are of the view that the issue is now not a serious problem. This view is supported by the studies by the New Zealand Forestry Research Institute (Rogers, 1997) and analysis of photographic evidence from 1962 to 1984 by Byers (1987).

Crowding has increasingly been a matter of grave concern in SNP especially during peak season (October and November) and spring season (March and April) (Rogers, 1997; Musa, 2002). As mentioned above, tourist arrivals to the SNP have been increasing at a phenomenal rate (13% yearly) and by now exceed the proposed carrying capacity of 15,000 tourists. Ghazali Musa (2002) describes that during peak season, every day there was an average of 400 tourists entering the Park, and this does not include porters, guides or animals (used for carrying trekkers' luggage). Traffic jams are often encountered along the trekking trails causing further widening to the track as well the creation of short-cuts (Nepal, 2000). Tourist numbers not only cause pressures to the service providers but also inflate the prices to the point that ordinary locals find unaffordable (Stevens, 1993).

Without any dissenting voices, many researchers have always reported waste and sewage disposal as a most serious impact of tourism in SNP (Pandey, 1994; Lachapelle, 1995; Rogers, 1997; Rogers & Aitchinson, 1998; Weaver, 1998; Nepal, 2000; Musa, 2002). Weaver (1998) points out that much of the waste disposal and sanitation problem in SNP is attribut-able to the behaviour and attitudes of the Sherpas themselves, rather than tourists. Lachapelle (1995) observes that many toilets in SNP are not maintained, are completely full and have effluent leaking into nearby water sources. Ghazali Musa (2002) reports that human excreta are a common sight on the ground of Namche weekly market, which is one of the most important cultural attractions in the Park. The exami-nation of SNP water sources also found that they are heavily contaminated by Coliform bacteria, which is enough to produce illness (Pandey, 1994; Lachapelle, 1995; Rogers, 1997). Contaminated water sources, unhygienic sanitary practices together with ignorance of public health consequences as a result of the low literacy rate result in many food-borne diseases, such as diarrhoea and hepatitis A among others, being endemic. Thus, all tourists in SNP are at risk of getting ill.

The other important issue that is relatively neglected by tourism research in SNP is health and safety. A study by Pandey (1994) demon-strates that tourists are not satisfied with the availability of information centres and signposts. There are some trekkers who have disappeared in the Park and who have never been found. Health issues among tourists in SNP is one of the main concerns currently being addressed by several non-governmental organizations such as Kathmandu Environmental and Educational Project, Himalayan Rescue Association and the Himalayan Trust. It is also a matter of concern among service providers (Gurung *et al.*, 1996). Pandey (1994) stated that almost half of tourists (46.7%) reported that they had some health problems such as diarrhoea, head-ache, altitude sickness and respiratory infection. Health ailments have reduced the satisfaction level of 50% of the visitors surveyed by Pandey. Pandey (1994) acknowledges the lack of local knowledge and awareness regarding hygiene and sanitation and safe waste and sewage disposal. Pandey (1994) finds visitors were highly satisfied with the visit. In his view visitors expected these poor conditions and they did not affect their satisfaction, as anticipated expectations of a destination are a determinant of the actual satisfaction.

All the studies conducted in SNP are of the Park and of the local people. Even though tourists have contributed substantially to the development of the region, and foreign aid has increased the social well-being of the local community, there has been no study looking solely at the welfare of the tourists. Pandey (1994) puts equal emphasis on tourists and local people in measuring their attitudes towards tourism development in SNP. The apparent neglect in researching the needs of the tourist has to be addressed as part of the sustainable development of tourism in SNP. This would help to ensure that tourist motivations are fulfilled and their holidays provide the satisfaction they hope for and also contribute to the sustainability of tourism in the region (Figure 8.1). Health is beyond any doubt one the most important issues faced by tourists in SNP. The sheer isolation of the mountains also removes tourists from easy access to health facilities, and such health facilities as there are may be limited.

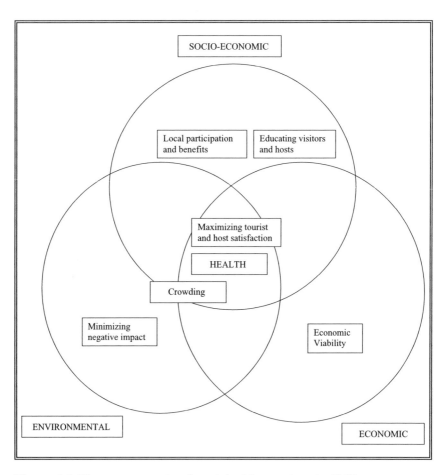

Figure 8.1 The components of sustainable tourism in SNP

Health Issues in High Altitude Regions

Most studies of tourist health have been conducted in low altitude environments. Thus, it is widely assumed that the most common travel-associated ailment is diarrhoea (Clark & Clift, 1996; Cartwright, 1996; Rudkin & Hall, 1996; Steffen, 1997). However, in two separate medical reports by Maundalexix (1992) and Pollard and Murdoch (1997), mountain sickness is stated to be the most common complaint among trekkers in the SNP (67% and 84% respectively). In 1997, 67% of hospital admissions at Kunde (the only hospital in SNP) among tourists were due to mountain sickness (Heydon, 1998). However, a significant feature of mountain sickness is that it is totally preventable by recognizing the symptoms and avoiding certain risky behaviours.

A high altitude destination is defined as any place at 2500 metres and above (Ward *et al.*, 1995; Pollard & Murdoch, 1997). The major effect of high altitude upon human physiology is the decrease in oxygen pressure and consequently the decreased content of oxygen in the arterial blood (Hultgren, 1997). The low oxygen concentration subsequently received by the body causes symptoms of acute mountain sickness (AMS). A definition of AMS was proposed by a consensus committee that met at the International Hypoxia Symposium in 1991 as 'in the setting of a recent gain in altitude, the presence of headache and at least one of the following symptoms: gastro-intestinal (anorexia, nausea, vomiting), fatigue or weakness, dizziness or light-headedness, difficulty in sleeping (insomnia)' (Hultgren, 1997: 219). Acclimatization is the process by which individuals gradually adjust to the low pressure of oxygen at high altitude (Pollard & Murdoch, 1997). Therefore, mountain sickness symptoms can be avoided by taking a slow and gradual ascent to the high altitude in order to allow sufficient time for the body to adjust to the gradual reduction in oxygen pressure. The incidence of mountain sickness is observed as being higher in organized groups with Shlim and Gallie (1992) arguing that this is caused by the competitive spirit of group members. At high altitude, alcohol, sleeping pills and narcotics should be avoided as they may slow down the breathing pattern while sleeping at night, and this will contribute to mountain sickness (Zafren, 2000). Two dangerous progressions of acute mountain sickness are HAPE (high altitude pulmonary oedema) and HACE (high altitude cerebral oedema). The former gives severe lung symptoms while the latter shows the signs of brain involvement. Both conditions warrant immediate descent. Ignoring the symptoms can be fatal.

Diarrhoea is one of the most common ailments experienced by tourists in SNP (Ali, 1991; Pandey, 1994; Heydon, 1998). This is mainly due to improper sewage systems, unsafe water supply and lack of knowledge regarding proper hygiene and sanitation in food preparation (Musa,

2002). Lachapelle (1995) expresses concern on serious shortcomings relating to the way in which lodges manage human waste. There is no effective monitoring system for human waste management in SNP. Namche, for example has a high and growing concentration of residents and tourists with no effective sewage system. According to Pandey (1994), rivers and streams in SNP are increasingly contaminated because of the lack of sanitary waste disposal. Of SNP population, 95% is hepatitis A positive, which is a strong indicator of the appalling hygiene (Heydon, 1998). This should therefore warn tourists that they have to be very careful while consuming food and drink in SNP.

In high altitude the exposure to dry air may injure the lining of the respiratory system and cause the symptoms of coughing and respiratory infection (Zafren, 2000). Due to low oxygen pressure any illnesses or injuries at high altitude will take a longer time to heal (Zafren, 2000). Harris *et al.* (1998) state that with increased elevation, the temperature will drop and expose the tourist to hypothermia and frostbite. The increase of elevation will result in the increase of UV exposure causing susceptibility to sunburn and therefore skin cancer. Other common medical conditions especially among mountain climbers are accidents (e.g. fall) and snow blindness (Shlim & Gallie, 1992; Pollard & Murdoch, 1997).

Research Justification

As discussed in the literature review, tourism in SNP inflicts considerable impacts which threaten its future sustainability. The review reveals that the main interest in tourism research and publications has been the impact of tourism on SNP itself either environmentally or the sociocultural changes inflicted on the region as the result of the tourism. Despite the magnitude of health impact on tourists who visit the region as reported by medical literature, there has been no research on this aspect of tourism and its place as an important component of sustainable tourism management. The main aim of this study is therfore to investigate travel health and sustainable development relationships in a peripheral high altitude region via examination of the factors shown in Figure 8.2 and their interrelationships.

Methodology

Data collection was achieved by a personally administered self-completion questionnaire. The content of the questionnaire aimed to explore the aspects of demographic profile, travel motivation, travel anticipation, health ailments and tourist satisfaction, and the interconnections of these aspects. The demographic profiles measured were nationality, age, gender, types of travel, high altitude experiences, forms

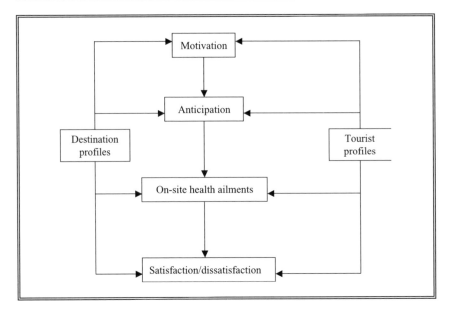

Figure 8.2 Travel health experience

of accommodation, educational attainment, season of travel and the use of porters. Thirty motivational variables were included in the survey based on a review of relevant literature, informal interviews, personal experience from fieldwork in the region and pilot testing. The variables were adapted from both general travel motivations (Moutinho, 1987; Prentice, 1993) and more specific travel motivation in mountain settings (Bratton *et al.*, 1979; Ewert, 1985), which includes the motivation of travel to SNP by Pandey (1994). Tourists were asked to provide their pre-travel preparation in terms of travel insurance, immunization and travel information. Tourists were also given the list of symptoms to be ticked should they have experienced those symptoms while travelling in the region. Overall satisfaction was measured using the five-point Likert scale. Seventeen individual variables of satisfaction were also measured using the five-point Likert scale. Open-ended questions were provided in the form of the most important activities, the best and the worst aspects of their visit and general comment.

Questionnaires were distributed personally by the researcher at the Jorsalle Entrance of SNP. A total of 750 questionnaires were given out to those who had completed their trek in the Park during three separate seasons (rainy, peak and winter seasons) in 1999, over a period of nine months. The sample was chosen randomly and only a maximum of ten tourists were given questionnaires in one day. Respondents were given the option of returning the completed questionnaire either by hand or by mail at various places: the Lukla Airport (the main airport exit out of SNP), the Himalaya Lodge in Lukla and several designated offices in Kathmandu. Four hundred and forty-eight usable questionnaires were returned and the response rate was calculated as 59.7%. Data were analysed using SPSS Version 10. Various statistical methods such as frequency analysis, chi-square, *t*-test and factor analysis were applied in order to investigate the connections and the significance of the findings.

Results

Demographic profiles

The greatest number of tourists to SNP as shown in Table 8.2 is from UK (20.4%). This is followed by USA (18.1%), Australia (9.6%), France (6.7%) and Spain (6.3%). These statistics are quite similar to the secondary data from the SNP entrance (Table 8.1), except for the low representation of Japanese tourists (2.7%) due to the use of only English questionnaires. Thus the sample of this study is a close representation of tourist arrivals in SNP.

Tourists from Europe represent the largest group in SNP (56.4%). North America represents 21.3% of the total tourists while Australasia 13.5%. 'Others' represent 8.8% of the total tourists in SNP.

Males constitute 60.6% of the tourists to SNP and females 39.4%. The majority of tourists in SNP are young. Most (42.0%) are within the 20–29 years, while 27.6% are within 30–39 years age group. The result differs from the secondary data where the biggest age representation is from 30–39 years. The higher percentages of females in this study compared to the secondary data (36.7%) and those with the age group of 20–29 may indicate that female and young tourists are more willing to respond by returning the completed questionnaires.

Most tourists to SNP are graduates (43.2%) or postgraduates (24.1%). The majority of tourists are first-timers (91.5%) and only some of 8.5% are repeat tourists. Organized groups constitute 38.8% of all tourists while FITs (free and independent travellers) constitute 61.2%. Most tourists (79.0%) in SNP stay in teahouses or lodges while 19.4% stay in tents. The majority of FITs (93.4%) stay in teahouses and lodges as opposed to 58.1% organized group tourists ($\chi^2 = 84.530$ df=3, $p \leq 0.001$). The services of porters are used by 62.9% of tourists.

In rating high altitude experience, the majority of tourists – 51.8% – consider themselves as 'novice'. 'Intermediate' (experience) tourists constitute 35.9% while only 12.3% rate themselves as 'experienced' tourists. Novice tourists are greater among the age group of 20–29 years old, and 'experienced' tourist are mainly from 30–39 years old

Table 8.2 Tourist arrivals in SNP by nationality

Tourist arrivals by nationality (n = 447)	Percentage
UK	20.4%
USA	18.1%
Australia	9.6%
France	6.7%
Spain	6.3%
Germany	4.7%
New Zealand	3.8%
Switzerland	3.6%
Holland	3.1%
Canada	3.1%
Japan	2.7%
Sweden	2.2%
Denmark	2.2%
India	1.3%
Ireland	1.1%
Czech Republic	1.1%
Finland	1.1%
Belgium	0.9%
Korea	0.9%
Others	6.9%

(χ^2 = 32.781 df = 10, $p \leq$ 0.001). Males tend to rate themselves higher in terms of high altitude experience than females (χ^2 = 6.945 df = 2, p = 0.031). The majority of trekkers (81.3%) enter SNP by flying to Lukla and trek to the Jorsalle Entrance. Of the other trekkers, 16.3% walk from Jiri, while 2.5% enter through Tashilabca. Since Lukla Airport is situated well above high altitude level (2600 meters), tourists do not have opportunity to acclimatize gradually to high altitude. Most tourists in SNP (76.3%) have never been to high altitude before coming to the Park. Only 23.7% had experience in high altitude in the past.

Travel Motivation

The top five motivations among tourists to SNP are 'to enjoy scenic beauty' (4.67), 'to trek/climb mountains' (4.33), 'to widen one's experience' (4.17), 'to view Sagarmatha' (4.16) and 'to encounter wilderness/

untouched nature' (3.96) (see Table 8.3). This observation is almost similar to Pandey (1994) who found 'trekking', 'viewing scenery' 'to see Mount Everest' and 'experiencing culture' as the top four reasons for visiting SNP.

Risk-taking motivations that predispose travellers to the incidence of mountain sickness are not considered as the main motivation of the visits to SNP. Travel for the element of 'risk' is generally not an important motivation (mean = 2.70). However, a gentler wording of risk-taking motivation, for example 'to be adventurous', is rated fairly high (mean = 3.80). This is concomitant with Bratton *et al.* (1979) who state that tourists are not actively seeking risk, but rather enjoying the adventure activity wherein the element of risk is a component of their recreational activities. Travel motivation 'for spiritual reasons' (2.84) and 'to be closer to God' (2.01) are among the lowest motivations to visit SNP. This is similar to Pandey's (1994) finding that only 4.0% of tourists visited SNP for spiritual and religious reasons. Tourists to the region are also less motivated by the need to be 'alone' (2.84), which signifies a strong social dimension among tourists.

Motivation items in this study have been chosen based on literature, personal conversation and pilot testing. The items are classified into several meaningful and correlated groups using factor analysis. Bartlett's test of sphericity is significant (χ^2 = 2782.835 df = 190, $p \leq 0.001$) and Kaiser-Meyer Olkin is 0.802, and these prove that the sample is adequate for factor analysis. Several motivation variables are excluded during the analysis as they do not contribute a strong connection to the grouping. As presented in Table 8.4, six motivation components are derived with a cumulative percentage of rotation sums of squared loadings of 65.951%. These are 'risk-taking motivation', 'cultural', and 'spiritual', 'to get away', 'sightseeing' and 'social'. All factor loadings of the motivation variables that contribute to motivation components are greater than 0.60, which indicates that each item has strong contribution to the groups (components) to which they belong.

Reliability coefficient alpha test shows strong internal consistency for 'risk-taking motivation' (0.8491), 'cultural' (0.7768) and 'spiritual' (0.8302). However internal consistency for 'to get away' (0.6197) is moderate, and is weak for 'sightseeing' (0.4694) and 'social' (0.3129). Thus in further statistical analysis, the results from using the last two motivation components have to be treated with caution.

Travel Anticipation

Some 85.0% of tourists to SNP purchase travel insurance while 12.5% do not. The percentage of tourists who do not know whether or not their travel is covered by insurance is 2.5%. Less educated tourists are

Table 8.3 Travel motivation of tourists in SNP

Motivation	N	Mean	SD
To enjoy scenic beauty	445	4.67	0.63
To trek/climb mountains	447	4.33	0.88
To widen my experience	445	4.17	0.95
To view Sagarmatha	447	4.16	0.98
To encounter wilderness/untouched nature	448	3.96	1.02
For a totally new and different experience	448	3.84	1.15
To take photographs	446	3.81	1.12
To be adventurous	447	3.80	1.08
To appreciate flora/fauna	446	3.79	1.04
To get away from life's pressure	447	3.74	1.19
To meet and socialize with local people	447	3.72	1.01
To enjoy the company of friends and family	446	3.72	1.21
For my personal development	444	3.64	1.18
To relax and rejuvenate	444	3.61	1.15
To learn about Sherpa culture	445	3.47	1.03
To enjoy a leisurely walk	445	3.35	1.25
To test my physical strength and endurance	447	3.30	1.27
A break from modern technology	446	3.29	1.31
To visit gompas and monasteries	446	3.24	1.09
To do things which only few could do	444	3.15	1.26
To meet and socialize with other trekkers	447	3.00	1.15
To learn how to cope with difficult situations	443	2.99	1.19
To test against challenges of nature	447	2.93	1.29
To experience solitude	443	2.85	1.31
To learn about Buddhism	446	2.84	1.25
To test my mental skill	446	2.76	1.28
To experience the element of risk	447	2.70	1.22
For spiritual reasons	448	2.26	1.35
To be alone	446	2.84	1.25
To be closer to God	447	2.01	1.29

Note: Measured by the five-point Likert scale (1 = not at all interested, 2 = not interested, 3 = neutral, 4 = interested and 5 = very interested). In bold letters are the risk-taking motivations.

Table 8.4 Motivation components derived from motivation variables by factor analysis of tourists to SNP

Motivation variables	Motivation components					
	Risk-taking motivation	Cultural	Spiritual	To get away	Sightseeing	Social
To test my physical strength and endurance	0.902					
To test against challenges of nature	0.873					
To test my mental skill	0.819					
To undertake strenuous activities	0.656					
The element of risk involved	0.609					
To learn about Sherpa culture		0.828				
To learn about Buddhism		0.750				
To meet and socialize with local people		0.718				
To visit gompas and monasteries		0.710				
For spiritual reasons			0.872			
To be closer to God			0.866			
A break from modern technology				0.769		
To get away from life's pressure				0.727		
To view Mount Everest					0.745	
To take photographs					0.729	
To enjoy the company of friends and relatives						0.744
To relax and rejuvenate						0.652
Reliability coefficient alpha	0.8491	0.7768	0.8302	0.6197	0.4694	0.3129

more likely to purchase travel insurance ($\chi^2 = 18.918$ d$f = 10$, $p = 0.041$). Before travelling to SNP, the majority of tourists (78.3%) had immunization and 21.7% had not. Age, sex, educational attainment and type of travel do not have a significant relationship with level of immunization.

The majority (85.0%) of tourists to SNP had access to information regarding health precautions and health consequences of visiting the area while 15.0% did not have access to this information. Among those who received information regarding health precautions they rate very low on 'spiritual' ($t = -2.932$ d$f = 426$, $p = 0.004$). The major source of health information (70.5%) of tourists to SNP is travel books (see Table 8.5). This is followed by doctors/paramedics (42.6%), friends/relatives (35.1%) and own experience (23.7%).

These findings are markedly different from Clift *et al.* (1997) where they found most health advice to tourists came from doctors/paramedics (66.4%) from general practitioners and 43.4% from nurses). They also found lower reliance on friends and relatives (23.9%), compared with this study (35.1%). In SNP even though Nepal has made it compulsory for trekking agents to distribute health information to trekkers (Musa, 2002), only 17.2% of trekkers obtained information from them. Travel agents gave health information to only 10.5% of the tourists to SNP. This is a much lower percentage than in Clift *et al.* (1997) who found that 23.0% gained information from travel agents. Himalayan Rescue Association

Table 8.5 Health information sources of tourists to SNP

Information sources	*Frequency*	*Percentage*
Travel books	315	70.5
Doctors/paramedics	190	42.6
Friends/relatives	157	35.1
Own experience	106	23.7
Internet	105	23.5
Trekking agents	77	17.2
Travel agents	47	10.5
Information centre	37	8.3
Brochures	32	7.2
Himalayan Rescue Association (HRA)	14	3.1
Video	7	1.6
Sagarmatha Pollution Control Committee (SPCC)	5	1.1

(HRA) which is one of the main non-governmental organizations responsible for providing health facilities in SNP and educating tourists on safe trekking only reached 3.1% of the trekkers.

Most tourists in SNP are self-sufficient in terms of first-aid treatment. 82.0% of the tourists carry their own first-aid kit. Tourists also noted (21.6%) that someone in their group carried a first-aid kit. FITs (85.2%) are more likely to carry a first-aid kit than organized tours (77.0%) (χ^2 = 4.865 df = 1, p = 0.027). The most common items carried in the first-aid kit by tourists to SNP are plasters/bandages (81.8%). This is followed by diarrhoea treatment (79.0%) and painkillers (72.7%). Acetazolamide, which is the only proven drug to prevent mountain sickness, is carried by 40.0% of tourists.

Health Ailments Experienced in SNP

In general, 88.9% of tourists visiting SNP experience one or more health ailments. Table 8.6 lists details of the kinds of ailments experienced by tourists in SNP and marks in bold those that are symptoms of mountain sickness. Headache, which is the main symptom of mountain sickness, is the most common ailment experienced by tourists in SNP (61.0%). The incidence of headache is much higher than indicated in other travel health studies such as the 42.7% among students in New Zealand (Ryan & Robertson, 1997), 20% among British tourists in Malta (Clark & Clift, 1996) and 14.2% among British tourists to the Gambia (Clift *et al.*, 1997). The higher incidence of headache can be further differentiated by the fact that the incidence of the ailment is strongly related to the consumption of alcohol among tourists sampled by Ryan and Robertson (1997) and Clark and Clift (1996). In this study 87% of those who drink alcohol 'never' drink more alcohol abroad than they do at home.

Since headache is the essential symptom for AMS diagnosis (Table 8.6 notes the symptoms of mountain sickness in bold), for the purpose of discussion, headache is assumed to indicate AMS. It is important, however, to bear in mind that the incidence of AMS symptoms should be lower or at most equal to the incidence of headache because not everyone present with a headache can be assumed as having AMS (refer to earlier definition of AMS).

Table 8.7 indicates that younger age groups are more likely to experience headache (AMS) than older age groups (χ^2 = 21.244 df = 5, p = 0.001). Of tourists under 20 years, 74.4% of them experience the symptom as opposed to 56.9% of those within 30–39 years and only 41.2% of those within 50–59 years. This observation supports the research of Hackett and Rennie (1976), Hultgren (1997) and Roach *et al.* (1995) who note that young tourists are more susceptible to AMS than older tourists. There is no significant relationship between the incidence of

Table 8.6 Ailments experienced by tourists in SNP (in bold are the symptoms of mountain sickness)

Symptoms	*Percentage* (n = 448)
Headache	**61.0%**
Shortness of breath on exertion	**49.1%**
Muscle strain/pain	42.3%
Fatigue	**37.8%**
Cough	37.4%
Diarrhoea	37.2%
Insomnia	**36.7%**
Loss of appetite	**33.8%**
Stomach discomfort	31.5%
Sore throat	24.5%
Joint pain	21.7%
Sunburn	16.9%
Backache	15.5%
Dizziness	**15.3%**
Vomiting	**14.9%**
Blisters	14.6%
Respiratory infection	10.8%
Fever	9.75
Shortness of breath at rest	**9.2%**
Cuts/bruises	7.0%
Loss of balance	**6.1%**
Confusion	**2.5%**
Hypothermia	2.5%

AMS and gender. This observation supports Pollard and Murdoch (1997) and Dietz (2000) who found that AMS equally affects males and females. There is no significant difference between the incidence of headache in tourists who are FITs and tourists in organized groups. This finding differs from Shlim and Gallie (1992) who found that AMS is experienced more by group tourists than independent tourists. Headache is suffered more by 'novice' tourists (67.5%) as opposed to 56.3% 'intermediate' and 47.3% 'experienced' tourists (χ^2 = 9.952 df = 2, p = 0.007). The use of porters is not significantly related to the incidence of headache.

Table 8.7 Tourists experiencing headache in SNP according to age group

Age group (years)	Frequency	Percentage
Below 20	29	74.4
20–29	118	66.7
30–39	70	56.9
40–49	38	62.3
50–59	14	41.2
60 and above	1	11.1

Apart from headache and shortness of breath on exertion, tourists to SNP experience other mountain sickness symptoms: fatigue (37.8%), insomnia (37.7%), loss of appetite (33.8%) and dizziness (15.3%). Some tourists may have experienced severe symptoms of mountain sickness (HAPE and HACE). Shortness of breath at rest is experienced by 9.2% of the tourists while loss of balance and confusion are experienced by 6.1% and 2.5% respectively.

Health symptoms are activity related. Since all the tourists are trekkers, a substantial number of tourists experienced symptoms like muscle pain (42.3%), joint pain (21.7%) backache (15.5%), and blisters (14.6%). The incidences of musculoskeletal pain are significantly less among those who perform regular exercise ($\chi^2 = 14.043$ $df = 3$, $p = 0.003$), 'experienced' tourists in high altitude ($\chi^2 = 12.464$ $df = 2$, $p = 0.002$) and those who use the services of porters ($\chi^2 = 4.033$ $df = 1$, $p = 0.045$). Soft tissue injuries (sunburn, blisters, cuts/bruises and frostbite) are experienced by 30.6% of the tourists to SNP. The incidence of soft tissue injuries is higher among younger tourists ($\chi^2 = 34.479$ $df = 5$, $p \leq 0.001$). Tourists on mountaineering parties are more likely to suffer soft tissue injuries compared with other tourists (60.0% and 30.0% respectively, $\chi^2 = 4.153$ $df = 1$, $p = 0.042$). Those who have the service of porters are less likely to suffer soft tissue injuries compared with those who have not (26.7% and 37.4% respectively).

Diarrhoea is experienced by 37.2% of tourists, which is concomitant to the 30–40% estimated by the World Health Organization (Rudkin & Hall, 1996). The incidence of diarrhoea is greatest among the younger age group, less common in the middle age group and gradually more common again in the older age group ($\chi^2 = 14.913$ $df = 5$, $p = 0.011$): 1–20 years (46.2%); 21–30 years (42.4%); 31–40 years (38.2%); 41–50 years (18.0%); 51–60 years (26.5%); and 60 years (44.4%). The incidence of diarrhoea is higher during the rainy season (40.8%) than during the peak (36.4%) and winter seasons (34.6%). The incidences of other gastro-intestinal symptoms (vomiting and stomach discomfort) are also more common during rainy season (44.4%) compared with 37.1% during the peak season and 29.6% during the winter season. The higher incidence of diarrhoea and other gastro-intenstinal symptoms during the rainy season could be attributed to the greater chances, at that time, of sewage contamination into food preparation. 'Experienced' tourists experience significantly lower incidence of diarrhoea (20.0%) compared with 40.7% among 'novice' and 38% 'intermediate' experience tourists ($\chi^2 = 8.215$ df = 2, p = 0.016). Those who had immunization experience a significantly higher incidence of diarrhoea compared with those who are not immunized (43.2% and 14.6% respectively, $\chi^2 = 26.463$ df = 1, p ≤ 0.001).

A cough is experienced by 34.4% of tourists, which could be due to the dryness of high altitude, and which irritates the respiratory system. During the winter season 66.7% of tourists suffer respiratory symptoms compared with 39.3% during the peak season and 31.0% during the rainy season ($\chi^2 = 43.134$ df = 2, p ≤ 0.001). Those who are immunized are more likely to have respiratory symptoms than those who are not (49.6% and 35.4% respectively, $\chi^2 = 6.053$ df = 1, p = 0.014).

The use of porters is not significantly related to the incidence of any mountain sickness symptom but significantly reduces the incidence of musculoskeletal pain and soft tissue injuries. The motivation in certain tourists 'to get away' is significantly associated with high incidence of mountain sickness. Tourists with 'spiritual' motivation, despite lacking in preparation, have significantly lower symptoms of mountain sickness. Risk-taking motivation is not related to a higher incidence of mountain sickness symptom.

Tourist Satisfaction

Tourists experience high level of satisfaction with their holiday in SNP: 61.7% of tourists rate their experience as 'very satisfied', 31.2% 'satisfied' and only 7.2% rate their satisfaction as 'neutral' to 'very dissatisfied'. Satisfaction arises from a number of factors (see Table 8.8). Tourists to SNP rate their satisfaction highly on 'nature beauty' (4.70), porters (4.37), activities (4.36), local friendliness (4.21) and guides (4.19). Items rated between neutral and satisfied are food/drink (3.83), accommodation (3.78), health (3.73), track condition (3.62), health facilities (3.21), weather (3.17) and information centre (3.00).

The two most unsatisfactory items for respondents are information signposts (2.77) and toilets (2.40). Non-applicable items have most frequency for 'porters' (125) and guides (135) since a great many tourists use the services of neither porters nor guides. The frequency of non-applicable items such as health information (79), information centre (92)

Table 8.8 Satisfaction of tourists in SNP with the listed items

Satisfaction items	VD	D	N	S	VS	NA	Mean	SD
Nature beauty	6	1	15	78	344	1	4.70	0.68
Porters	3	4	43	90	179	125	4.37	1.02
Activities	6	5	28	189	215	1	4.36	0.77
Local friendliness	4	11	57	183	185	3	4.21	0.84
Guides	4	18	47	85	155	135	4.19	1.17
Food/drink	5	32	101	202	103	1	3.83	0.91
Accommodation	5	31	108	205	90	3	3.78	0.90
Your health	13	46	98	176	109	1	3.73	1.04
Track condition	14	14	112	201	73	1	3.62	0.98
Health facilities	13	47	189	75	37	79	3.21	1.36
Weather	64	97	75	103	99	3	3.17	1.40
Information centre	18	75	161	71	20	92	3.00	1.48
Information signposts	34	105	163	57	15	45	2.77	1.35
Toilets	108	132	131	62	10	2	2.40	1.09

Note: The mean is calculated after the non-applicable variable is recoded as missing value. The items are measured using a six-point Likert scale (1 = very dissatisfied (VD), 2 = dissatisfied (D), 3 = neutral (N), 4 = satisfied (S), and 5 = very satisfied (VS) and 6 = not applicable (NA)).

and information signposts (45) may indicate that many of the tourists either do not notice or do not encounter such amenities. The main contribution to satisfaction (the items that most tourists rate as 'very satisfied') are activities, nature beauty, guides and local friendliness. The less favourable levels of satisfaction (items rating 'neutral' to 'satisfied') are accommodation, health, food/drink, information centre and track condition. The greatest source of dissatisfaction is toilets: most people rate them as 'dissatisfied' to 'neutral'. Health facilities and signage are not significantly related to the satisfaction items, which is probably due to the failure of respondents to answer the questions on these items in the questionnaires. Many tourists have no views on health facilities and do not encounter or observe signage.

As mentioned earlier, tourist satisfaction in SNP is mainly derived from the beauty of nature, activities, local friendliness and the services of porters and guides. This finding is further supported by the open-ended question on the best aspect of the tourists' visit. The top three answers are 'the beauty of scenery and sites' (48.2%), 'viewing the

Himalayas' (27.5%) and 'meeting and socializing with locals' (24.2%). Tourists experience higher satisfaction in the winter season and by those who use the services of porters. In winter, SNP receives the lowest number of tourists, and mountain peaks are normally clear of clouds.

Among aspects of SNP that are rated rather unfavourably in the individual variable ratings are health information, information centres, signposts and toilets. Table 8.9 shows the worst aspects of tourists' visits to SNP according to the response in the open-ended question.

Getting sick is the worst aspect of the visit to SNP (28.0%). Toilets in general are also among the worst experiences in SNP (26.0%) because they are generally dirty and smelly. Rubbish and litter disturb 17.0% of tourists. Crowding is among the worst of the social impacts in SNP (12.2%) especially during the peak season. Tourists also observe unsanitary and unhygienic practices among service providers (9.2%).

Is Tourism in SNP Sustainable?

Ecotourism is currently seen as a sustainable option for mountain tourism development (Inman & Luger, 1998). In the last decade there has been considerable proliferation of ecotourism definitions and the trend will likely continue. According to Fennel (2001: 403), 'the principle among the reflux of definitions is the sense that we have either not got it right, or that there ought to be different rules for different geographical reasons'. From a content analysis of 85 ecotourism definitions Fennell (2001) found that the seven most frequently mentioned elements were: nature-based, conservation, reference to culture, benefits to locals, education, sustainability and impact.

Table 8.9 Worst aspects of tourists' visit to SNP

The worst aspects of SNP	*Percentage of cases (n = 393)*
Getting sick	28.0%
Toilets	26.0%
Rubbish/litter	17.0%
Too many people	12.2%
Cold	11.2%
Rain	10.4%
Dirty/poor/muddy trails	9.7%
Unhygienic practices/poor sanitation	9.2%
Food	8.4%

Robinson (1997) states that SNP is an example of ecotourism development in which local participation is sought in development plans including the protection of natural resources. Weaver (1998), despite agreeing that Nepal is a prime example of an ecotourism destination, stresses that tourism development in SNP has a serious impact that might not be compatible with ecotourism. Rogers (1997) who conducted a detailed survey on 33 villages in the area from 1993–1996, argues that due to the overwhelming impact of tourism, SNP cannot be described as a model for ecotourism. The perennial issues of deforestation and the disposal of human and consumer waste, alone, are incompatible with the ideals of ecotourism. Rogers and Aitchinson (1998) describe several serious problems in waste management in SNP such as dead bodies on mountain peaks, human and material waste on mountaineering and trekking peaks especially at the base camps, litter produced by residents, tourists and support staff and also poor sanitation practices by many lodges.

The impact of tourism in SNP is usually discussed in terms of the impact on the natural environment and local culture. It should be stressed that a negative impact on tourists such as health and safety is equally important. This is especially so in SNP, a destination in a high altitude peripheral area of a less developed country, where poor sanitation and unhygienic practices subject tourists to many food-borne diseases, and the altitude exposes many to mountain sickness symptoms. All the diseases frequently experienced by nine out of every ten tourists in SNP are preventable. Thus, education is an important component of ecotourism policy that should be delivered more intensively than it is at present to tourists and locals alike. Even though most tourists are buying their way to SNP through travel agents and trekking agents, health information is disseminated only by 17.2% and 10.5% respectively. The HRA, which provides lectures on high altitude sickness prevention to the tourists reaches only 3.1% of the tourists, while another NGO, the Sagarmatha Pollution Control Committee, which actively educates tourists in SNP, provides information to only 1.1% of the tourists. Therefore, health should be regarded as a major focus in ensuring sustainable tourism development in SNP.

Health is applicable to all the components of ACE. Adventure has the element of danger as a primary attraction, which puts trekkers and mountaineers in SNP at risk of getting sick especially from mountain sickness, musculoskeletal pain and accidents. Culturally, the influx of tourists in SNP has changed the provision of food and toilets. Menus are quickly adapted to those tourists who travel in their own environmental bubbles. Since the refrigerator is uncommon, food storage is unsafe. Food hygiene, preparation and handling leave much to be desired. Thus tourists are exposed to food-borne diseases such as diarrhoea and vomiting. Modern toilets, which are built for tourist use, are often not properly maintained due to lack of water accessibility in the mountains. The use of traditional toilets, which use dried leaves to cover the excreta, may offer better benefits and the advantages need to be recognized by the tourist. They are not only less odorous but their end product could be used as fertilizer. Poorly maintained modern toilets perhaps are among the highest source of tourist dissatisfaction in SNP (Musa, 2002).

A satisfactory holiday is crucial for tourism sustainability. Researchers in SNP, with the exception of Pandey (1994), have never measured tourist satisfaction. It is often assumed that tourists are overwhelmed with natural beauty and accept the various ailments incurred in the mountains as a part of the price to be paid for their holiday experience (Pandey, 1994; Heydon, 1998). In measuring overall satisfaction, especially in natural settings, satisfaction is rated high regardless of the unpleasant experiences encountered. The fact is probably easily explained by 'coping' strategy, whereby tourists often focus on satisfactory elements of their holiday while rating overall satisfaction in order to maintain their holiday satisfaction (Higham, 1996). The overall satisfaction in this study, as well as in Pandey's (1994), was high, possibly for the same reason. However, in this study, on closer inspection, in the ratings of individual satisfaction variables as well as the responses to the open-ended questions, tourists report considerable unsatisfactory experiences such as being sick, bad toilet conditions, and lack of information centres and signposts. These issues need to be addressed in order to provide higher customer satisfaction, which will subsequently enhance the sustainability of tourism in SNP.

Socially, tourism development in SNP has improved the living standards, health care system and education of the Sherpas (Rogers, 1997; Rogers & Aitchison, 1998). However, it appears that this improvement has received little financial contribution from the Government of Nepal itself. Much of the social improvement in SNP is due to foreign aid. The main medical establishments in SNP (Kunde Hospital and Periche Health Post), are both run by non-governmental organizations that are heavily dependent on foreign donations. Most of the schools are also run by foreign aid and donations. The over-reliance on foreign sources lessens the obligation and undermines the will of the government to do things on its own, and such dependency is said by MacLellan *et al.* (2000) to permeate almost every level of society. Government contributes little to the development of the local community in the region even though substantial revenues have been collected each year from the escalating number of visitors entering the Park. Rogers (1997) points out that in 1996–1997, only 2% of the income from the entrance fees and trekking permits was channelled back to the local community. Nepal (2000) argues that tourism benefit in SNP is not equally distributed. Villagers away from the main tourist routes remain poor and live far below the poverty line (Nepal, 2000). It is also believed that most of the wealth belongs to only a few local elites (Musa, 2002). All these facts indicate that tourism in SNP is actually not economically sustainable by itself in its present form. Without the aid from foreign donations, tourism development in SNP may not be as flourishing as it is today.

Conclusions

SNP provides a useful field for analysis of a peripheral high altitude ACE destination and its sustainability. This chapter highlights health as a neglected but important area to be included in tourism management and policy in high altitude destinations in general, and in SNP in particular.

Ecotourism and its sustainability in SNP require the inclusion of the following components: local participation/benefits, economic viability, education dissemination, tourist satisfaction and the minimizing of tourism impact. In minimizing negative tourism impact all environmental, cultural, economic and social impacts should be given weight according to their severity. Regarding social impact, health and safety and crowding are the most serious issues in SNP. Health issues are not only important for the local but also for the tourist. Because of the nature of the location and the types of activities engaged in, health needs must be seen as a core element in achieving sustainability in SNP (see Figure 8.1).

Many aspects of SNP provide evidence that tourism in the region is not sustainable and not compliant with ecotourism principles. The most widely publicized tourism impacts, albeit controversial, are deforestation and cultural modification. The region suffers the impact of crowding and inflation. Tourism and infrastructure development in SNP are heavily reliant on foreign donations and aid. The revenue gained from tourism, rather than benefiting the local population in general, seems to be of more benefit to central government and local elites who own the lodges and hotels in the region. Waste and sewage management are still the perennial issues and locals are still either not practising or are not aware of proper hygiene in food preparation and daily life.

In reviewing ecotourism, in terms of minimizing tourism impact, there is a considerable neglect in assessing the impact of tourism activity on tourists themselves. The focus has always been on minimizing environmental and cultural impact. In SNP, not to speak of other peripheral area tourist destinations, the notion of ecotourism and its sustainability should include equal emphasis on minimizing social impact especially on the health and safety of the tourist, particularly through improved education. The region has not just endemic food-borne diseases but also subjects tourists to suffering mountain sickness symptoms.

Although often used as an icon of ACE destination, tourism in SNP, at present, is not sustainable and not compliant with ecotourism principles. Impacts such as deforestation, cultural modification, crowding, waste and sewage management and also the region's over-reliance on foreign aid and donations, are major issues of concern. Finally, this chapter has emphasized that, particularly in such high-altitude environments as that of SNP, tourist health issues should also be a core consideration in sustainable tourism development, judging from both the volume and the severity of ailments experienced by tourists in the region.

References

Adams, V. (1992) Tourism and Sherpa. *Annals of Tourism Research* 19 (3), 534–554.

Ali, A. (1991) *Status of Health in Nepal*. A report produced from Resource Centre for Primary Health Care, Nepal and South-South Solidarity, India.

Baker, G.C. (1993) *Nepal-Sagarmatha Forestry Report 1993 Visit*. Rangiora: New Zealand Forest Research Ltd.

Barracharya, S.B. (1998) The Annapurna Conservation Area Project. In East, P., Luger, K. and Inman, K (eds) *Sustainability in Mountain Tourism-perspectives for the Himalayan Countries* (Part 3 (1)). Delhi: Book Faith India.

Belk, R.W. (1993) Third world tourism: Panacea or poison? The case of Nepal. *Journal of International Consumer Marketing* 5 (1), 27–68.

Bjoness, I.M. (1983) External economic dependency and changing human adjustment to marginal environment in the high Himalaya, Nepal. *Mountain Research Development* 3 (3), 263–272.

Bratton, R., Kinnear, G. and Korolux, G. (1979) Why people climb mountains. *International Review of Sports Sociology* 14 (2), 23–36.

Brower, B. (1991) *Sherpa of Khumbu: People, Livestock and Landscape*. Delhi: Oxford University Press.

Byers, A. (1987) An assessment of landscape change in the Khumbu region of Nepal using repeat photography. *Mountain Research and Development* 7 (3), 77–81.

Cartwright, R. (1996) Tourists' diarrhoea. In Clift, S. and Page, S.J. (eds) *Health and the International Tourists* (Chapter 3). London: Routledge.

Clark, N. and Clift, S. (1996) Dimension of holiday experiences and their implication: A study of British tourists in Malta. In Clift, S. and Page, S.J. (eds) *Health and the International Tourist*. London: Routledge.

Clift, S., Grabowski, P. and Sharpley, R. (1997) British tourists in the Gambia: Health precaution and malaria prophylaxis. In Clift, S. and Grabowski, P. (eds) *Tourism and Health: Risks, Research and Responses*, (pp. 97–116). London: Pinter.

Cockerell, N. (1997) International tourism report No. 1 – Nepal. *Travel and Tourism Intelligence* 1, 40–57.

Dietz, T.E. (2000) *High Altitude Medicine Guide*. Available at: www.high-altitude-medicine.com (accessed 17 November 2000).

Draper, J. (1988) The Sherpa transformed: Towards a power-centred view of change in the Khumbu. *Contribution to Nepalese Studies* 15 (2), 139–162.

Ewert, A. (1985) Why people climb: The relationship of participant motives and experience level to mountaineering. *Journal of Leisure Research* 17 (3), 241–250.

Fennell, D.A. (2001) A content analysis of ecotourism definitions. *Current Issues in Tourism* 4 (5), 403–419.

Fisher, J.F. (1990) *Sherpas: Reflection on Change in Himalayan Nepal.* Delhi: Oxford University Press.

Furer-Haimendorf, C.V. (1984) *The Sherpas Transformed: Social Change in a Buddhist Society.* New Delhi: Sterling Publisher.

Gurung, H. (1991) *Tourism Carrying Capacity in the Mountain Regions of Nepal.* Kathmandu: UNDP.

Gurung, C. and DeCoursey, M. (1994) The Annapurna Conservation Area Project: A pioneering example of sustainable tourism? In Cater, E. and Lowman, G. *Ecotourism: A Sustainable Option?* (Chapter 11). Chichester: Wiley.

Gurung, G., Simmons, D. and Devlin, P. (1996) The evolving role of tourist guides: The Nepalese experience. In Richard, B. and Hinch, T. (eds) *Tourism and Indigenous People* (Chapter 5). London: International Thompson Business Press.

Hackett, P.H. and Rennie, D. (1976) The incidence, importance, and prophylaxis of acute mountain sickness. *Lancet* 2, 1149–1154.

Harris, M.D., Terrio, J., Miser, W.F. and Yetter, J.F. (1998) *High Altitude Medicine,* published by American Academy of Family Physicians, 15 April 1998. Available at: http://www.aafp.org/afp/980415ap/harris.html (accessed 12 March 2001).

Heydon, J. (1998) *Annual Report from Kunde Hospital.* Kathmandu: The Himalayan Trust.

Higham, J. (1996) Wilderness perception of international visitors to New Zealand. Unpublished Ph.D. thesis, Centre for Tourism, University of Otago, New Zealand.

Hinrichson, D., Lucas P.H., Coburn, B. and Oprety, B.N. (1983) Saving Sagarmatha. *Ambio* 12, 203–205.

Houston, M.D. (1987) Deforestation in Khumbu. *Mountain Research and Development* 7, 76.

Hultgren, H. (1997) *High Altitude Medicine.* Stanford: Hultgren Publications.

Inman, K. and Luger, K (1998) Ecotourism and village development – the Oeko Himal strategy for sustainable tourism. In East, P., Luger K. and Inmann, K. (eds) *Sustainability in Mountain Tourism-Perspectives for the Himalayan Countries.* Delhi: Book Faith.

Jefferies, B. (1982) Sagarmatha National Park: The impact of tourism in the Himalaya. *Ambio* 11 (5), 274–281.

Lachapelle, P. (1995) *A Report of Human Waste Management in Sagarmatha National Park.* Kathmandu: School for International Training.

Ledgard, N.J. (1994) *Nepal – Sagarmatha Forestry Report 1994 Visit.* Rangiora: New Zealand Forest Research Institute.

MacLellan, L.R., Dieke, P.U.C. and Thapa, B.K. (2000) Mountain tourism and public policy in Nepal. In Godde, P.M., Price, M.F. and Zimmermann, F.M. (eds) *Tourism and Development in Mountain Regions* (Chapter 9). Wallingford: CABI Publishing.

Maundalexix, A. (1992) High altitude medicine practice at HRA in Manang (11,000 feet) and Periche (14,000 feet). In *High Altitude Medicine and Physiology, Proceedings of Congress on High Altitude Medicine and Physiology.* Kathmandu, Nepal, 8 April 1992.

Moutinho, L. (1987) Consumer behaviour in tourism. *European Journal of Marketing* 21 (10), 5–44.

Musa, Ghazali (2002) An investigation of travel health experiences in high altitude environment: Case studies of Sagarmatha National Park, Nepal and Tibet, China. Unpublished Ph.D. thesis, Department of Tourism, University of Otago, New Zealand.

Nepal, S. (2000) Tourism in protected areas: The Nepalese Himalaya. *Annals of Tourism Research* 27 (3), 661–681.

Pandey, M.B. (1994) International visitor attitudes to Sagarmatha (Mt Everest) National Park. Unpublished thesis submitted to Lincoln University in fulfilment of the thesis required for the degree of Master of Parks and Recreation Management, Canterbury, New Zealand.

Parker, T. (1993) Nature tourism in Nepal. In Nenon, J. and Durst, P. (eds) *Nature Tourism in Asia: Opportunities and Constraints for Conservation and Economic Development* (pp. 21–30). Washington, DC: Forestry Support Programme.

Pawson, I.G., Stanford, D.D. and Adams, V.A. (1984) Effects of the modernization on the Khumbu region of Nepal changes in population structure, 1970–1982. *Mountain Research Development* 4 (1), 73–81.

Pollard, A.J. and Murdoch, D.R. (1997) *The High Altitude Medicine Handbook*. Oxford: Radcliff Medical Press.

Prentice, R. (1993) Motivations of the heritage consumer in the leisure market: An application of the Manning-Haas demand hierarchy. *Leisure Sciences* 15 (4), 273–290.

Roach, R., Houston, C. and Honigman, B. (1995) How well do older persons tolerate moderate altitude? *West Journal Medicine* 162, 32–36.

Robinson, D.W. (1992) Social-cultural impacts of mountain tourism in Nepal's Sagarmatha National Park: Implications for sustainable tourism. In Thorsell, J. (ed.) *World Heritage Twenty Years Later: 4th World Congress on the National Park and Protected Areas* (pp. 123–131). Gland: IUCN.

Robinson, D.W. (1997) Strategies for alternative tourism: The case of tourism in Sagarmatha (Everest) National Park, Nepal. In France, L. (ed.) *Sustainable Tourism*. London: Earthscan.

Rogers, P. (1997) Tourism, development and change in Sagarmatha National Park and its environs. Unpublished thesis submitted to the University of Wales for the Degree of Philosophy Doctor, University of Wales, Aberystwyth.

Rogers, P. and Aitchinson, J. (1998) *Towards Sustainable Tourism in the Everest Region of Nepal*. Kathmandu: IUCN Nepal & ICPL.

Rudkin, B. and Hall, C.M. (1996) Off the beaten track. In Clift, S. and Page, S.J. (eds) *Health and the International Tourist* (pp. 89–107). London: Routledge.

Ryan, C. and Robertson, E. (1997) New Zealand student-tourists: Risk behaviour and health. In Clift, S. and Grabowski, P. (eds) *Tourism and Health: Risks, Research and Responses* (pp. 119–138). London: Pinter.

Sherpa, M.N. (1982) *Sherpa Culture: Ways of Life, Festivals and Religion of the Sherpa People*. Kathmandu: KMTNC.

Shlim, D.R. and Gallie, J. (1992) The causes of death among trekkers in Nepal. The HRA and clinics, Kathmandu, Nepal. In *High Altitude Medicine and Physiology, Proceedings of Congress on High Altitude Medicine and Physiology*. Kathmandu Nepal, 8 April 1992.

Simmons, D.G. and Koirala, S. (2000) Tourism in Nepal, Bhutan and Tibet: Contrast in facilitation, constraining and control of tourism in the Himalayas. In Hall C.M. and Page, S. (ed.) *Tourism in South and South East Asia-Issues and Cases* (pp. 256–267). Oxford: Butterworth-Heineman.

Steffen, R. (1997) The epidemiology of travel-related health problems. In Clift, S. and Grabowski, P. *Tourism and Health: Risks, Research and Responses* (pp. 27–37). London: Pinter.

Stevens, S. (1993) *Claiming the High Ground*. Los Angeles: University of California Press.

Stevens, S. and Sherpa, M.N. (1992) Tourism impact and protected area management in Highland Nepal: Lessons from SNP and ACAP. Paper presented at *IUCN 4th World Congress on National Parks and Protected Areas*, Caracas, Venezuela.

Ward, M.P., Milledge, J.S. and West, J.B. (1995) *High Altitude Medicine and Physiology* (2nd edn). Cambridge: Chapman and Hall Medical University Press.

Weaver, D.B. (1998) Ecotourism in Nepal. In Harrison, D. (ed) *Ecotourism in the Less Developed World* (Chapter 6). Wallingford: CAB International.

Zafren, K. (2000) Mountain sickness and other hazards in the Nepal Himalayas. Available at: www.nepalonline.net/hra/ (accessed 17 December 2000).

Zurick, D.N. (1992) Adventure travel and sustainable tourism in the peripheral economy of Nepal. *Annals of the Association of American Geographers* 82, 608–628.

Chapter 9
Second Home Tourism in the Swedish Mountain Range

DIETER K. MÜLLER

Introduction: Second Homes in Mountain Areas

Second home tourism has recently attracted renewed interest all over the Western world (e.g. Buller & Hoggart, 1994; Kaltenborn, 1997a, 1997b, 1998; Halseth, 1998; Müller, 1999, 2002a, 2002b; Williams & Kaltenborn, 1999; Flognfeldt, 2002; Williams & Hall, 2002). The emergence of new forms and patterns of production also entailed new patterns of consumption favouring for example short breaks and second home tourism (Williams & Hall, 2002). In particular, areas on the outskirts of metropolitan areas that allow for frequent access have benefited from the demand for second homes, while peripheral areas mainly attract second home owners who have an emotional link to the area (Müller, 2002b). Amenity-rich peripheral areas also tend to attract second home owners with remote origins.

Mountain areas are part of these amenity landscapes and hence, they are also areas of significant social and economic change. Formerly regions of extensive agriculture and forestry, mountain areas have been particularly hit by economic restructuring (Pettersson, 2002). This occurred, in great part, as a result of their peripheral locations in relation to major population concentrations. Changes included depopulation, loss of employment opportunities and an increasing average age among the remaining population. Tourism has created opportunities for these areas and helped to turn some mountainous areas into prosperous regions (Godde *et al.*, 2000). In Europe, the Alps in particular benefited considerably from tourism and with certain skiing resorts becoming well-known tourist destinations.

Hotels and apartment buildings usually cater for the accommodation of tourists. However, at least in the Scandinavian context, it is apparent that tourists also choose to purchase a second home for private use in order to secure access for visits to the mountain range (Jansson & Müller, 2003). In some municipalities the second home population boosts the number of inhabitants on average by up to 20% (Müller & Hall, 2003). It is however unclear who these seasonal residents are. It is expected that distance functions as a social filter enabling mainly well off households to purchase second homes in the mountains. In addition, it is suggested that the mountain range is highly heterogeneous in terms of second home development.

The purpose of this chapter is to analyse second home ownership in the Swedish mountain range. The main objective is to scrutinize the relationship between the second home owners' primary residences and the destination and its impact on the composition of the second home owner population. Finally, the chapter discusses what impact the unequal access to second home ownership in the mountains has on the destination.

Second Homes and the Pleasure Periphery

By the turn of the 20th century second homes were already built in areas perceived as wilderness (Coppock, 1977; Löfgren, 1999). Designs reminding owners of frontier development were often used in constructing the cottages. In Scandinavia, British hunters and anglers initiated the construction of cottages and sometimes of luxurious hunting villas to serve their sporting purposes (Sillanpää, 2002). This idealization of the countryside, and wilderness areas in particular, was a result of the increasing urbanization and a growing awareness of the value of wilderness for heritage and ecology (Hall, 1992; Bunce, 1994).

The wilderness experience comprises several aspects all tempting tourists to spend time in remote places. Reviewing the academic work on wilderness Hall and Page (2002: 259) identify the following components of the wilderness experience: aesthetic appreciation, religion, escapism, challenge, history/romanticism, solitude, companionship, discovery/learning, vicarious appreciation, and technology. Mountain areas fit well into the description of wilderness, and consecutively their touristic utilization can be traced back in the 18th century (Nilsson, 2001). Although mountain areas initially were perceived as wilderness, one may argue that the ongoing development during the 20th century converted them into modern tourist resorts leaving almost no notion of wilderness behind. However, it is obvious that the perception of wilderness differs between tourists (Higham, 1998; Hall & Page, 2002). Therefore, Hall (1992) suggests a wilderness continuum featuring growing wilderness quality with increasing remoteness and primitiveness of the visited area (see Chapter 1).

As shown elsewhere second homes can provide an opportunity to achieve some kind of wilderness experience. Jaakson (1986) provided a comprehensive overview over the meaning of second home tourism. Inversion from everyday life appears to be one main attraction of the second home. This inversion regards not only the focus on leisure opposed to work, but also a general relaxation and informality in the second home. Moreover, second home ownership can be interpreted as a step 'back-to-nature' often related to ideas of pioneer life and a rejection of modernity (Jaakson, 1986; Williams & Kaltenborn, 1999). Although the majority of second home owners are satisfied with staying in the countryside, some adapt the surrounding of the second home to their image of nature and others also regress towards a simple rustic lifestyle (Jaakson, 1986; Müller, 1999). Hence, second home ownership can be seen as a means to experience wilderness and the components noted above.

Nevertheless, by no means can all second homes be characterized in that way. The touristic development of the mountains meant that an increasing number of people could reach such areas. The development of ski resorts in particular generated new interest and boosted mountain tourism. The available accommodation initially comprised hotels and boarding houses, but since the 1960s second homes have become a significant contribution to the local accommodation sector (Nilsson, 2001). Although some of the second homes are used commercially, many owners prefer to use their properties exclusively for themselves (Jansson & Müller, 2003).

Consequently, second homes in the mountain areas provide more than just access to wilderness experiences. Instead, the commodification of the mountain experience due to such things as alpine skiing and snowmobile driving required the establishment of new accommodation opportunities in the pleasure periphery. Second homes are one means satisfying this new demand. Hence, the establishment of second homes in the mountain areas has also meant a democratization of mountain tourism by allowing a larger number of people to participate in tourism.

Fredman and Heberlein (2001) report an overall increase in mountain tourism in Sweden since 1984, mainly related to alpine skiing. They offer three explanations for this growth: changes in Swedish society allowing for short trips, media influences focusing on outdoor experiences, and Swedish achievements in competitive winter sports. Changes also comprise the spatial distribution of tourism. Tourism is now more concentrated to the southernmost parts of the mountain range that have alpine skiing resorts, meanwhile the more peripheral areas suffer from a decline.

Butler (1998) describes this process as a shift from traditional to modern activities. Sandell (1997; see also Kaltenborn *et al.*, 2002) uses the concept of eco-strategies to characterize the different perceptions of environment that form the foundations for various activities within the environment. In his terminology, alpine skiing fits well into the 'Factory' category, representing a view that is positive towards an almost unlimited use of the environment for entertainment and production. The traditional second home in the mountain range allowing admiration of the scenery is more an expression of the category of 'Museum', i.e. visiting without leaving traces. The shift from a museum strategy to a factory strategy implies larger impacts on the environment but also on the local communities.

Second Home Patterns and the Geography of Amenity-rich Areas

Recent changes in the production system entailed that landscapes with high amenity values increasingly attracted migration and tourism (Fountain & Hall, 2002; Williams & Hall, 2002). Growth in leisure time, teleworking and an increasing number of retired households has intensified demand for attractive living environments. Mountain areas obviously contain considerable amenity values and hence, they have attracted migration and tourism sometimes causing severe environmental problems (Glorioso, 2000).

What is perceived as an amenity is individual and hence, it has to be investigated empirically. In the case of second homes, amenities can be related to the place where the second home is located. Second home living in itself can also be considered an amenity (Jaakson, 1986). Hence, the spatial distribution of second homes cannot be seen as a blueprint of the geography of amenity values. Instead, many second home owners tend to prefer a second home in the vicinity of the primary residence allowing for frequent visits (Wolfe, 1951; Bell, 1977; Müller, 2002a). Müller (2002a) therefore distinguishes between second homes for weekend purposes and second homes for vacation purposes. The location of the first is mainly dependent on the location of the primary residence. Consequently, the demand for second homes decreases with increasing distance from the primary residence. The patterns follow a distribution usually expressed by a distance–decay function. In contrast, the location of second homes for vacation purposes is geographically independent from the location of the primary residence. Instead, it can be argued that their spatial patterns correspond with the geographical distribution of amenity-rich areas inviting for vacations. Hence, amenity-rich areas can be identified as the residuals between an observed second home pattern and a distance–decay function representing a theoretical second home pattern (see Figure 9.1). Observing second home patterns with that in mind enables the assessment of the amenity values of the popular destination areas.

The components that characterize an attractive second home location are difficult to identify. Earlier studies suggest a mixture of environmental aspects such as rural landscape, existing settlements, and lake or

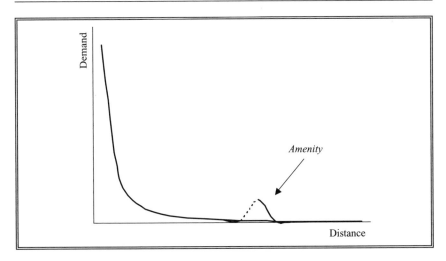

Figure 9.1 Second home demand and amenity-rich areas

river view, and spatial aspects, such as a limited distance between primary residence and second home (Aldskogius, 1968, 1969; Burby III *et al.*, 1972; Bell, 1977; Müller, 2002). In the mountains it can be expected that alpine skiing facilities will influence the location patterns of second homes. Purpose-built second homes are concentrated at resorts, while converted primary residences are more equally spread representing the historical settlement pattern.

Elite Spaces?

The concentration of second homes in the pleasure periphery raises questions regarding their impact on the local community. A comprehensive assessment of this question lies outside the frame of this chapter (see Hall & Müller, 2004). However, the impact of second home development on rural change has been debated widely and with substantial controversy (e.g. Jordan, 1980; Fritz, 1982; Shucksmith, 1983; Buller & Hoggart, 1994; Deller *et al.*, 1997; Gallent & Tewdwr-Jones, 2000; Müller & Hall, 2003). The impacts of second home development on property values and taxes have been a particularly intriguing issue. The vicinity of amenities and the concentration of demand for second homes in certain mountain resorts obviously implie increasing property values. In other contexts this is usually mentioned as reason for the displacement of primary residents (Gallent & Tewdwr-Jones, 2000). However, in the context of the present chapter, this question seems to be of minor interest only, simply because second homes in mountain areas are often purpose-built rather than replacing existing housing stock. Moreover, socio-economic decline of such regions entails that tourism is usually welcomed (Jenkins *et al.*, 1998; Pettersson, 2002).

It is also sometimes argued that second home tourism is elitist and without doubt increasing property values function as social access filters (Halseth, 1998; Gallent & Tewdwr-Jones, 2000). This notion should however be seen in context of regional or national political and socio-economic circumstances. In the Nordic countries second home ownership is so common that this notion certainly lacks validity. Nevertheless, on a local level competition can force certain potential second home owners into cheaper areas. Consecutively, mountain resorts and other amenity-rich areas are transformed into highly segregated elite spaces. To further assess the accuracy of these ideas, focus is placed on second home ownership in the Swedish mountain range.

Methodology and Definitions

The paper is based on a comprehensive geographical database containing information on about 500,000 second homes in Sweden, 1991–1996. The database, based at the Department of Social and Economic Geography, Umeå University, is especially designed by Statistics Sweden and combines individual data for each property such as property value and area and individual data for their owners. Moreover, every post in the database is linked to a geo-reference that makes it possible to conduct an analysis based on a geographical information system (GIS). Hence, the definition of second homes is the one applied by Statistics Sweden. That implies that the second home owners themselves have to decide on the status of the property in the annual property taxation. Moreover, second homes have to be of cottage or villa type.

The definition of mountains employed for this paper is mainly determined by practical reasons. A database on land use in Sweden provided by Swedish *Lantmäteriet* was used to identify areas above the timberline. These areas were then completed with a 10km buffer delimitating the area here referred to as mountains.

The relationship between primary residences and second homes are charted below in order to identify the mountain as an amenity-rich area. This is done for a sample of Swedish urban regions. Thereafter, second homes in the mountain range are compared with all second homes in Sweden in terms of dimensions such as value and the characteristics of owners. Finally, the focus is turned to the mountain resort Sälen.

Second Homes in the Swedish Mountain Range

The overwhelming importance of the distance between primary residence and second homes can be easily visualized by charting the relationship between the number of second homes and the distance from the second home owners' primary residences. A linear regression model explains the logarithm of the amount of second homes in all 10km zones measured from the home districts of all second home owners. For all second homes in Sweden the regression coefficient r^2 takes the value 0.975 and hence, it can be stated that almost all variation in second home patterns can be explained by distance. Of course, this average value hides regional variations and hence, the situation is also charted for second home owners from a number of urban regions. Figure 9.2 shows, for example, for Umeå in northern Sweden a higher concentration of second homes exists about 300 to 400km from the city. This area can be found in the mountain area. Similarly, the second home concentrations for the other selected cities can be found in the mountain ranges causing regression coefficients departing somewhat from the national average.

Also the overall pattern in Sweden shows a concentration of second homes in the mountain area, although coastal locations dominate the pattern (Figure 9.3). Altogether 21,427 second homes or 4.3% of all Swedish second homes are located within the mountain area. A significant share of those owning a second home in the mountains also has their primary residence in the mountain range. The number of second home owners residing outside the mountains is 17,918 or 83%. The majority of those have their primary residence in one of the coastal cities of northern Sweden or in Stockholm and the Lake Mälaren area. Owners also come from minor settlements in the interior parts of northern Sweden.

Moreover, the map showing the Swedish second home patterns indicates clearly that second home tourism in the Swedish mountains is concentrated to a limited number of resorts that usually feature alpine skiing facilities. These properties are also of rather high value and exclusive to rather affluent households only.

Surprisingly, the assessed property values of the second homes in the mountain range are below the national average (Table 9.1). The explanation of this has to be looked for in the overall pattern of second homes in Sweden, where coastal locations are most desirable. Moreover, considering the strong relationship between demand and distance to the primary residence then coastal areas are favoured, because the majority of the Swedish population can be found there. Hence, coastal areas form the dominant amenity-rich areas in Sweden, while mountain areas have to be considered as peripheral amenity-rich areas. In contrast, assessed building values, i.e. the part of the assessed taxation value referring to the building of the property, for mountain homes are more similar to the national average. This indicates that second homes in the mountains are of a rather good standard, not at least because the average property area is smaller than the national average.

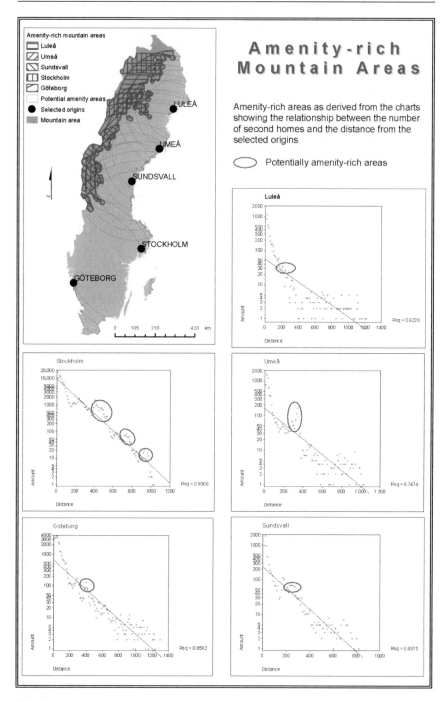

Figure 9.2 Amenity-rich mountain areas

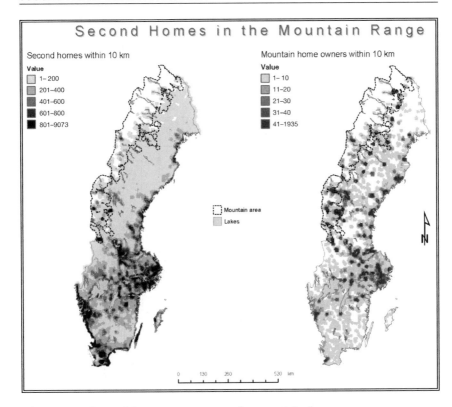

Figure 9.3 Second home patterns and mountain home owners

However, differences between second home owners residing inside and outside the mountain area are obvious. Assessed property values and building values are considerably higher for second homes owned by households residing outside the mountain area meanwhile the average property size is larger among those second homes owned by local owners. This is also apparent in spatial terms, where outside owners are concentrated to the limited number of areas with high assessed property values.

Second home owners

Mountain home owners residing outside the area are on average more affluent than the average second home owner household and particularly than the owners residing inside the area. When classifying the second home owners households according to income classes representing 10% of all Swedish households, it becomes obvious that the richest class in particular is present in the mountain resorts. In addition, households with incomes between 264,657 SEK and 334,945 SEK are strongly

Table 9.1 Characteristics for mountain second homes owned by households residing outside and inside the mountain areas and for the national average

	Assessed property values (SEK)			Assessed building value (SEK)			Property area (m²)		
	Outside	Inside	All	Outside	Inside	All	Outside	Inside	All
25% quartile	76,000	38,000	95,000	80,000	65,000	76,000	1350	1500	1355
Median	155,000	81,000	180,000	118,000	94,000	111,000	1652	1980	1965
75% quartile	252,000	165,000	291,000	173,000	143,000	165,000	2120	2702	2890
Mean	182,000	118,000	220,000	140,000	120,000	137,000	2199	2900	2999
Std deviation	140,000	113,000	181,000	89,000	83,000	99,000	8594	4368	6009
< 50,000 SEK				4363	1599	132,130			
No data	8	3	361	8	3	361	917	315	33,038
N	17,910	3506	498,583	13,547	1907	366,453	16,993	3191	465,545

represented in the mountain area but also in the overall group of second home owners. The lowest income class shows the highest figures, which can be explained by the fact that there are many retired households in this group, many of which continue to own their formerly permanent home in the mountain region, although they are unable to use it themselves. Household incomes of owners residing inside the mountain areas are significantly lower than those of the other owners. Second home owners residing outside the mountain area are considerably better educated than those residing inside the area and also better than the national average. From this analysis it can therefore be concluded that the established patterns regarding the second home owners and their households indicate that second home ownership in the mountain area is mainly a privilege for rather affluent and well-educated households.

Second homes in Sälen

Sälen is one of the most prominent winter resorts in Sweden. Moreover, as it is the southernmost and closest resort to the Stockholm metropolitan area, it generates a considerable share of tourism in the area. The area is also known for its rather easy alpine skiing and cross-country skiing tracks that attract skiers from all age groups. The resort is primarily managed by Skistar, a company that runs several alpine resorts in the southern part of the Swedish mountain range and recently invested a considerable amount of money to boost winter sport tourism in the area.

Altogether there are 2157 second homes in the area (Figure 9.4), these second homes are of a much higher standard than average in the

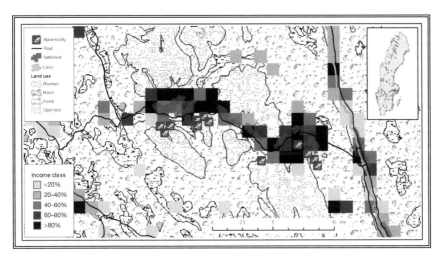

Figure 9.4 Second home owners in the Sälen resort

mountain area (Table 9.2). The mean assessed property value is 193,000 SEK, higher than the average in the mountain area and also 123,000 SEK higher than the national average. The same pattern can be found with respect to building values. The average property area is however much smaller than the national average indicating that second homes are purpose-built and not former primary residences.

Table 9.2 Second home owners' disposable household incomes, 1996. Each class is representing 10% of all Swedish households

Income class (upper borders in SEK)	Outside (%)	Inside (%)	All (%)	Sälen (%)
178,589	26.4	47.1	35.1	21.8
197,237	5.1	5.4	6.0	4.0
226,644	8.3	8.6	9.0	7.3
264,657	12.1	9.9	11.5	9.9
306,973	13.3	8.4	11.4	11.2
334,945	7.7	3.9	5.8	6.9
360,048	5.0	1.7	3.9	4.7
385,151	4.2	1.4	2.9	4.7
395,909	1.3	0.5	1.0	1.1
> 395,909	15.4	3.0	9.5	26.1
No data	1.2	10.9	3.9	2.2
Total	100.0	100.0	100.0	100.0

Table 9.3 Second home characteristics in Sälen

	Assessed property value (SEK)	Assessed building values (SEK)	Property area (m²)
25% quartile	289,000	131,000	1156
Median	381,000	195,000	1396
75% quartile	455,000	272,000	1641
Mean	375,000	213,000	1543
Std deviation	153,000	121,000	1815
N	2157	2157	2157

Table 9.4 Educational level for all Swedish second home owners, owners residing outside and inside the mountain areas and for owners in Sälen, 1995

Education	All	Inside	Outside	Sälen
No data	13.1	19.5	6.2	6.4
Elementary school	17.5	23.3	14.3	12.7
Secondary school	6.8	6.6	6.7	7.0
High school ≤ 2 years	22.6	27.2	22.4	18.5
High school > 2 years	12.4	9.4	14.0	17.0
University ≤ 2 years	11.4	7.3	14.9	15.1
University > 2 years	14.9	6.4	19.8	21.8
Ph.D.	1.3	0.3	1.6	1.4
Total	100.0	100.0	100.0	100.0

In addition, Sälen's second home owners are more affluent than the national average and the average for the mountain area. Altogether more than 26% of the second home owners in Sälen belong to the top 10% of the Swedish households in term of income (Table 9.3), and more than 50% of the second home owners have an university degree (Table 9.4). Hence, Sälen really forms a relatively exclusive destination. The concentration of highly educated and affluent households can also be traced in the local geography of the area. The affluent households are concentrated to the central parts of the resort and in particular to the alpine skiing facilities, meanwhile less affluent households reside in more peripheral locations and in the close-by river valley (Figure 9.4).

Conclusion

The study shows that mountains are perceived as amenity-rich areas attracting second home owners to an extent that cannot be explained by simple distance–decay functions. Nevertheless, second home patterns are related to the urban fields of the nearby urban areas. Consequently, owners residing in the cities along the Gulf of Botnia are more likely to own a second home in the northern mountain range, while owners from the Stockholm metropolitan area are mainly present in the southern parts of the mountains. The mountain areas are however by no means the only amenity-rich region in the country. Instead, second homes in the mountain area are less expensive than the national average. Demand is far greater in the vicinity of the metropolitan areas and the coast.

However, the study also illuminates that the mountain area is by no mean homogenous, at least regarding its attractiveness for property investments. Although the overall patterns indicate a rather modest demand for mountain homes, it can be confirmed that certain resorts attract highly affluent and educated households converting the resorts in exclusive spaces dominated by alpine skiing. Hence, it is reasonable to ask whether it is the mountains as such that attract second home tourism. Instead, it can be assumed that it is the combination of alpine and Nordic skiing that forms the main amenity of second home tourism in the mountain range. The amenity value of the area is therefore mainly related to an activity and not just the scenery. Hence, second home tourism fits well into what Butler (1998) lists as modern activities in the countryside, or what Sandell (1997) considers a factory strategy.

The present situation indicates that second home areas, at least in the mountain resorts, form a component of a commodified pleasure periphery. The purchase of a property in these places is not cheap and hence, continuous access is limited mainly to affluent households. Second homes for rent and other accommodations are however also available for other households. Cheaper properties are primarily available outside these places. That makes the mountain range a highly segregated area. Affluent groups control alpine resorts, meanwhile less well-off groups can mainly afford more peripheral areas. Second home tourism is thus far from being just a nostalgic regression. It is also an expression of power relations and contributes consecutively to create a blueprint of urban patterns of social exclusion within peripheral leisure and tourism spaces.

This conclusions of this chapter should however not be seen deterministically. More research is needed to clarify the role of second home tourism for changes in the periphery, since second home tourism still provides the precondition for admiring mountain scenery. Second homes outside the alpine resorts allow the experience of solitude, escapism, romanticism and other factors listed as part of the wilderness experience by Hall and Page (2002: 259). Nevertheless, a nostalgic conceptualization of second home tourism fails to capture its true variety and complexity.

References

Aldskogius, H. (1968) Studier i Siljanområdets fritidshusbebyggelse. *Geografiska regionstudier* 4. Uppsala: Kulturgeografiska institutionen.
Aldskogius, H. (1969) Modelling the evolution of settlement patterns: Two studies of vacation house settlement. *Geografiska regionstudier* 6. Uppsala: Kulturgeografiska institutionen.
Bell, M. (1977) The spatial distribution of second homes: A modified gravity model. *Journal of Leisure Research* 9, 225–232.
Buller, H. and Hoggart, K. (1994) *International Counterurbanization: British Migrants in Rural France.* Aldershot: Ashgate.

Bunce, M. (1994) *The Countryside Ideal: Anglo-American Images of Landscape.* London: Routledge.

Burby III, R.J., Donnelly, T.G. and Weiss, S.F. (1972) Vacation home location: A model for simulating the residential development of rural recreation areas. *Regional Studies* 6, 421–439.

Butler, R. (1998) Rural recreation and tourism. In Ilbery, B. (ed.) *The Geography of Rural Change* (pp. 211–232). Harlow: Longman.

Coppock, J.T. (1977) Second homes in perspective. In Coppock J.T. (ed.) *Second Homes: Curse or Blessing?* (pp. 1–16). Oxford: Pergammon.

Deller S.C., Marcouiller, D.W. and Green, G.P. (1997) Recreational housing and local government finance. *Annals of Tourism Research* 24, 687–705.

Flognfeldt Jr, T. (2002) Second home ownership: A sustainable semi-migration? In Hall, C.M. and Williams, A.M. (eds) *Tourism and Migration: New Relationships between Production and Consumption* (pp. 187–281). Dordrecht: Kluwer.

Fountain, J. and Hall, C.M. (2002) The impact of lifestyle migration on rural communities: A case study of Akaroa, New Zealand. In Hall, C.M. and Williams, A.M. (eds) *Tourism and Migration: New Relationships between Production and Consumption* (pp. 153–168). Dordrecht: Kluwer.

Fredman, P. and Heberlein, T. (2001) *Changing Recreation Patterns among Visitors to the Swedish Mountain Region 1980–2000.* Paper prepared for the TTRA conference 'Creating and Management Growth in Travel and Tourism', Kiruna, Sweden, 21–23 April 2001. Östersund: Etour.

Fritz, R.G. (1982) Tourism, vacation home development and residential tax burden: A case study of the local finances of 240 Vermont towns. *American Journal of Economics and Sociology* 41, 375–385.

Gallent, N. and Tewdwr-Jones, M. (2000) *Rural Second homes in Europe: Examining Housing Supply and Planning Control.* Aldershot: Ashgate.

Glorioso, R.S. (2000) Amenity migration in the Sumava bioregion, Czech Republic: Implications for ecological integrity. In Godde, P., Price, M. and Zimmermann, F.M. (eds) *Tourism and Development in Mountain Regions* (pp. 275–295). Wallingford: CABI.

Godde, P.M., Price, M.F. and Zimmermann, F.M. (2000) Tourism and development in mountain regions: Moving forward into the new millennium. In Godde, P.M., Price, M.F. and Zimmermann, F.M. (eds) *Tourism and Development in Mountain Regions* (pp. 1–25). Wallingford: CABI.

Hall, C.M. (1992) *Wasteland to World Heritage: Preserving Australia's Wilderness.* Melbourne: Melbourne University Press.

Hall, C.M. and Müller, D. (eds) (2004) *Tourism, Mobility and Second Homes: Between Elite Landscape and Common Ground.* Clevedon: Channel View.

Hall, C.M. and Page, S.J. (2002) *The Geography of Tourism and Recreation: Environment, Place and Space* (2nd edn). London: Routledge.

Halseth, G. (1998) *Cottage Country in Transition: A Social Geography of Change and Contention in the Rural-Recreational Countryside.* Montreal: McGill-Queen's University Press.

Higham, J. (1998) Sustaining the physical and social dimensions of wilderness tourism: The perceptual approach to wilderness management in New Zealand. *Journal of Sustainable Tourism* 6, 26–51.

Jaakson, R. (1986) Second-home domestic tourism. *Annals of Tourism Research* 13, 367–391.

Jansson, B. and Müller, D.K. (2003) *Fritidsboende i Kvarken.* Umeå: Kvarkenrådet.

Jenkins, J.M., Hall, C.M. and Troughton, M. (1998) The restructuring of rural economies: Rural tourism and recreation as a government response. In

Butler, R., Hall, C.M. and Jenkins, J. (eds) *Tourism and Recreation in Rural Areas* (pp. 43–67). Chichester: Wiley.

Jordan, J.W. (1980) The summer people and the natives: Some effects of tourism in a Vermont vacation village. *Annals of Tourism Research* 7, 34–55.

Kaltenborn, B.P. (1997a) Nature of place attachment: a study among recreation homeowners in southern Norway. *Leisure Sciences* 19, 175–189.

Kaltenborn, B.P. (1997b) Recreation homes in natural settings: Factors affecting place attachment. *Norsk Geografisk Tidsskrift* 51, 187–198.

Kaltenborn, B.P. (1998) The alternate home: Motives of recreation home use. *Norsk Geografisk Tidsskrift* 52, 121–134.

Kaltenborn, B.P., Haaland, H. and Sandell, K. (2002) The public right of access – some challenges to sustainable tourism development in Scandinavia. *Journal of Sustainable Tourism* 9, 417–433.

Löfgren, O. (1999) *On Holiday: A History of Vacationing*. Berkeley: University of California Press.

Müller, D.K. (1999) *German Second Home Owners in the Swedish Countryside: On the Internationalization of the Leisure Space*. Umeå: Department of Social and Economic Geography.

Müller, D.K. (2002a) German second home development in Sweden. In Hall, C.M. and Williams, A.M. (eds) *Tourism and Migration: New Relationships between Production and Consumption* (pp. 169–186). Dordrecht: Kluwer.

Müller, D.K. (2002b) Second home ownership and sustainable development in northern Sweden. *Tourism and Hospitality Research* 3, 343–355.

Müller, D.K. and Hall, C.M. (2003) Second homes and regional population distribution: On administrative practices and failures in Sweden. *Espace, Population, Societe* 2 (forthcoming).

Nilsson, P.Å. (2001) Tourist destination development: The Åre valley. *Scandinavian Journal of Hospitality and Tourism* 1, 54–67.

Pettersson, Ö. (2002) *Socio-economic Dynamics in Sparsely Populated Areas*. Umeå: Department of Social and Economic Geography.

Sandell, K. (1997) Naturkontalt och allemansrätt: om friluftslivets naturmöte och friluftlandskapets tillgänglighet i Sverige 1880–2000. *SGÅ* 73, 31–65.

Shucksmith, D.M. (1983) Second homes: A framework for policy. *Town Planning Review* 54, 74–193.

Sillanpää, P. (2002) *The Scandinavian Sporting Tour: A Case Study in Geographical Imagology*. Östersund: Etour.

Williams, A.M. and Hall, C.M. (2002) Tourism, migration, circulation and mobility: The contingencies of time and place. In Hall, C.M. and Williams, A.M. (eds) *Tourism and Migration: New Relationships between Production and Consumption* (pp. 1–52). Dordrecht: Kluwer.

Williams, D.R. and Kaltenborn, B.P. (1999) Leisure places and modernity: The use and meaning of recreational cottages in Norway and the USA. In Crouch, D. (ed.) *Leisure/Tourism Geographies* (pp. 214–230). London: Routledge.

Wolfe, R.J. (1951) Summer cottages in Ontario. *Economic Geography* 27, 10–32.

Part 3: Island, Coastal and Marine Environments

Chapter 10

Maximizing Economic Returns from Consumptive Wildlife Tourism in Peripheral Areas: White-tailed Deer Hunting on Stewart Island/Rakiura, New Zealand

BRENT LOVELOCK AND KEVIN ROBINSON

Introduction

Stewart Island, New Zealand's 'third island', is located at the foot of the South Island, accessible across 30km of some of the roughest seas surrounding the nation. The island has a wonderful resource of dense rainforest, diverse bird life and a beautiful coastline that has attracted tourists for well over a century. Thus it was appropriate, if not a little belated, that New Zealand's fourteenth national park, Rakiura National Park, was officially opened on the island on the 9 March 2002.

The announcement of a national park was the result of five years of debate between various stakeholders on the island and across the country. However, the initial proposal of national park status outraged some groups including hunters who visit the island in substantial numbers. Indeed, half of the 450 submissions on the initial national park proposal came from hunters, worried that with a change in status of the land, they would no longer be allowed to hunt white-tailed deer (Asher, 2001). Currently, hunters from all over New Zealand (and some from overseas) come to the island to hunt the only accessible herd of white-tailed deer in the country. However, national parks legislation states that introduced plants and animals (such as deer) shall as far as possible be exterminated, raising the fear among hunters that recreational hunting was going to be abandoned, and the deer herd exterminated as a result of the new status in land.

Hunters supported their case for maintaining the deer herd by arguing that the potential loss of recreational hunting on the island would impact heavily on tourism and the associated economic benefits that hunting tourism brings to the local community (Department of Conservation, 1997b). While deerstalkers presented the potential benefits of hunting white-tailed deer, the conservation movement drew attention to the damage done by deer to the forest and other ecosystems on the island. Thus, while hunting currently remains as is under the new national park status, its long-term future is anything but assured, with a strong lobby for elimination of deer, backed in part by conservation policy stating that deer should be eradicated if or when feasible on Stewart Island (Department of Conservation, 1997a; Royal Forest and Bird Protection Society, 1999).

The Future of the Deer Herd

To a certain extent, the outcome of this debate is a microcosm for the future of deer and other game animal populations in New Zealand. New Zealand is in a different position to many other parts of the world that offer game hunting, in that all of the mammalian game species are introduced species, and pose very serious threats to indigenous ecosystems that have evolved in the absence of mammalian herbivores. Thus all of New Zealand's seven species of deer, plus other game animals such as pigs, tahr and chamois are all officially considered pests under the *Wild Animal Control Act* (New Zealand Government, 1977). Despite such recognition and other legislation that unequivocally states that introduced species in national parks should be eliminated (New Zealand Government, 1980), the government has adopted an ambiguous position on the issue. While in the past deer control has been a major preoccupation of some natural resource management agencies, increasingly the government has been happy to leave the control of game herd populations to recreational hunters and commercial meat recovery operators. However, the efficacy of these control measures has been brought into question by an increasingly vocal and politically connected conservation lobby.

While in most parts of the country the elimination of deer would be logistically challenging to say the least, Stewart Island, because of its isolation and manageable size, and because of the high quality of its native flora and fauna, presents a good case for a 'deer-free' refuge. Strengthening the case is the demonstrated extent of the damage caused by deer on the island. Additional arguments against the retention of a herd include the fact that recreational deer hunting is, at best, only a marginally effective deer control measure on the island – this relating mainly to accessibility issues for hunters, the difficult nature of the forest, plus the deer's natural cunning and ability to avoid hunters. Furthermore, commercial meat recovery as a control measure is not viable due to the smaller size of white-tailed deer.

Thus while a strong national lobby exists for the retention of recreational hunting on Stewart Island, the case largely hinges around demonstrating the economic value of the white-tailed deer herd to the local community, and more broadly to New Zealand. The local community of about 400 permanent residents generally supports the retention of the herd. Many local (island) hunters argue their case either in terms of 'traditional rights' to hunt deer, or through the subsistence value of the deer meat (venison) that they bring home. However, a stronger case may be built in terms of the expenditures of hunter-tourists who come from outside of the island's economy and who may ultimately contribute to the incomes of island residents. Such an income stream is unquestionably desirable, particularly for an economy such as Stewart Island's whose traditional commodity base (crayfish and blue-cod) may be unsustainable in terms of meeting the community's future needs. Thus in the transition to a service-based economy, hunting-tourism may become an increasingly important contributor.

Questions remain, however, over the magnitude of hunting-tourism expenditure and the extent to which it may contribute sustainably to such a destination's micro-economy. Stewart Island, as with many such island and peripheral economies, faces the challenges of maximizing the economic benefits of tourism when saddled with the burdens of isolation, reliance on outside economies, and having a tourism sector in its infancy.

The Economic Value of Hunting-tourism

Many studies into the economic value of hunting or of game herds have been undertaken throughout the world. The motivations for undertaking such research are varied. Perhaps the best-known of these studies are those performed in Africa, demonstrating the value of game herds, as a means of advocating the creation and maintenance of protected areas (e.g. Baldus, 1990; Child 1995; Hosking, 1996; Wilkie & Carpenter, 1999). Wilkie and Carpenter write of safari hunting being a significant and sustainable source of income to offset the costs of maintaining protected areas in central Africa. For example, Cameroon would need to attract only 4% of Safari Club International members travelling to Africa to generate a revenue stream of US$750,000 per year in trophy fees. And the authors note that in general, southern African countries capture up to 50% of the proceeds of safari hunting. From a community point of view, Shackley (1996) describes the CAMPFIRE (Communal Areas Management Programme for Indigenous Resources) programme in Zimbabwe. This programme enables rural communities to make money, through the hunting-tourists, from animals that would otherwise be poached because they were pests.

Perhaps on a more comparable note with Stewart Island is much of the research undertaken in North America. During the 1970s and 1980s in particular, many studies were undertaken in the United States on the value of game herds and hunting – generally to help guide resource allocation decisions for publicly managed lands (e.g. Charbonneau & Hay, 1978; Martin & Gum, 1978; Schoenfeld & Hendee, 1978; Sorg & Nelson 1986; Swanson *et al.*, 1989). Comparable research has been undertaken more recently in response to economic changes and transition from commodity-based economies (e.g. timber) in regional America (e.g. Guaderrama *et al.*, 2000). Another aspect of hunting research is that it focuses, in this era of cost-recovery and user-pays, on the economic benefits and costs, to public agencies, of certain forms of recreation/tourism such as hunting (e.g. Meyer *et al.*, 1998). In a similar vein, research has helped assign economic value to the hunting experience to assist game managers with allocating hunting opportunities (e.g. Akabua, 1996; Scrogin, 1999). Finally, in the context of sustainability, some studies have been undertaken to examine hunting's contribution (in economic terms) to sustainable natural area management (e.g. MacGregor, 1998).

Encouragingly, the majority of hunting studies demonstrate a high economic value associated with hunting, whether measured in terms of expenditure, efficiency, net willingness to pay, or consumer surplus. For example, Swanson *et al.*'s (1989) study of southeast Alaskan big game hunting estimated a total hunting value of US$7.2 million per annum. Similarly, Burger *et al.*'s (1999) study of bobwhite hunting in the southeastern United States estimated hunter expenditure at U$95 million, deriving an economic impact figure of US$193 million per annum.

However, a number of key issues emerge from the above body of work relating to the potential of destinations to maximize gains from hunting-tourism and recreation. The first point of note is the fallibility of staking a tourism or economic strategy upon natural populations of game animals – populations that are subject to natural and induced fluctuations. For example, in Burger *et al.*'s (1999) study, regional declines of the game species have contributed to declining hunter participation. This resulted in the loss or diversion of US$13 million of economic impacts between 1991 and 1992.

Perhaps a more worrying concern is the questionable ability of hunting-tourism derived income to serve as a replacement for more traditional commodity-based returns. While hunting may be highly valued in terms of 'willingness to pay' for the experience, the actual tangible financial benefits for regions, localities and the individuals residing within them may be minimal. This relates to the nature of the hunting-tourism expedition. Hunting-tourism involves hunters coming from outside of their normal area of residence and staying overnight to engage in hunting. In contrast to other forms of tourism, some studies have shown that hunting-tourists, while perhaps having a high rate of overall trip expenditure, may contribute little to the locality where they actually engage in their hunting. This is because most expenditure on equipment, food and other items is made in their home region. While at the hunting location, because hunters often are self sufficient in terms of accommodation and catering, there is little potential return while on-site. For example, in Guaderrama *et al*.'s (2000) study of the contribution of hunting and other forms of tourism as a replacement for timber harvesting and manufacturing as an economic base in Valley County, Idaho, a major share of recreation purchases are made outside of the county. The authors concluded that because of this, a huge increase in tourism would be needed to financially compensate for the loss of timber harvest and manufacturing. Furthermore, because of the increase in visitor numbers, in all likelihood, the quality of the visitor experience could not be maintained. Naturally, for an activity such as hunting, it is important that numbers are kept at safe levels. A similar study (Meyer *et al*., 1998) in Clark County, Idaho, revealed that spending by hunters within the county amounted to only 16% of total trip spending. Interestingly, while this was greater than that of two other categories of recreationists (camper/fishers and snowmobilers) hunters also demanded more services (and thus financial outlay) from local government, in terms of items such as assistance and rescue. Thus in the domestic North American hunting-tourism model we see a focus of the economic activity being on the location of residence of the hunter-tourists rather than the locality of the hunting itself. This appears to differ substantially from the benefits of safari hunting described in Africa. The difference seems to hinge upon the reliance of hunters in the latter location, because of their unfamiliarity with the destination, upon local providers of accommodation, transport, guiding and after-kill services (e.g. trophy mounting). In fact this reliance may be essential for the safety of hunters in that environment. This is not necessarily the case in the domestic model above.

Therefore, it seems that tourism providers in hunting localities can adopt two obvious strategies to maximize the retention of hunting-tourism income. The first being to maximize hunters' reliance on their services, such as accommodation or guiding. This could be done through demonstrating the real advantages of using such services (e.g. access to better trophies, more likelihood of achieving a kill within a given time-frame, and safety) or through simply generating the perception that such services are essential – whether they are or not in reality being a different matter. The second strategy is to make it more efficient and convenient for hunters to obtain their hunting equipment/supplies at or nearby the hunting locality. However, there are inherent obstacles to these strategies being implemented. First, the very motivation for the hunting experience is largely one of self-reliance, 'man-alone' or man against nature (e.g. Hendee, 1974 in Schoenfeld & Hendee, 1978). Thus, for many, even the majority of domestic hunters, this would preclude the use of many such services. Second, is the nature of the hunting locality. Generally, the more significant game herds are found in more remote or peripheral areas – often areas that have little in the way of shops and other services, let alone the specialty services required to fulfill some of the equipment needs of hunting-tourists. The investment required in infrastructure and services may simply be too great for many such peripheral locations.

The Stewart Island Study

By any definition, Stewart Island is a peripheral area. It suffers from geographical isolation, is distant from core areas of activity, has poor access to and from markets, and suffers from economic marginalization caused by a decline in a traditional industry (in this case fishing) (Brown & Hall, 2000). The island is also peripheral not only in terms of its distance from the core, but also the high cost of access/transport, and its sparse population. Like many other peripheral areas, maximizing and retaining the benefits of tourism expenditure are problems faced by the Stewart Island community.

Stewart Island is the southernmost of New Zealand's three major islands and is cut off from the rest of Southland (the closest region on the 'mainland' and a peripheral area in its own right) by the 30km stretch of Foveaux Strait (Figure 10.1). The island is about 75km long by 45km wide, its 1746 square kilometres mainly comprising rainforest, with pockets of lowland swamp and scrub. The island is unsuitable for intensive farming and derives its income from commercial fishing, aqua-culture and tourism (Sorrell, 1999). Most of the land (93%) is Crown owned, and administered by the central government agency responsible for protected area management in New Zealand, the Department of Conservation (DoC) (Department of Conservation, 2002).

The island's only settlement is Oban, located in Halfmoon Bay, with a resident population of 384 people (Statistics New Zealand, 2002). The town has a small but growing tourism infrastructure, comprising mainly B&Bs, backpacker accommodation and second homes but is severely limited when it comes to retail facilities. Oban has always been primarily a fishing settlement, but has increasingly become a popular gateway tourist destination, particularly for those visitors interested in the outdoors and natural history. An attraction for many visitors to the island is the rich wildlife, particularly the forest and marine birdlife, which are found in numbers and diversity generally greater than the mainland. For instance, the island is one of the few places in New Zealand where tourists may readily encounter a kiwi in its natural environment.

Figure 10.1 Stewart Island

Currently, visitor numbers are in the vicinity of 30,000 per annum, with the majority of these being international visitors. Tourism is estimated to be growing at the rate of 10 to 15% per annum on the island. Indeed, because of this growth, tourism in Southland (the region to which Stewart Island belongs) is accelerating at a faster rate than anywhere else in New Zealand except Queenstown, the country's premier alpine resort (Brook, 2001). With the new land status and attraction of a national park, visitor numbers are expected to grow even faster, with estimates varying from 65,000 to up to 150,000 visitors per annum within 15 years (Allen, 2000). Visitation is highly seasonal, with many visitors also remaining spatially concentrated around Oban over the summer months, participating in a range of nature tourism activities such as bush walking, bird watching, fishing, diving and sea kayaking. In this new national park, the DoC maintains a network of tracks (245km) and huts, used mainly by trampers and hunters. The most popular tramping routes are the Rakiura Great Walk (three days) and the Northern Circuit, a challenging ten-day trip around the northern part of the island. Much of the southern part of the island is very remote, rugged and inaccessible by most means.

Transport to the island is provided by a catamaran ferry service (about one hour) from the mainland port of Bluff, and an airlink from Invercargill, the nearest city on the mainland. In addition, a number of operators, based both in Oban and at Bluff operate charter boat services, to Oban or other parts of the island. Air charter is also available (from Invercargill) to some locations where there are beaches safe enough to land a small aircraft. From Halfmoon Bay, a number of boat operators provide transport to various parts of the island.

The proposal to establish a national park on Stewart Island has coincided with or fuelled a number of studies that have addressed tourism on the island. In 1997, the New Zealand Tourism Board (1997) and Department of Conservation (1997a, 1997b) undertook research regarding the development of Stewart Island and rationalization of protected area lands. One factor that emerged from both studies was the potential positive economic impacts that would be associated with the island becoming a national park. The New Zealand Tourism Board report identified strategies to enhance the returns from tourism on the island, and included hunting-tourism within their scope, as a means of contributing to this goal.

Hunting on Stewart Island

Hunters travel all the way to Stewart Island primarily because of the attraction of being able to hunt white-tailed deer in the only accessible herd of this species in New Zealand. White-tailed deer (*Odocoileus virginianus*) are native to North America, and were released on the island in 1905 for hunting. The herd has thrived, and now Stewart Island boasts some of the best white-tailed hunting in Australasia.

Part of the attraction of white-tailed deer for hunters, apart from being a different species from the main species of deer hunted in New Zealand (red deer) is their reputation for being extremely elusive. This characteristic is well demonstrated by the average number of days spent by hunters to be successful in bagging a white-tailed deer, which is high at around ten days per kill (Lovelock, 1987).

However the nature of the hunting experience on the island is also different to that of most mainland locations. Part of this is the 'island' experience. But also the characteristics of the environment, with rugged coastlines, dense bush, plus interesting birdlife (and the chance to see a kiwi), combine with the opportunities to fish and dive (most hunting blocks border the sea) to produce a unique hunting experience. The mode of travel to and from the island and the hunting block, whether by small plane landing on a beach, or by boat around a rough coastline, is also likely to be an important part of the trip for many hunters.

Many hunting blocks are quite remote from Oban and require some considerable investment in time (and money) to get to. The most remote blocks, in the south of the island, require several hours of travel by charter boat to get to, while even the most accessible may be an hour or two by boat from Oban, or half anhour by plane from Invercargill. Walking is not often considered as a mode of transport by hunters on the island, mainly because of their limited time, the amount of equipment they often require, and also because many hunters would simply prefer to invest the physical effort into hunting rather than tramping the long distances required to access their blocks.

Permits are required for all hunting on Stewart Island, and are available through a booking system from the DoC or the Rakiura Maori Land Trust for the limited number of Maori-owned hunting blocks. Hunting permits are free of charge, but small charges apply for hunters wishing to stay in DoC huts. Recently, a series of additional smaller huts have been established in a number of blocks by a hunter trust specifically for hunters, and a small charge applies for the use of these.

Published research on hunting on the island is limited. Most hunting-related research has focused on the quality of the natural resource and on deer population dynamics rather than the activities of hunters. However, hunter returns from 1997 to 2000 (New Zealand Deerstalkers Association, 2000 in Robinson, 2002) indicate that each year about 500 permits are issued for hunting parties, with an average number of about four hunters per party. Most hunters visit the island in the late summer or autumn, to maximize their chance of attaining a trophy buck. Although hunters stay on average about a week, only about two deer are killed per party. Research on hunter expenditure is more sparse. A hunter study undertaken in 1980–1981 by the New Zealand Deerstalkers Association concluded that hunters made an important contribution to the Stewart Island economy, spending about NZ$150,000 on accommodation, boat and aircraft hire, and supplies (Burton & Howden, 1982). More recently, the hunter returns mentioned above have provided very basic data on hunter expenditure, estimating the average cost per hunter per trip to be around NZ$500 (New Zealand Deerstalkers Association, 2000 in Robinson, 2002).

Study Methodology

A self-completion survey was determined to be the most appropriate and efficient means of collecting data on hunter expenditure relating to their trips to the island. Between October 2001 and April 2002, a total of 110 self-completion survey questionnaires were provided for hunters who had permits to hunt the DoC blocks on the island. An incentive to participate was offered in the way of a draw for the prize of a hunting magazine subscription. With the co-operation and assistance of DoC, an initial 70 questionnaires were posted to hunters with their hunting permits. These were completed and returned by one member of the party after they had undertaken their hunting trips. A low initial response rate (29%) from this approach necessitated a further, alternative means of distributing the questionnaire. The remaining 40 questionnaires were mailed to hunters randomly selected from those who had already been issued with a DoC hunting permit earlier in 2001.

The survey questionnaire comprised five sections with 33 items in total. The majority of items were closed choice, with five open-ended items included that related to specific expenditure and the costs of hunting on Stewart Island in general. The first section focused on hunters' modes of transport to the island and to their hunting blocks, and the costs of this. Section Two required hunters to estimate their party's expenditures on supplies (food, beverages and hunting equipment). Respondents identified the places of purchase of their supplies. Section Three explored expenditure specifically on Stewart Island. Respondents were asked if they, or members of their party, or their family or friends (on an associated trip) visited the island. Reasons for visiting or not visiting were sought, along with expenditure estimates. The following section sought information on the party's hunting block, its location and the party's selection rationale. The final section elucidated information on the composition, origin and experience of the hunting party and length of the hunting trip.

Pre-testing of the questionnaire was undertaken on colleagues, and a pilot of the revised version undertaken with a small number of hunters known to the researchers. A potential problem with this approach to data collection was identified in terms of recall error, but to some extent this was felt to be compensated for by respondents being able complete the questionnaire in their own time and potentially consult with members of their hunting party in order to provide more accurate responses.

The overall response rate for the survey was 48%, with 53 questionnaires returned. At this point, the exploratory nature of this study should be acknowledged. The small overall sample size (10% in terms of the average number of permits issued each year for hunting parties) may limit the ability to generalize broadly for this population from the data presented. Although non-response bias was not thoroughly investigated, there is no indication from the nature of the responses that the sample was non-characteristic of hunter-tourists to Stewart Island. The sample corresponds well in terms of information on party composition and trip length gained from basic kill returns and the earlier New Zealand Deerstalkers Association study (Burton & Howden, 1982; Department of Conservation, 2002). The DoC was also provided with a copy of the survey results and did not identify any issue with respect to non-representativeness of the sample.

Data analysis was undertaken using the statistical programme *SPSS* (Version 10.1). Responses to open-ended questions were transcribed from the questionnaires and coded according to a progressively developed set of themes.

Hunter and Hunting Trip Characteristics

Hunting parties on average comprised 5.5 members, although a significant proportion of parties were quite large, with seven hunters or more (26.4% (14)). This in part reflects the considerable expense of travel to the island and the response of hunter-tourists whereby they form larger groups and thus reduce travel costs.

Hunters from the south of the South Island predominated in the survey, with most hunters coming from Otago, Southland and Canterbury respectively. Collectively these three regions contributed 77.4% of hunters. A small number of hunters came from the North Island (7.5% (4)) with three hunters travelling from overseas (5.7%).

The average length of stay for hunters was 7.1 days. However, more than half the hunting parties surveyed stayed over a week hunting on the island. This extended length of stay relates to the distance and expense of getting there, with hunters maximizing their stay. The length of stay also relates in part to the difficult nature of the hunting on the island, with white-tailed deer being renowned for their elusiveness. On average a hunter requires ten days to bag a deer (Lovelock, 1987). Many hunters are, however, return visitors, with only 15.1% (8) of respondents making their first hunting trip to the island.

The hunters surveyed had chosen hunting blocks over most of the island, the exceptions being the blocks administered by the Rakiura Maori Land Trust (permit holders for these blocks were not surveyed). Hunting blocks were generally selected for a variety of reasons, with no individual reason standing out as being substantially more important than the rest. Common reasons for choosing blocks included their location and accessibility either by plane or boat, their accommodation facilities (usually a DoC hut) and their hunting reputation. Only one party chose a block because they considered it a 'cheap option', and although fishing was often stated as a reason for choosing a block, it was seldom the main reason.

Hunter Expenditure

Transport

The most common mode of transport used by Stewart Island hunter-tourists was commercial boat, 66% (35) of hunting parties choosing to travel by this form. For this item, 'commercial boat' includes both the scheduled service from Bluff to Oban, as well as the many charter boat services available, based in both Bluff and Oban itself. For most hunters, (73.6% (39)) the mode of transport identified in Table 10.1 conveyed them directly to their hunting block. Only about one quarter of hunting parties travelled to Halfmoon Bay (Oban).

For those parties that travelled to Halfmoon Bay, further transport was required to get to their hunting block. This transport was mainly in the form of commercial charter boat or water taxi, although a number of parties used private boats to get to their blocks. One party was flown to their block by commercial plane from the 'airport' at Oban. The commercial operators transporting hunters on to their blocks from Oban were generally Stewart Island based.

In terms of the commercial transport service used to travel to the island, two or three operators dominated, including the 'Foveaux Express', the scheduled service from Bluff to Oban (34.6% (18)), the Southern Isle (19.2% (10)) and Southeast Air (13.2% (7)). Just over half (55.8% (29)) of the hunting trips utilized transport operators that were based on Stewart Island, the remainder concentrated in Invercargill (Southeast Air), with a smaller number of trips being made with operators based in Bluff and elsewhere.

Respondents indicated the reasons for choosing their modes of transport. Most respondents identified a combination of factors that contributed to their decision, including price, convenience, block location, party size, availability and time. The most commonly identified primary

Table 10.1 Mode of transport to Stewart Island

	Frequency	*Percentage*
Commercial plane	12	22.6%
Private plane	1	1.9%
Commercial boat	35	66.0%
Private boat	2	3.8%
Helicopter	1	1.9%
Other	2	3.8%
Total	53	100.0%

reason for choosing the mode of transport was convenience (47.2% (25)). In this sense, it appeared that an important aspect of 'convenience' was the minimization of the number of legs of travel. Block location (18.9% (10)) and, interestingly, price (15.1% (8)) were somewhat less important considerations. Hunter-tourists surveyed spent a total of NZ$51,760 on transport to their hunting block (Table 10.2). The average expenditure per party was NZ$977 and per person NZ$184. By far the greatest transport expenditure was on transport directly to the hunting block, relatively little being spent on transport to Halfmoon Bay and from there to the block.

Hunting equipment

Hunting-tourism is a very specialized form of special interest tourism that requires special equipment, relating to the performance of the hunt itself, and to survival in an often hostile natural environment. In this study 'hunting equipment' comprised rifle, ammunition and related products, and tent, sleeping bag, outdoor clothing, footwear, navigational and survival gear. Hunting equipment was purchased from a variety of locations, including the home location, Invercargill (the nearest metropolitan centre to Stewart Island) and the island itself. However, the hunters' home locations were by far the most common main location of purchase (75.5% (40)), followed by Invercargill (24.5% (13)). Only one respondent reported making a hunting equipment purchase from Stewart Island, and this was not considered the main location of purchase.

The main reason given by respondents for not purchasing their equipment from the island was convenience (64.2% (34)). As noted above,

Table 10.2 Transport expenditure

Expenditure category	Total expenditure ($)	Average expenditure per party ($)	Average expenditure per person ($)
Transport to Halfmoon Bay	$6060	$433 (*n* = 14)	$106 (*n* = 57)
Transport from Halfmoon Bay to hunting block	$4100	$456 (*n* = 9)	$100 (*n* = 41)
Transport straight to hunting block	$41,600	$1066 (*n* = 39)	$185 (*n* = 225)
Total transport expenditure	$51,760	$977 (*n* = 53)	$184 (*n* = 282)

most hunting parties travelled directly to their hunting block, not visiting Oban on the way. This obviously precludes the purchase of equipment at Oban for most hunters. However, another reason for not purchasing hunting equipment at Oban, was that it simply is not available, or at least not to the knowledge of the survey respondents (15.1% (8)). There is one general store in Oban, but it holds only a limited range of equipment related to outdoor recreation.

Most respondents spent relatively little on hunting equipment for their trip, 67.9% (36) spending less than $100. The relatively low average expenditure on hunting equipment reflects the fact that most hunters, unless hunting perhaps for the first time, would already have a comprehensive inventory of hunting equipment that they would use for various hunting expeditions throughout the year. Having said that, a small number of respondents reported spending over NZ$500 on equipment. The total expenditure on hunting equipment specifically for the Stewart Island trip amounted to NZ$7800, or NZ$147 per party.

Food and beverage supplies

The home region was again the most common primary location for the purchase of food supplies (54.7% (29)). However, food was also commonly bought in Invercargill as well, with 43.4% (23) of parties reporting that city as their main location for expenditure on food. Most parties report multiple sourcing for their food supplies. In all likelihood, many hunting parties would bring some staple food and specialized 'outdoor' food products (e.g. freeze-dried and energy products) from their home regions, and would purchase fresh food (meat, dairy products, bread, fruit and vegetables) from Invercargill because of convenience. This especially applies to that significant proportion of hunter-tourists who travel considerable distances from throughout the South Island and further afield.

Only one respondent identified Stewart Island as the main location of expenditure on food, with another indicating some food purchase there. The main reason (64.2% (34)) that this was the case, is because of the inconvenience of making food purchases from the island – again relating to most parties being transported directly to their hunting blocks. Likewise, block location was recorded as a reason for not purchasing food from the island. There was also the perception that food products were expensive on the island.

In a similar vein, the main location of purchase for beverages (this item related mainly to the popular purchase of alcoholic beverages) was the home region (50% (26)) followed closely by Invercargill (40.4% (21)). Purchases in Bluff and Stewart Island were reported by a small number of respondents. Alcohol is readily available from the hotel at Oban, but,

Table 10.3 Expenditure on food and beverages

Expenditure category	Total expenditure ($)	Average expenditure per party ($) (n = 53)	Average expenditure per person ($) (n = 282)
Food supplies	$21,810	$412	$77
Beverages	$16,390	$309	$58
Total food and beverage expenditure	$38,200	$721	$135

Note: All figures in NZ$.

as for food purchases, convenience (50.9% (27)), block location (26.4% (14)) and expense (13.2% (7)) were listed as the main reasons for not purchasing beverages from the island.

Total expenditure on food and beverages amounted to NZ$38,200, equating to $721 per party or $135 per person (Table 10.3). This expenditure appears relatively low in terms of average domestic tourist spending on food and beverages (Gravitas, 2002). The total expenditure per hunter per day on food and beverages was around $19. However, hunter-tourists generally supplement their purchased food supplies with food products they obtain from their hunting and associated fishing activities. This is partly due to taste, partly tradition, in that shot deer are not 'wasted', and also due to the need to have fresh meat during a long hunting expedition that may last up to ten days – a period over which meat transported to the island will not remain fresh and edible. Survey respondents were asked to assign a monetary value to the food products they consumed that were obtained from hunting and fishing while on the island. Most parties (86.8% (46)) consumed food obtained from hunting and fishing, with an average value per party of NZ$179. The total value of food sourced from hunting and fishing was not inconsiderable at NZ$9,470. An interesting aspect of the expenditure data was the relatively high spending on beverages (75%) as a proportion of spending on food. This likely relates to the expense of purchasing alcoholic beverages and their centrality in the hunting-tourism experience.

Non-hunting travel companions

As indicated above, from the transport data, relatively few parties travelled to Halfmoon Bay on the way to their hunting blocks. However, a higher percentage (47.2% (25)) of respondents indicated that they *did* visit Halfmoon Bay while on the island, suggesting that they made their visit on their return from their hunting blocks. The main reason that most hunters did not visit Halfmoon Bay was the location of their block. Visiting Halfmoon Bay for hunters who have blocks to the far south of the island, or in the north or the west would add considerable time and cost to the trip to their hunting block. Such a visit would only be cheap and easy, and perhaps necessary for those with blocks in the central Paterson Inlet area. However, a significant number of respondents (15.1% (8)) indicated that there were members of their travel party who did not travel to the hunting block but visited Halfmoon Bay. Respondents estimated that the collective expenditure of their non-hunting companions was in the vicinity of NZ$525, quite a small amount. Unfortunately there was no data collected on the actual number of visitors in this category, or the activities they engaged in at Halfmoon Bay.

Hunter-tourists were asked about their own expenditure while visiting Halfmoon Bay – expenditure over and above that already detailed under transport, equipment, food and beverage supplies. The main categories would thus be accommodation, catered meals and souvenirs. Their estimate of expenditure totalled NZ$1725, or an average of NZ$216 per party.

Total Expenditure

Total hunter expenditure, including that of non-hunting friends and companions was NZ$100,010, equating to NZ$1887 per party or NZ$355 per hunter (Table 10.5). When divided by the average length of stay on the island of 7.1 days, this equates to an average daily spend of NZ$50. If these figures are applied to the total number of hunting parties visiting the island each year, then based on the 581 permits issued on the year 2000, the total expenditure on Stewart Island hunting-tourism would reach as high as NZ$1.1 million.

However, the proportion of hunter expenditure on the island was relatively small. Table 10.5 records the expenditure on Stewart Island and outside the island for each category of expenditure. Notably, as illustrated in Figure 10.1, transport is the only item that contributed a significant amount to the island, 57% of total transport expenditure going to island-based operators. Equipment, food and beverage expenditures all contributed little to the island relative to total hunter expenditure on these items.

In reality, however, the proportion of total trip transport costs going to the island would be less than that indicated by these results, as the survey did not generate data on the costs of getting from the hunters' home locations to the point of embarkation (usually Invercargill or Bluff)

Table 10.4 Total hunter expenditure

Expenditure category	*Total expenditure ($) (n = 53)*	*Average expenditure per party ($) (n = 53)*	*Average expenditure per hunter ($) (n = 282)*
Total transport expenditure	$51,760	$977	$184
Hunting equipment	$7800	$147	$28
Total food and beverage expenditure	$38,200	$721	$135
Island expenditure incl. family/friends	$2250	$42	$8
Total expenditure	$100,010	$1887	$355

Note: All figures in NZ$.

Table 10.5 Stewart Island and non-island expenditure

Category of expenditure	*Stewart Island expenditure ($)*	*Stewart Island expenditure as a % of total category expenditure*	*Non-island expenditure ($)*	*Total expenditure for category ($)*
Transport	29,505	57.0%	22,255	51,760
Equipment	75	0.1%	7800	7875
Food	150	0.7%	21,810	21,960
Beverages	270	1.6%	16,390	16,660
Other	1725	n/a	n/a	n/a
Family/Friends	525	n/a	n/a	n/a
Total	32,250	32.1%	68,255	100,505

Note: All figures in NZ$.

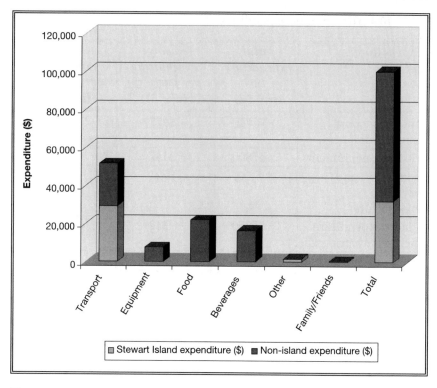

Figure 10.2 Stewart Island and non-island expenditure

for transportation across Foveaux Strait to their hunting blocks. In a similar way, the other costs of accommodation and food, which were incurred from the time that hunters' left their home locations to the point of embarkation for the island, were not recorded. Thus if the study were to consider the *entire* trip rather than just the Stewart Island component, the proportion of overall trip expenditure that went to Stewart Island businesses would likely be even lower than that indicated. Also, it should be noted that this study has not taken into account any leakage of tourism-generated income out of the island economy. This figure is likely to be significant because of the small size and lack of diversity of the local economy and limitations in its ability to meet the complete goods and services needs of the tourism sector.

Discussion and Conclusions

This study of Stewart Island hunter-tourist expenditure illustrates well the problems faced by small, isolated, peripheral communities when attempting to use tourism as a means of generating economic returns. Hunting is a popular form of tourism on the island and will likely continue to be so in the future, however the economic benefits to the island from hunting tourism are minimal. Average daily spend at NZ$50 is considerably lower than that for domestic tourists, based upon expenditure data for domestic visitors to Southland, which is NZ$81 per night (Gravitas, 2002). By far the biggest proportion of hunter expenditure is off the island. The underlying reason for this is the physical nature of the destination in terms of its distance from the mainland, its ruggedness and the difficulty of access (in terms of both time and expense) to hunting blocks. These characteristics, along with the small scale of the retail community and the lack of retail choice on the island dictate that hunters travel directly to their blocks, often bypassing Oban, purchasing their food and equipment from their home towns or the mainland points of embarkation.

Ironically, it is these very characteristics, the natural and social isolation of the island, that attract hunters to the destination in the first place. The difficult nature of the crossing of Foveaux Strait, the seasickness, or the challenges of landing in a light aircraft on a remote and rugged beach are integral parts of the Stewart Island hunting experience. Similarly, if Oban was a substantially larger, more typical New Zealand town, in all likelihood that proportion of hunters who choose to visit the centre would no longer be attracted: thus the 'paradox of peripherality' appears to hold true for this destination (Brown & Hall, 2000: 3).

The study also confirms the findings of researchers in other parts of the world (e.g. Meyer *et al.*, 1998; Guaderrama *et al.*, 2000) that the contributions of hunting-tourism may be limited because the focus of the economic activity is the location of residence of the hunter-tourists rather than the locality of the hunting itself. In support of this tendency, comments made by many survey respondents indicated that everything is pre-purchased and packaged before leaving home. In the case of Stewart Island there appears to be two loci of expenditure, the home residence and the point of embarkation for the trip from the mainland to the island. This is due to the nature of the island destination, requiring a trip of at least two legs. As most hunters originate from the south of the South Island, they travel by car to the points of embarkation. But because of the high cost of transport across Foveaux Strait, they tend to form reasonably large groups as a strategy to reduce costs. These groups, however, pose logistical problems in terms of transporting the large amount of equipment and food required. Thus the purchase of food, at least, is often undertaken at the place of embarkation.

Although this does not benefit Stewart Island itself, there are economic benefits to the wider political/economic region within which the destination lies. For example, Stewart Island falls within the Southland

District, so expenditure within Southland District would in some way benefit the island – for example through local government taxation that may ultimately contribute to the costs of infrastructural development on the island. Unfortunately, Invercargill and Bluff, the main points of embarkation and expenditure for hunter-tourists are outside of the Southland District, so may not provide benefits in this manner – but that is not to deny the broader regional benefits of additional tourism expenditure in Stewart Island's closest urban neighbour.

In terms of strategies to generate greater economic returns from hunting-tourism, there are limits to the extent to which Stewart Islanders may make gains. As discussed above, destinations may try to maximize hunters' reliance upon services, such as transport, accommodation and guiding. In the case of the island, there are many transport operators based on the island. But there are also a number of operators based at Bluff or Invercargill, who are at an advantage in terms of the total steaming distances required to access hunting blocks, and who compete very effectively for a share of the transport dollar. Some of the larger transport operators, though, do employ staff on the island, and thus contribute in the way of direct, indirect and induced income to the island economy. Focusing on accommodation is probably a less effective strategy, as most hunters do not make the visit to Oban, where there is already an extensive range of accommodation. Furthermore, accommodation in the Crown-owned hunting grounds is provided by the DoC at a minimal cost. One strategy suggested by the New Zealand Tourism Board is to organize an annual hunting competition event, staged over a number of weekends, with Oban as the focus of the event, thus capturing hunter-tourists and associates in this way (New Zealand Tourism Board, 1997). In a similar vein, the encouragement of non-hunting companions to accompany hunters could be lucrative, and fostered through the development and promotion of packages that offer accommodation and activities for this sector, centred on Oban.

Guiding services do have potential for generating island income, but mainly for international hunter-tourists who may have a greater acceptance of this service than their domestic counterparts. Currently only a small number of international hunter-tourists visit the island, but it seems that there may be potential to promote the island more to international hunters, at least from Australia, where white-tailed deer are not available for hunting (however, it is a commonly hunted species in North America).

The strategy of making it more convenient for hunters to purchase their equipment and supplies from Oban also faces challenges. As noted above, few hunters are tempted, or need to visit Oban, it being more convenient to purchase from home or the point of embarkation. Also it is doubtful if Oban retailers could be competitive or even have access to the range of goods required, because of issues of scale.

Collectively, these issues challenge the extent to which hunting-tourism in its present format can contribute to the economic sustainability of a peripheral area such as Stewart Island. Furthermore, the findings of this study undermine the current argument of deerstalkers in support of the retention of the white-tailed herd. Rather than relying upon a neo-liberal argument for the retention of hunting, based solely on the (limited in this case) economic benefits that hunting brings to the community, hunters may be able to develop a stronger case centred around some other premise, for example their 'traditional rights' to hunt.

References

Akabua, K.M. (1996) *Economic Valuation of Nontimber Resources Under a Lottery Rationing System: The Case of Moose Hunting in Newfoundland.* Ph.D. thesis, University of Alberta. Available at: http://wwwlib.umi.com/dissertations/fullcit/ (accessed 19/9/00).

Allen, D. (2000) Conservation Board to support Stewart Island impact study. *Southland Times*, 11 August, p. 17.

Asher, J. (2001) From island to Rakiura National Park. *Southland Times*, 12 May, p. 1.

Baldus, R. (1990) The economics of safari hunting. *Internationales Afrika-Forum* 26 (4), 361–366.

Brook, K. (2001) Concerns in paradise. *Southland Times*, 6 July, p. 5.

Brown, F. and Hall, D. (2000) Introduction: The paradox of peripherality. In Brown, F. and Hall, D. (eds) *Tourism in Peripheral Areas* (pp. 1–6). Clevedon: Channel View Publications.

Burger, L.W., Miller, D.A. and Southwick, R.I. (1999) Economic impact of northern bobwhite hunting in the southeastern United States. *Wildlife Society Bulletin* 27 (4), 1010–1018.

Burton, R.N. and Howden, D.T. (1982) *Hunter Usage Survey: Stewart Island 1980–1981.* N.p.: New Zealand Deerstalkers Association.

Charbonneau, J.J. and Hay, M.J. (1980). Determinants and economic values of hunting and fishing. *Forty-Third North American Wildlife Conference.*

Child, G. (1995) Hunting for conservation. In Child, G. (ed.) *Wildlife and People: The Zimbabwean Success. How the Conflict between Animals and People Became Progress for Both* (pp. 180–209). Harare: Wisdom Foundation.

Department of Conservation (1997a) *Stewart Island / Rakiura National Park Investigation: Discussion Document.* Invercargill: Department of Conservation, Southland Conservancy.

Department of Conservation (1997b) *Stewart Island / Rakiura National Park Investigation: Report to the New Zealand Conservation Authority.* Invercargill: Department of Conservation, Southland Conservancy.

Department of Conservation (2002) *Department of Conservation Policy Statement on Deer Control.* Available at: http://www.doc.govt.nz/Conservation/002~Animal-Pests/Policy-Statement-on-Deer-Control/002~Introduction.asp (accessed 29 March 2002).

Gravitas (2002) *New Zealand Domestic Travel Survey 2000.* Wellington: Tourism Research Council.

Guaderrama, M.C., Meyer, N., Harp, A. and Taylor, R.G. (2000) *Replacement of Timber Harvest and Manufacturing with Recreational Visitors as Economic Base Case of Valley County, Idaho.* Moscow, Idaho: Department of Agricultural Economics and Rural Sociology, University of Idaho.

Hosking, S. (1996) Official statistics on the income generated by the hunting industry in South Africa. *South African Journal of Wildlife Research* 26, 103–106.

Lovelock, B.A. (1987) *Northern Stewart Island Wild Animal Survey 1986.* Inevrcargill: Department of Conservation.

MacGregor, H.G. (1998) The economic value of deer hunting and its distribution in the Fundy Model Forest, 1994 (*Odocoileus virginianus*, New Brunswick). MF thesis, University of New Brunswick, Canada.

Martin, W.E. and Gum, R.L. (1978) Economic value of hunting, fishing and general rural outdoor recreation. *Wildlife Society Bulletin* 6 (1), 3–7.

Meyer, N., Harp, A. and McGuire, K. (1998) *Economic Impacts and Fiscal Costs of Public Land Recreation in Clark County, Idaho.* Moscow, Idaho: Department of Agricultural Economics and Rural Sociology, University of Idaho.

New Zealand Government (1977) *Wild Animal Control Act 1977.* Wellington: Government Print.

New Zealand Government (1980) *National Parks Act 1980.* Wellington: Government Print.

New Zealand Tourism Board (1997) *Stewart Island Tourism Strategy: A Strategy for Sustainable Growth and Development.* Wellington: New Zealand Tourism Board.

Robinson, K. (2002) Hunter visitation to Stewart Island: An exploratory estimation of expenditure. Unpublished dissertation for graduate diploma in Tourism, Department of Tourism, University of Otago, Dunedin, New Zealand.

Royal Forest and Bird Protection Society (1999) Help create a new national park. *Conservation News* 115 (August), 3.

Scrogin, D.O. (1999) *Individual and Aggregate Approaches for Valuing Lottery-rationed Big-game Hunting Privileges in New Mexico.* Ph.D. thesis, Universty of New Mexico. Available at: http://wwwlib.umi.com/dissertations/preview_all (accessed 19/9/00).

Schoenfeld, C.A. and Hendee, J.C. (1978) *Wildlife Management in Wilderness.* Pacific Grove, CA: The Boxwood Press.

Shackley, M. (1996) *Wildlife Tourism.* London: International Thomson Business Press.

Sorg, C.F. and Nelson, L.J. (1986) *Net Economic Value of Elk Hunting in Idaho.* United States Department of Agriculture, Forest Service Resource Bulletin RM-12. Fort Collins, CO: USDA Forest Service, Rocky Mountain Forest and Range Experiment Station.

Sorrell, P. (ed.) (1999). In *The Cyclopedia of Otago and Southland* (Vol. 2) (pp. 1147–1150). Dunedin: Dunedin City Council.

Statistics New Zealand (2002) *2001 Census of Population and Dwellings: Final Counts 2001.* Available at: http://www.stats.govt.nz/ (accessed 21 March 2002).

Swanson, C.S., Thomas, M. and Donnelly, D.M. (1989) *Economic Value of Big Game Hunting in Southeast Alaska.* USDA Forest Service Resource Bulletin RM-16. Fort Collins, CO: United States Department of Agriculture, Forest Service, Rocky Mountain Forest and Range Experiment Station.

Wilkie, D.S. and Carpenter, J.F. (1999) The potential role of safari hunting as a source of revenue for protected areas in the Congo Basin. *Oryx* 33 (4), 339–345.

Chapter 11

The Economic Benefits of an Ecotourism Project in a Regional Economy: A Case Study of Namuamua Inland Tour, Namosi, Fiji Islands

FILIPO TOKALAU

Introduction

A global definition of ecotourism is yet to be accepted (Higham & Luck, 2001), however, there is a general consensus that one of the special features of ecotourism is its ability to stimulate economic development therefore empowering local people through earning income and employment. From that standpoint, economic benefit is one of the objectives of using ecotourism as a development strategy.

Many developing countries have, since the 1980s, turned to ecotourism as a source of foreign exchange (Cater, 1993; Cater & Lowman, 1994; Tourism Resource Consultants, 1999). It is the backbone of the Galapagos Islands and Costa Rican economies (Honey, 1999), and a major contributor to other Central American countries specifically Belize (Lindberg & Enriquez, 1997). Panacea aside, Fiji adopted tourism because of the income and employment opportunities it offers. It is now Fiji's largest foreign exchange earner bringing in F$521 in 2001 (*Fiji Post*, 2000). Tourism is directly and indirectly responsible for around 45,000 jobs in 1998, which was equivalent to approximately 32% of the total labour force (*Fiji Post*, 2000).

With tourism, Fiji envisages to utilise and take advantage of its strengths in which it has a comparative advantage (Bull, 1995). These include the mystique and clean environment, friendly and safe atmosphere and an ideal position in the Pacific for sea and air route systems. Globally, Fiji potentially stands to benefit from rises in the world's discretionary income and cost reduction in air travel given that demand for travel and leisure are income and price elastic (Bull, 1995). This means that a slight rise in world income coupled with some reduction in costs will lead to an appreciable rise in tourist arrivals.

The major purpose of this chapter is to assess the extent to which the Namuamua Inland Tour (NIT) project is generating tangible benefits to the local communities. It also demonstrates that ecotourism is an engine for economic development at the 'grass-roots level' in the peripheral regions of Fiji. A more subtle but benign objective is filling-in an informational gap that could be conducive to policy making for rural development in peripheral island economies.

The Ecotourism Sector

This chapter uses a definition of ecotourism developed for the Fijian situation, that is:

> a form of nature-based tourism which involves responsible travel to relatively undeveloped areas to foster an appreciation of nature and local cultures, while conserving the physical and social environment, respecting the aspirations and traditions of those visited and improving the welfare of local communities. (Harrison & Brandt, 1997)

Fiji has a comparative advantage on the supply side of ecotourism. It is endowed with the serene physical environment and has a unique local culture (USP, 1980; Harrison, 1997) coupled with the friendliness and hospitality of its people (MTT, 1997) and the safety of Fiji's forest (Weaver & King, 1996).

Ecotourism as business practice is a relatively 'old' phenomenon in Fiji yet adoption of the concept is 'new'. Although not called 'ecotourism', appropriate nature-based tourism strategies were initially implemented in the late 1970s and early 1980s and promoted as an alternative development strategy relative to that of mass resort tourism (Harrison, 1997). Strengthening of the institutional framework of ecotourism has been ongoing.

Economic analysis of ecotourism is scant in Fiji despite there being a number of ecotourism sites (Harrison, 1997). However, there are unsupported claims that ecotourism has increased incomes for instance in the villages of Nakavika (Bricker, 2001), and Bouma and Abaca (Corbett, 2000). This chapter attempts to present a partial economic analysis on NIT, a largely 'home-grown' and riverine-based ecotourism project. It was implemented in 1990 to improve the livelihood of communities in the upland region of Navua with the assistance of the government and Sun Tours, a local inbound travel operator (Tuinalele, 1995: 3).

Research Site

Namuamua is a remote village located in the interior of Namosi Province in Viti Levu. Viti Levu is the biggest island of the Fiji archipelago, where the capital Suva is located. The village is situated on the bank of the Navua River about 16 kilometres upstream from Navua town. Namuamua has 46 households with around 290 villagers including civil servants and school children. Being the administrative centre of the Upper Navua area, which covers ten villages, Namuamua has a primary school, a health centre, an agricultural extension centre and a radio telephone station. Housing, most of which is wooden and concrete, is of a decent standard. There are a number of Fijian *bures* and prominent among these are the tourists' 'meeting house', and 'nerve centre' for village tourism activities.

There is running water with the river being utilised mainly for washing. Power is supplied by a community-owned diesel generator, albeit on an intermittent basis and supplemented by benzene/kerosene lights. However, a number of individuals have their private generators. While most Namuamuans are Catholics and Methodists, a small number belong to other denominations. The village is accessible by road and by river. The Beqa feeder road is serviced by community-owned lorries but the river is more favourable and significantly cost-effective for local commuters. Coupled with its serene environment, the river provides an enjoyable experience for tourists.

Subsistence agriculture is still the predominant source of income in Navua upland region where surpluses are marketed in Navua for income earning. Agricultural and cropping systems have changed a little partly because of the intrinsic nature of crops. However, with monetisation, Namuamuas are increasingly turning to some semi-cash farming. The marketable crops include *yaqona* (*Piper methysticum*), *taro* (*Colocasia esculenta*), *tapioka* (*Manihot esculenta*) *dalo-ni-tana* (*Xanthosoma sagittifolium*) and *duruka* (*Saccharum edule*) (Parham, 1972). Remittance is insignificant in the scheme of things given that only a limited number of Namuamua villagers live and work elsewhere.

Most, if not all, of the villagers are engaged in tourism related activities in one way or another as Namuamua village is a popular destination that hosts two tour businesses. The project under study is one of them. NIT exclusively provides employment for the *mataqali* of *Nabukebuke* (Tuinalele, 1995: 4). A *mataqali* is an agnatically related social unit, usually a lineage of the larger clan and it is also the recognised landowning unit in Fiji (Ravuvu, 1983). Kusitino Matakibau, a member of the *mataqali* initiated, operates, manages and owns NIT. He resides in Navua town.

The Tour

The tour usually originates in Lautoka, Fiji's second city where tourists are picked up along the way at the hotels along western Viti Levu and Coral Coast. Tourists who want to visit Namuamua get off at Navua town where the actual tour begins. The one-and-half to two-hour boat trip upstream the Navua River provides an exhilarating experience as the boat cruises through the fast flowing rapids, lush unspoilt Namosi forests, scenic waterfalls and sometimes through serene rock pools and gorges. At times when the water levels are low, the journey can be longer, arduous and risky yet exciting thanks really to the experience of the punt operators. Depending on the day and circumstances, the river environment can be a hub of activities for fishing, gardening, watering of animals, washing, playing and boating.

The arrival of the tourists at the village is marked by the beating of the *lali*. Young warriors dressed in traditional costumes of *masi* (*Brousonetia papyrifera*) and leaves await the arrival of tourists to escort them into the *bure* or meeting house. Once inside, a guide from the village explains to the visitors the sacredness of *yaqona* ceremony before they are accorded with the Fijian welcoming tradition. Towards the end of the ceremony, the *bilo* or *yaqona* bowl is passed to all tourists. For most, if not all, this will be their first ever experience of tasting *yaqona*. After the ceremony, the guides take the tourists on a village tour. This trip highlights the focal points of interests in the village such as the scenic views, the village green, health centre, and the school, as well as hearing the stories surrounding the establishment of the village's old and new sites.

On their return to the meeting house, the tourists are greeted to a spectacular spread of island food. A typical lunch will include a selection of vegetables, root crops and fresh fruits. Except for meat, most or all of the food are derived from the village gardens. At the end of the meal, the place is cleared for an afternoon of entertainment and dancing.

The men start the afternoon with a war-cry challenge followed by traditional dances or *mekes* – a combination of *wesi*, and *vakamalolo*. *Wesi* is a highly active dance where dancers use spears and fans and is performed exclusively by men. This is followed with the women with their *vakamalolo*, performed in a sitting posture. Finally, the local serenades where men folk of the village with guitar and clapping of hands set the pace for dancing. Tourists soon find themselves dancing with the villagers against the beat of some very popular local numbers. Then with the Fijian farewell song is sung, tourists are presented with a *salusalu* as they board the punts bound for Navua. A *salusalu* is made from colourful and scented flowers, is commonly worn around the neck and is often presented to a visitor as a sign of one's appreciation. At the Navua end, the Sun Tours coach awaits for the passengers to be transported to their respective hotels.

Method and Data

In order to obtain some indication on the size and value of tourism in the Namuamua region, a survey was undertaken in Namuamua village in 1997. Primary data on employment and income was elicited from employees through face-to-face interviews. A census of current employees was obtained through the assistance of the village head-man. Seventeen out of 24 were identified and these were individually approached to solicit their consent. As a means of getting some consistency, efforts were made to include former employees with four taking part in interviews. A significant number of the workers have been made redundant over the years largely due to 'social intra-relative frictions', an issue beyond the scope of this paper. Information from NIT was elicited through a 'self-completed' questionnaire.

Respondents were asked to provide information on the type of work they do and the incomes they earned from 1990 to 1997. Realising that employees sourced money from tourism in two ways, respondents were asked to declare their monthly wages as well as weekly revenues earned from sales of souvenirs and handcrafts. Other information collected included the respondents' main expenditures and how they allocate time in a typical tourist day. It is important to note that the tour is operational for three days of the week. This strategy was put in place to control the 'disruptive effects' of tourism on the village community (Tuinalele, 1995). Age and number of dependents were also included in the social bio-data of respondents.

NIT was requested to provide secondary data on tourist arrivals, tour fees, employment and its expenditures on village-related infrastructural development efforts. The opportunity cost of getting a comprehensive feedback from NIT was anticipated to be high so information regarding the business' expenditure on interests and profits and other commercially sensitive parameters were deliberately left out of the questionnaire.

Results and Discussions

Incomes

Tourism income is a function of tourists' arrivals, tour fees and sales from handcrafts. Tourist arrivals increased fivefold from 1920 in 1990 to 10,950 in 1997 (see Table 11.1). Children are assumed to make up 10% of the total annual visitors and pay a differential fee that is half that of the adult fee. Tour fees rose slightly between 1990 and 1995, then sharply from F$30 to F$40 in 1996 to 1997. Due to simultaneous rise in tour fees and tourist arrivals, gross income rose steeply from F$45,600 to F$416,100 in 1990 and 1997 respectively. This represented a ninefold rise in the project's gross revenue. Tourism in Namuamua was presumably just 'taking-off' in 1991. Tour receipts rose by 100% in the second year of operation. This is due to the combined effect of doubling of tourist numbers coupled with rigorous marketing via the Internet and in-flight advertising with Qantas Airlines.

Table 11.1 Tourist arrivals, employment, communal development
infrastructure, 1990–1997

Year	1990	1991	1992	1993	1994	1995	1996	1997
Tourist arrivals ('000s)	1.92	3.84	4.5	5.5	6.9	7.99	8.89	10.95
Employment – full-time – casual[1]	34 144	34 384	38 467	36 592	37 767	29 855	29 919	29 1129
Fee per – person[2] – boat[3]	25 60	25 60	27 60	27 60	30 60	30 70	40 70	40 70
Infrastructure						Electric generator Footpath Refrigerator		

Source: Namuamua Inland Tour, author's personal survey for NIT (1997); Ministry
of Tourism and Transport (1997)

Notes:
1 10% are children.
2 Per adult.
3 Return trip charges.

In order to determine the revenue from handcrafts sales, an income
and expenditure survey of NIT employees was carried out in 1997 (Table
11.2). On average an employee would have earned F$233 a month from
handcraft sales. By extrapolation handcraft sales increased from F$7920
in 1990, peaked in 1992 at F$8850 and fell to F$6760 in 1997. The precar-
ious trend is aligned to that of the rise and fall of number of employees
(full time).

Tour and handcraft receipts are initial incomes as they represent the
'first round of spending' of tourists where NIT's operator and souvenir
sellers are the primary benefactors. In order to gauge secondary income
that is generated, an analysis of costs incurred was undertaken. The
major operational costs for NIT for the period in question are presented
in Table 11.3. These include wages, transport (punt building, punt
charges, fuel and maintenance), food and drinks and other costs (construction of meeting *bure* and new toilet facility, and purchases of a
generator and refrigerator).

Tourism total (gross) income includes initial and secondary incomes.
Initial income is the sum of tour receipts and handcraft sales (Tables

Table 11.2 Average monthly income and expenditure for a typical
NIT employee, 1997

Income ($F)			Expenditure ($F)				
Salaries	*Handcraft*	*Farming*	*Handcraft*	*Household*	*Farming*	*Education*	*Church*
83	233	255	173	62	23	28	13
90^1	740^1	425^1	490^1	200^1	100^1	200^1	40^1
40^2	250^2	90^2	160^2	60^2	10^2	10^2	10^2

Source: Author's personal field survey (1997)

Notes:
1 Higher bounds.
2 Lower bounds.

Table 11.3 NIT's expenditure (F$ '000) 1990–1997

Costs	1990	1991	1992	1993	1994	1995	1996	1997
Transport								
– charges[1]	8.6	23.4	28	35.5	46	59.9	64.3	79
– others[2]	15.1	15.1	16.2	18.6	19.6	21.5	26.9	32.4
Food and drinks	3.2	3.2	3.2	3.6	3.8	4.8	5.8	7.9
Wages	12	12	14	14	15	18	20	24
Other costs[3]	1.4	1.4	1.4	1.4	1.4	2.3	2.3	2.3
Total	40.3	40.3	62.8	73.1	85.8	106.5	119.3	145.6

Source: Author's NIT and personal survey (1997)

Notes:
1 Punt charges.
2 Fuel, punt purchase and maintenance.
3 *Bure*, toilet facility, generator and refrigerator.

11.1 and 11.2). Secondary or indirect income is the summation of NIT's
operational costs and employees' handcraft expenditure at village level
(Tables 11.2 and 11.3). These are summarised in Table 11.4.

Beneficiaries

Tables 11.3 and 11.4 indicate the main income beneficiaries and their
respective but approximate shares. NIT's earnings are the difference

Table 11.4 Total income generated (F$ '000), 1990–1997

Income	1990	1991	1992	1993	1994	1995	1996	1997
Primary								
– tour	45.6	91.2	115.4	141.1	196.7	227.7	337.8	416.1
– handcraft	7.9	7.9	8.9	8.4	8.6	6.7	6.7	6.7
Secondary								
– tour	40.3	40.3	62.8	73.1	85.8	106.5	119.3	145.6
– handcraft	5.9	5.9	6.6	6.3	6.4	5.1	5.1	5.1
Total	99.7	145.3	193.7	228.9	297.5	346	468.9	537.5

Source: Author's NIT and personal survey (1997)

between total revenue and total cost. This grows from F$5300 to F$270,500 while employees' share rose from F$19,900 to F$30,900. Punt operators in Namuamua and nearby villages earned F$8600 in 1990. This was equivalent to 144 extra punts demanded at a rate of F$60 per punt. Punts operators earnings rose steeply to F$79,000 in 1997. In 1990, NIT was responsible for injecting approximately F$18,300 into the Navua business community by way of costs for fuel, maintenance, food and drinks and life saving equipment. This rose to F$40,300 in 1997. Business also benefited from construction of NIT's infrastructure that included the *bure*, a modern toilet facility, a generator and refrigerator. These cost approximately F$1400 in 1990. It is intriguing to note the multiplier effect (Bull, 1995) at work. Table 11.4 show that approximately F$150,000 was created in 1997 from an initial income of F$422,000 raising the total to F$572,000 in that year.

The Upper Navua region

In order to gauge the 'full impact' of tourism on Namuamua, a detailed account is undertaken. According to Lindberg (1993) the contribution of tourism depends not only onhow much money flows into the region, but also how much of what comes into the region stays in the region, thereby producing a multiplier effect. Therefore, to determine how much tourism income is injected into the village economy, an income and expenditure survey of NIT employees was also carried out (Table 11.2). Higher and lower bounds of income and expenditure are presented to elucidate the magnitude of differentials as 'an average' portrays a distorting picture of reality.

Incomes from tourism are attractive as they are significantly large by village standards where handcraft sales feature as the most promising in terms of financial returns. Table 11.2 indicates that a typical seller would earn as much as three times more from handcrafts than his/her salaried income. This supports other researchers' view that handcrafts can be a significant, and sometimes the primary source of tourism-related income for local communities (Linberg, 1993).

Monthly salaries range from F$40 and F$90 for women and men respectively. The salaries are not exploitatively depressing as income from souvenir sales significantly boosted total monthly income. However, the trend demonstrates one of the negative economic characteristics of the tourism industry *vis-à-vis* low remuneration, particularly for women (Mathieson & Wall, 1982, Lindberg & Enriquez, 1997).

Tourism augments farm income as 40% of the average employee's monthly income is contributed by tourism. *Taro* and *yaqona* are the two most productive crops, but the former exhibits higher productivity in terms of dollar per man-day. Crop productivity can be ascertained through gross margin analysis but is beyond the scope of this research. The ability to earn from subsistence farming differs significantly across families in Namuamua due to a multitude of motivating and other factors, including educational, entrepreneurial and attitudinal factors. Earnings from farming can be few and far between depending on the agronomical factors, size of farm, need for hard cash, and market conditions. Sustenance aside, data shows that farming (with F$255 monthly income) is still the backbone of Namuamua economy.

The community also benefits through meaningful investment in farming and education. Though primary education is to a large extent free, secondary education can be exorbitantly expensive. For example, at the time of the research a parental employer was paying around F$200 per term for his daughter's education. A typical entrepreneurial employee spends a maximum of F$100 in *taro* and *yaqona* production per month providing meaningful income to fellow villagers. Retailing *yaqona* is an easy and lucrative source of money in Namuamua as the village market is inexpensive, durable and stable.

On the expenditure side, approximately 56% of souvenir sales are re-spent on new stock. This is a leakage as the transaction is undertaken outside Navua. However, given that the linkages in the regional economy are quite robust, leakages from tourism are expected to be minimum.

A small portion of the household's expenditure is spent in village's retail stores for basic household items. Their small size aside, the shops are convenient in saving time and money while providing necessary food supplements. The majority of Namuamuans are Methodists so followers are expected to subscribe towards the *i Talatala's* (local preacher) allowance on monthly basis. Due to paucity of data, other household costs such as donations to the community and traditional functions, provincial tax and miscellaneous spending were left out from the analysis.

Tourism also appeared to trigger increases in entrepreneurial skills. Table 11.5 shows a variety of small business enterprises that were operating in 1997 and an analysis of their contribution to the village economy.

Handcraft selling is essentially a demand-driven business catering for tourists' need for souvenir and exotic memorabilia, appreciation of culture and the motivation to contribute to community's development. It is a bourgeoning enterprise and very suitable for women. Its contribution to the village economy is very significant as noted above. As handcraft vendors, women were able to up-skill themselves in budgeting and marketing, negotiations and banking. Unfortunately, these skills are traded off with the added burden of running the business that rendered them socially disadvantaged as they engaged themselves in their new trade.

With the high propensity of villagers to buy *yaqona* coupled with uncertainty in marketing conditions, more often then not, villagers would opt to sell their *yaqona* in the village. As labour is surplus with almost zero opportunity cost, income accrued from this venture is 'pure' profit. While men are often responsible for the harvesting and drying of *yaqona*, its marketing at the village level is undertaken by their female counterpart. Good money management is the only tangible explanation in such a clear division of labour regime.

At the time of research, five stores were owned and operated by NIT employees. Likewise, the majority of punt operating and grass cutting

Table 11.5 Analysis of small business enterprises, Namuamua village, 1997

Category	Number	Local earning/saving
Handcraft selling	14	Relatively large earning but moderate saving
Yaqona selling	Can be many at one time	Significant saving and increasing
Household store[1]	5	Some savings are retained
Punt operation	5	Little savings are retained, and increasing
Grass cutting	6	Small but contribute significantly to community
Labour	Some	Small but increasing

Source: Author's personal survey (1997)

Note: 1. Stores that sells more than five items of goods.

businesses were run and owned by NIT employees. Although no data was collected to substantiate the assertion that significant investment in these ventures came from tourism, it remains as a likely scenario. Punt operation existed before the advent of tourism in the Upper Navua regions but its demand really increases with the growth of tourism. Punts are affordable with lower risks than vehicular transport. With the availability of grass cutters, more villagers can be released to do other chores from communal cleaning where weeding is an important feature. This also raises the community's productivity to a significant degree.

Development projects

From 1995 to 1996 NIT invested a sum of F$8000 in Namuamua village development projects. These include the construction of concrete pathways in the village, the provision of a diesel generator to supplement lighting and a refrigerator for health centre. The concrete pathways provided safer alternatives for walking through the village, which can be hazardous given its site and location. Storage of the much-needed medicine in the village health centre is now possible with the availability of a refrigerator thus saving the government and the community a considerable amount of costs.

With the availability of electricity, the school is now able to run evening classes and study hours for children. Such an opportunity was not forthcoming under the legacy of benzene and hurricane lamps. Circumstantial evidence shows that the pass rates have been steadily increasing. A school informant attributes the success to a number of socio-economic and technological factors one of which is quality study time at night. The various projects have therefore contributed significantly to the socio-economic betterment of the village community, notwithstanding the absence of a proper social benefit–cost analysis.

Employment

NIT demands punt operators, tour guides, entertainers and food caterers. As Table 11.1 indicates, full-time but secondary employment rises marginally from 34 to 38 between 1990 and 1992 and then falls quite significantly to 29 in the ensuing years up to 1997. More than 50% of employees are women where they play multiple roles as guides, entertainers, food preparers and handcraft sellers. This is indicative of the feminisation of the industry (Matheison & Wall, 1982, Lindberg & Enriquez, 1997). Women are food caterers and entertainers. Though laborious and the work requires little skill, it is not that pessimistic a scenario in such circumstances as women are using tourism to their advantage to gain meaningful employment that has positive socio-economic ramifications for themselves, their families and the community at large (Hall & Page, 2000).

The fall in total number of full-time secondary employment is not consistent with the rise in tourism arrivals. Despite the ease of substitutability for labour, it is envisaged that one of the immediate repercussions is the loss of operational efficiency. The issue is intriguing and warrants some discussion and perhaps further research. Part-time employment increased almost tenfold from 144 to 1129 in 1990 and 1997 respectively. The term is restrictive in the sense that it used exclusively to include punt operators. It is envisaged that the business community in Navua would also benefited through employment generation.

Some incidence of induced employment arose when NIT employees hired fellow villagers to farm or do other chores for them. This 'extra' labour provides opportunity to cultivate more crops and may improve marginal productivity compared with household members (Forsyth, 1995). A small number of villagers are selling their labour in return for cash, and its significance in the village economy is increasing.

Time management

On a typical tourist day, NIT employees are expected to carry out their tourism duties as well as their day-to-day responsibilities to the households and community. In the absence of time management, the extra responsibilities demanded from the household would have adversarial effects on itself and the community. Fortunately, tourism introduced a management regime into a legacy where time was totally unstructured. Table 11.6 shows the division of labour in a typical Namuamauan household before and after tourism was introduced.

Table 11.6 Division of work and time management for a typical labourer pre- and post-tourism

	Pre-tourism		*Post-tourism*	
Task	*Household*	*Farming*	*Household*	*Farming*
Performed by	Women and children	Men	Men, women and children	Men, women and children
Timing	Unstructured	Unstructured	Structured 8–11 a.m. and 4–5 p.m.	Structured 8–11 a.m. and 4–5 p.m.

Source: Author's field survey (1997)

Time management has improved as employees adapt themselves to a structured system in carrying out their different roles. For example, on a typical tourist day, household and farming duties are scheduled prior to tourists' arrival and after their departure. Tourism-related duties are carried out at around 12.00 to 15.00. An ensuing effect is increases in marginal productivity of labour. Men and children are more productive as they actively engaged in household and farming duties some of which were 'outside' their domains.

Labour is in overabundant supply. This means that its opportunity cost is minimal or near zero. Children constitute a considerable portion of labour, which has very little economic value. With tourism, children's productivity is boosted as they carry out a greater role in farm production. As an example in 1997, labour cost F$10–12 per day while *taro* was commanding a price of $10 per bundle. Assuming zero inflation and discounting, a youth who plants 50 *taro* plants is worth F$50 gross return to his labour eight to ten years later. Farm-oriented activities also ensure that children and the rest of the family will continue to work in agriculture, as it is the mainstay of village life. It also reduces the family's dependence on income derived from tourism thereby cushioning its adversarial effects of seasonality and unpredictability (Wallace & Pierce, 1996).

The Way Forward

Notwithstanding the overarching importance of planning and management, NIT can increase its economic contribution to local communities and realise its business goal by repositioning. This can be carried out in several ways. First by improving quality of its service in the punt-guiding department. Punt operators are experienced boaters but ineffective information providers on the socio-physical environment of the tour including the flora and fauna. NIT can identify this bottleneck through a visitor survey. Interestingly Namuamua and nearby villages have reserves of reasonably educated youths who can become efficient tour guides. Should NIT see that this comes to fruition, then it will provide more employment for underemployed youths, as well as contributing to the revival of local knowledge, and socio-cultural renaissance.

NIT plans to expand its business into lodging. *Bures* as rest and guest houses would provide simple accommodation facilities enabling tourists to extend visits. *Bure* lodging can be a viable venture in a rural setting as building materials are cost effective, coupled with surplus and skilful labour. It increases tourist's expenditure, reduces the establishment costs markedly and increases economic contribution to the community. The added facilities are best located outside the village boundary. This would ensure some control on the negative impacts of tourists on the community whileallowing the village to maintain its authenticity (USP, 1980). In the absence of social impact analysis it is crucial that other control and management measures are required to ensure a minimum impact outcome.

Backward linkage with agriculture was weak and almost non-existent as there was little evidence of village-grown food on the tourists' menu. Food management is now taken over by the operator who sources it from the fresh food market in Navua. Rejuvenating the tourism–village garden link is fundamental to tourism in Namuamua. Though its total economic impact may not be significant, it will improve financial return to subsistence farmers, providing them with meaningful employment and diversifiying the means of income generating activities. In addition, it will also improve utilisation of land and maximise the use of government technical expertise. Market gardening therefore has the potential to reduce leakages and strengthen linkages thereby increasing tourism's economic contribution to the community.

Conclusion

The chapter provides a partial analysis of the economic benefits that an ecotourism project contributes to a local region as well as providing some baseline assessment of its impact on social and resource development in an upland region in Fiji. The fundamental findings are that ecotourism has improved the economic opportunities of local beneficiaries through income and employment generation, increased local entrepreneurship and improved proficiency in time management resulting in rises of labour productivity. Non-tangible benefits were improved health and education standards. Several options are mapped out for NIT to increase its economic contribution to the local region, broaden its entrepreneurial base and achieve some economies of scale in its operation. Given the increasing nature of competition in Upper Navua, it is in the region's interest that NIT explores those avenues.

Acknowledgement

This case study is the result of numerous hardworking and dedicated individuals. The author would like to thank the villagers of Namuamua for their comradeship and in particular the employees of NIT. Their enthusiasm and interest in tourism is the basis of this study. Thanks are due to the village headman, Aborosio Sovatabua for his guidance and perseverance, and to Kositiono and Maria Matakibau for their advice, support and friendship. A special *vinaka* goes to the University of the South Pacific for funding the research and to the Economics Department staff for their wisdom. I am also grateful to Ministry of Tourism for additional documents and support.

References

Bricker, K.S. (2001) Ecotourism development in the rural highlands of Fiji. In Harrison, D. (ed.) *Tourism and the Less Developed World: Issues and Case Studies* (pp. 235–249). Wallingford: CAB International.

Bull, A. (1995) *The Economics of Travel and Tourism*. Melbourne: Pitman.

Cater, E.A. (1993) Ecotourism in the third world: Problems for sustainable development. *Tourism Management* 14 (2), 85–90.

Cater, E.A. and Lowman, G. (eds) (1994) *Ecotourism: A Sustainable Option?* Chichester: Wiley.

Corbett, A. (1995) Tourism Resource Consultant, Wellington, New Zealand. Personal communication.

Fiji Post (2000) Tourism surpasses sugar, Sunday 4 August. Available at: www. fijilive.com/news/news.php3?art=o4/04e.hmtl (accessed 4 August).

Forsyth, T.J. (1995) Tourism and agricultural development. *Annals of Tourism Research* 22 (4), 877–900.

Hall, C.M. and Page, S. (2000) *Tourism in South and South East Asia, Issues and Cases*. Auckland: Butterworth Henemann.

Harrison, D. (1997) *Ecotourism and Villaged-based Tourism: A Policy and Strategy for Fiji*. Paper prepared for Ministry of Tourism, Transport and Civil Aviation. Suva: University of the South Pacific.

Harrison, D. and Brandt, J. (1997) Ecotourism in Fiji. Paper presented at the Pacific Science Inter-Congress 'Island in the Pacific Century', University of the South Pacific, Suva 13 July.

Higham, J. and Luck, M. (2002) Urban ecotourism: A contradiction in terms. *Journal of Ecotourism* 4 (1), 36–51.

Honey, M. (1999) *Ecotourism and Sustainable Development: Who Owns Paradise?* Washington, DC: Island Press.

Lindberg, K. (1993) Economic aspects of ecotourism. In Lindberg, K. and Hawkins, D.E. (eds) *Ecotourism, A Guide for Planners and Managers* (2nd edn), (pp. 87–117). Vermont: Ecotourism Society.

Lindberg, K. and Enriquez, J. (eds) (1997) *An Analysis of the Ecotourism's Economics Contribution to Conservation and Development in Belize* (Vol. 2). Washington, DC: WWF.

Mathieson, A. and Wall, G. (1982) *Tourism: Economic, Physical and Social Impacts*. Harlow: Longman Scientific and Technical.

MTT (Ministry of Tourism and Transport) (1997) *Fiji Tourism Development Plan*. Suva: Government of Fiji.

Parham, S.D. (1972) *Plants of Fiji*. Suva: Government Printery.

Ravuvu, A. (1983) *Vaka I Taukei: The Fijian Way of Life*. Suva: Institute of Pacific Studies, University of the South Pacific.

Tourism Resource Consultants (1999) *A Report on Pacific Ecotourism Workshop, at Taveuni, Fiji*. Prepared for the New Zealand Overseas Development Aid, Wellington: Tourism Resource Consultants.

Tuinalele, T. (1995) *Ecotourism Course Project: Namuamua Inland Tour*. A report prepared for the Department of Tourism, Fiji.

USP (University of the South Pacific) (1980) *Pacific Tourism: As Islanders See It*. Suva: Institute of Pacific Studies of the University of the South Pacific.

Wallace, G.N. and Pierce, S.M. (1996) Evaluation of ecotourism in the Amazon. *Annals of Tourism* 23 (4), 843–879.

Weaver, S. and King, B. (1996) Environmental management and Fiji tourism. *Journal of Pacific Studies* 19, 127–144.

Chapter 12
Growth of Beach Fale Tourism in Samoa: The High Value of Low-cost Tourism

REGINA SCHEYVENS

Introduction

Samoa is an independent Pacific Island nation with exceedingly beautiful beaches, rainforests and volcanic features, and is home to vibrant Polynesian communities living mainly in picturesque villages dotted around two main islands. It is seemingly another perfect island paradise, yet in the past Samoans have been reluctant to trade on their country's natural beauty and cultural features by encouraging tourism development. Threats to the country's agriculture sector led to a change of heart in the early 1990s, and tourism has since rapidly grown to become Samoa's main industry (Thuens, 1994; Twining-Ward & Twining-Ward, 1998).

Yet Samoa is also on the world's geographical and economic periphery, a small developing country in the middle of the world's largest ocean – the final place on earth to see the setting of the sun in the last millennium – and still dependent to some extent on aid disbursements from wealthier countries and remittances from Samoans living abroad. In this context it would be easy to equate Samoa's peripherality with vulnerability and powerlessness, however the reality of tourism development in Samoa belies such assumptions. What has emerged, in fact, is a largely home-grown tourism industry characterised by small- and medium-sized enterprises, which are owned mostly by Samoans. Unlike the three most popular Pacific Island destinations, Fiji, French Polynesia and New Caledonia, Samoa is not home to numerous large resorts catering to medium- to high-spending tourists, rather, the largest growth in recent years has been experienced in the budget beach *fale* accommodation sector, which is popular with both domestic and international tourists.

In providing for tourists on quite limited budgets, beach *fale* tourism in Samoa provides an interesting contrast to the 'high value, low volume' ecotourism ideal which assumes that it is in the interests of the natural environment and local communities that countries attract small numbers of higher spending tourists. This chapter suggests that budget beach *fale* tourism in Samoa could also be considered 'high value' in terms of community development if it involves cultural education of guests, the economic benefits are retained locally, it supports conservation of resources, and it allows for high levels of local participation and control.

The ideas herein are supported by a small, but growing, body of literature that challenges critiques of tourism in Third World contexts that suggest the industry is inherently exploitative and damaging to social and environmental systems. Recently a few organisations have chosen to specifically examine how tourism can enhance the well-being of local communities in less industrialised countries. From a development perspective, tourism should help to meet basic needs, enhance a community's sense of pride or dignity, contribute to self-reliance, and sustain their livelihoods (Scheyvens, 2002a). The 'Fair Trade in Tourism' movement would support such objectives, as they aim to ensure that a large proportion of tourist expenditure goes to the country, and the area, where they spend their holidays, thus maximising benefits for local people (Shah & Gupta, 2000). Along these lines also, we see the UK's Department for International Development and Overseas Development Institute commissioning studies on 'pro-poor tourism' (Ashley *et al.*, 2000), and at the World Summit for Sustainable Development in Johannesburg, 2002, the World Tourism Organisation launched their new project entitled 'STEP: Sustainable Tourism as a primary tool for Eliminating Poverty in the world's poorest countries'. While Samoa is not one of the world's poorest countries, it is lower on the United Nations Development Programme's Human Development Index than the likes of China, Peru or the Philippines (see http://hdr.undp.org). As such, it is worthwhile to ascertain the extent to which tourism has brought real benefits to people living in rural Samoan communities.

To begin, this chapter explores the way in which the tourism industry has evolved in Samoa, noting in particular how respect for *faaSamoa* and the land tenure system have limited large-scale growth of the industry. Next, the government's strategy of supporting a sustainable form of tourism development is considered. The main part of the chapter then draws on the author's recent fieldwork in Samoa (mid-2003) to outline the benefits of beach *fale* tourism for local communities, while also highlighting concerns about future changes in the industry.

The Nature of Tourism Development in Samoa

Until recently there has been ambivalence towards tourism development in Samoa, which is strongly tied to the people's history of resistance to outside interference in their politics, economy and culture.

Protecting *faaSamoa*

Samoans have never accepted foreign domination. In 1899, an agreement between Germany and the USA saw the Samoan islands split, with Germany taking control of Western Samoa. The colony fell into New Zealand hands at the start of the First World War, but this imposed control was not welcome. A non-violent rebellion against New Zealand rule, the Mau movement, became active in the 1920s and 1930s: 'The Mau not only rejected colonial authority but turned away from Western development and culture' (Stanley, 2000: 460).

Western Samoan made history in 1962 by becoming the first Pacific Island territory to gain independence. While Samoa faced 60 years of political rule by outsiders, the colonial period failed to undermine the people's cultural independence or *faaSamoa* (Twining-Ward & Twining-Ward, 1998). *FaaSamoa* refers to the traditional way of life of the Samoan people, and respect for *faaSamoa* is a key reason why Samoa has taken a cautious attitude towards tourism (Fairburn-Dunlop, 1994): there is 'concern that this may have adverse consequences upon the dignity, self-reliance, traditional customs, authority structure and morals of rural people' (Meleisea & Meleisea, 1980: 42). The guarded approach to tourism is evidenced in various efforts to control tourism, which date back to at least 1919. As noted in the *Lonely Planet* guidebook when referring to the picturesque volcanic crater of Lake Lanoto'o: 'In 1919 local traders suggested that a road be built to the lake to allow easy access to holiday-makers, but proponents of "controlled tourism" saw to it that the idea remained only a suggestion' (Talbot & Swaney, 1998: 115).

It is argued that *faaSamoa* attitudes still 'mould the industry', thus for example, in hotel floorshows male dancers are just as prominent as female dancers, 'rather than the South Seas image of sarong-clad dusky maidens wiggling their way through frenzied hulas' (Fairburn-Dunlop, 1994: 129). And although a lot of modified craft items are offered for sale to tourists, authentic craft items such as traditional tapa cloth have been kept for the Samoan people's own use and ceremonial exchange (Fairburn-Dunlop, 1994: 138–9; Meleisea & Meleisea, 1980). In the interests of *faaSamoa* also, foreigners who are being intrusive or driving too fast through villages, may find themselves subject to negative behaviour from children, including the throwing of stones or baring of bottoms (Stanley, 2000: 466).

Land tenure issues

The same reluctance to cede land and resources to outside interests, which was apparent at the time of the Mau movement, has been applied to the tourism sector today. Around 81% of land is held in customary tenure, including most coastal land desired by tourist developers (Twining-Ward & Twining-Ward, 1998: 269). There are two options for customary land: while it cannot be sold or transferred, developers can gain access to it through a 30-year lease or through joint ventures. In practice, however, 'the communal nature of land holding and consensus decision-making . . . hinder the smooth development of tourist initiatives' (Fairburn-Dunlop, 1994: 132). Financial institutions are often reluctant to lend money for tourism investments on customary land, as this is seen as high-risk (ADB, 2000: 187–8). Customary land tenure has thus provided a considerable constraint to development of large, coastal resorts (Pearce, 1999), as Peteru (1998: 36) laments:

> Attempts to bring in big hotel chains including Marriot and Sheraton flopped after reaching ground breaking stage, several times, when landlords started haggling for more money. [Samoa has thus gained a reputation] as a difficult place to do that kind of business.

Lack of landowner interest in land deals with large outside corporations means the tourism industry in Samoa seems destined for the moment to be dominated by small-scale, locally-owned and operated initiatives. Only one of the four hotels with over 50 rooms is foreign owned, and it has been suggested that: 'Tourism in Samoa is almost exclusively a family business' (Twining-Ward & Twining-Ward, 1998: 266).

Government Support for Sustainable, Controlled Tourism Development

In the 1970s and 1980s the government was reluctant to encourage tourism development, thus, for example, they were at first averse to building a full-scale airport for wide bodied jets (Meleisea & Meleisea, 1980). While expansion of Faleolo International Airport did begin in 1983, and the Samoa Visitors' Bureau was established in 1984, tourism was low on the official list of priorities (Twining-Ward & Butler, 2002).

Active promotion of tourism by the government did not begin until the 1990s when they were spurred on to find development alternatives after the devastation caused by two cyclones (in 1990 and 1991) and taro leaf blight (in 1993) which destroyed almost the entire crop of this staple – and main foreign exchange earner – on both main islands (Twining-Ward & Twining-Ward, 1998: 262). Yet even then they did not want to encourage mass tourism or the development of large-scale resorts, rather, they implemented the 1992–2001 Tourism Development Plan (TDP) which stresses that 'tourism in Samoa needs to be developed in an environmentally responsible and culturally sensitive manner, follow a policy of "low volume, high yield", and attract discerning and environmentally aware visitors' (Government of Western Samoa & Tourism Council of the South Pacific 1992, cited in Twining-Ward & Twining-Ward 1998: 263). It is unlikely that the constant stream of budget tourists who hang out in beach *fales* today would be seen as either 'high yield' or 'discerning'.

Despite the lack of aggressive marketing of tourism, visitor numbers grew from around 20,000 in 1970, to almost 48,000 visitors in 1990, and over 88,000 visitors in 2001 (Page & Lawton, 1996; Twining-Ward & Butler, 2002). The key source markets for Samoa are American Samoa (35%), New Zealand (30%), Australia (10%), USA (10%), and Europe (10%) (Stanley, 2000: 462), but an important note is that Samoans who are returning to visit friends and relatives (VFR) slightly outnumber other tourists (ADB, 2000: 184). Tourism is now the largest industry in Samoa, and by 1998 it contributed 16% of Samoa's gross national product, higher than remittances from Samoans overseas, and four times more than agriculture (Twining-Ward & Twining-Ward, 1998).

Sustainable tourism comes through as a key approach in the aims of the new Tourism Development Plan (TDP) (2002–6), which states:

> Sustainable tourism development will be undertaken at a rate, and in ways that will:
>
> - generate continuing economic benefits throughout Samoan society
> - contribute to a general improvement in the quality of life in Samoa
> - reflect, respect and support fa'aSamoa
> - conserve and enhance the country's natural and built environments; and
> - enhance tourists' experiences of Samoa'. (Government of Samoa, 2002: 17)

Rather than simply adopting sustainable tourism rhetoric, which is probably evident in the TDPs of numerous countries, Samoa has embraced the concept of sustainable tourism in ways that directly reflect respect for the well-being of Samoan people:

> What is distinctive about the Samoan case is the way in which the country's strong social and cultural traditions – the faaSamoa – have been incorporated in government tourism policies and the ways in which these policies are being implemented through the NTO [National Tourism Office] in their attempts to foster local participation in the development process. (Pearce, 1999: 154)

Respect for *faaSamoa* is evident in the government's promotional activities. Tourism marketing draws particular attention to its cultural and environmental attractions, rather than playing on the typical 'beach paradise' stereotype common for Pacific Island destinations. The national carrier, Polynesian Airlines, was severely berated by members of the public and ended up withdrawing an advertisement that used a scantily clad woman as part of its promotional efforts (Fairburn-Dunlop, 1994: 129).

The Evolution of the Beach *Fale* as a Samoan Tourism Icon

The TDP for 1992–2001 mentioned above had a marketing strategy that 'entails seeking out higher spending leisure tourists . . . in main source markets' (cited in Pearce, 2000: 196). However, the most notable tourism growth area has been the beach *fale* sector, which provides budget accommodation and meals to both international tourists (including backpackers, adventuresome tourists of all ages, surfers and Samoans resident abroad who return to visit friends and family) and domestic tourists (including church and family groups, public and private businesses on 'retreats', and expatriates). For approximately US$15–20/night (all monetary values are presented in US$, based on the conversion rate for December 2003 of Samoan Tala $1 = US$0.35), patrons get their own open beachside *fale* (essentially a hut without walls), bedding, light and mosquito net, access to shared facilities, and two meals. There is also a market for domestic day visitors who like to picnic on beaches near to Apia on weekends, paying US$5 per carload or US$20 per vanload of people. This price covers both the right of access to the beach (Samoans have traditionally compensated others when using resources not owned by their own family) and use of the facilities (*fales* and bathrooms).

There were 44 registered beach *fale* operations by December 1999, mostly on the island of Upolu, which is home to the country's capital, Apia. Certainly their growth as commercial establishments is a recent phenomenon, as Meleisea and Meleisea mention only one example of beach *fale* tourism in their 1980 paper on tourism in Samoa, Piula, where the Methodist church constructed basic facilities and a *fale* and made these available to visitors for a small fee. However, beach *fales* have existed in a non-commercial sense for a much longer period of time, as they were constructed by families for their own leisure purposes, for example, as a place to rest in on a Sunday afternoon after a morning in church and the traditional large Sunday lunch. As explained by a Peacecorp worker currently living in Samoa, beach *fales* are '. . . places where [Samoan] people hang out . . . oh, and by the way, you [tourists] can pay to use them too' (Male Peacecorp worker, July 2003).

Most commercial beach *fales* were developed in the early 1990s after the cyclones and taro blight, as an alternative economic development initiative (Twining-Ward & Twining-Ward, 1998: 267). Grants from AusAID's Tourism Development Fund to construct toilet and shower facilities for guests were an added incentive at the time. Beach *fales* also offered an attractive option for Samoans returning from overseas and wanting to use their money to establish an economic venture near to their families in the rural areas. Many constraints to the development of more up-market tourism ventures were either not of concern to the budget sector, or seen as an advantage. Importantly, beach *fales* are owned by local families so there are no concerns about leasing land or negotiating joint ventures.

The New Zealand government through NZAID has provided significant support for tourism development in Samoa, including beach *fale* ventures (Hall & Page, 1996: 180–5; Terra Firma Associates, 2001: 4). Prior to 2002, bilateral aid was dispersed through NZODA (New Zealand Official Development Assistance), although for the sake of simplicity, the term NZAID will be used to cover all bilateral aid from NZ to Samoa. Direct support for beach *fales* has included funding two seminars for beach *fale* owners (in 1998 and 1999), which involved consultation on the *Samoa Beach Fale Owners' Manual*. They have also supported community awareness programmes whereby 'villagers' awareness of the nature and potential of tourism has been heightened . . . and advisory services are offered' (Pearce, 1999: 150–1). NZAID established a Tourism Support Fund in 1999 to provide advice and financial grants to tourism operators: this has been very popular with beach *fale* owners who can get dollar for dollar reimbursements for improving their infrastructure, such as ablution blocks.

The beach *fale* experience is rated highly by the growing urban middle classes in Samoa who seek leisure activities on the weekends. They are particularly weeks booked by domestic visitors over school holiday periods and Christmas time, but at other times of the year well-known beach *fale* businesses can be booked out thanks to corporate and government groups using their facilities for team building and strategic visioning exercises. In addition, beach *fales* have provided international visitors with a unique experience (Twining-Ward & Twining-Ward 1998: 264). As one guidebook notes, beach *fales* are

> an excellent way to combine hiking, snorkeling, swimming, surfing, and just plain relaxing with a sampling of Samoan life . . . . As well as being great shoestring places to stay, they're a wonderful introduction to Samoan culture. (Stanley, 2000: 470, 495)

A number of tourists interviewed in the process of my fieldwork commented that the open sided nature of beach *fales* was a culturally appropriate form of accommodation: 'The set up is open plan: it promotes mixing and sharing – that's the Samoan way – not like when I was in Australia' (Young Samoan man, June 2003), and most international tourists stressed that their experience of staying in beach *fales* far exceeded their expectations:

I've had 16 years of travel experience and nowhere else in the world is there something like this. It's just an amazing form of accommodation ... there's a real sense of belonging and partnership [with the Samoan culture] that you don't get from other forms of accommodation'. (Middle-aged male tourist from New Zealand, July 2003)

Benefits of Budget Beach *Fales* for Rural Communities

While not everyone is aware of or interested in what beach *fales* have to offer, it is clear from speaking to beach *fale* owners and other villagers that tourism associated with beach *fales* has fostered community development in a number of ways in Samoa. Often it provides a means of sustainable economic growth in the context of few alternative livelihood strategies (Terra Firma Associates, 2001: 50). As one female beach *fale* owner explained 'I started this business because I didn't want my family to live on scraps ... We pray all the time but God won't give us things unless we work for them'. The benefits of beach *fales* for local communities are discussed below, focusing on economic, social, environmental and political development.

Many people assume that tourists on a budget spend little money on their travels overall, when in fact their contribution to the local economy can be significant for a number of reasons. First, free and independent tourists such as backpackers typically stay longer than other groups of tourists, thus while their daily expenditure may not be high, the total amount of money they spend can be considerable (Scheyvens, 2002a). This is why some beach *fale* owners prefer international guests, as they stay longer and spend more money than domestic tourists. Those catering more to domestic day visitors can still earn significant amounts of money, however, as witnessed by daily takings of up to US$350 at Matareva Beach. It should also be noted that domestic tourists are not as fickle as international tourists and the domestic market is less subject to seasonality, plus domestic tourism conserves foreign exchange, so there are advantages in governments promoting this sector rather than the more 'glamorous' international market (Scheyvens, 2002a).

Second, because tourists staying in beach *fales* do not demand luxurious, imported goods, owners can maximise the use of local products and services, which has multiplier effects for the economy. For example, beach *fale* owners often purchase fruit, vegetables and seafood from extended family members or other villagers, and when constructing the *fales*, they tend to purchase locally made blinds, string and mats, as well as hiring the services of the village plumber, carpenter and electrician. As one owner explained, 'Money should be left in my village rather than going elsewhere'. Another noted: 'Our idea is to help the community. We buy food products from villagers – if you need fish, arrange it with a fisherman. The same goes for building materials'. They employ mainly family members, but will take on extra staff during busy periods.

Third, because of the adventuresome nature of many international tourists visiting Samoa and their interest in culture, the tourists tend to seek out more remote areas where other tourists do not go (Twining-Ward & Twining-Ward, 1998), thus spreading their money over a wider geographical area. This can mean that economically deprived regions, which have cultural or natural features of interest to adventurous tourists, also benefit directly from the tourism industry.

Beach *fales* provide villagers with an opportunity to diversify their livelihood options, thus spreading a family's economic risk. Thus if the price for bananas goes down or an aunty loses her job in Apia, economic prospects for the family are still promising if they own a beach *fale* enterprise. Beach *fales* also fit in well with other rural livelihood strategies, so that whether a family member works on the plantation or in the beach *fale* kitchen that day can depend on bookings. While during busy periods beach *fales* may provide most of a family's income, even successful beach *fale* ventures may need to call on other livelihood strategies at less popular times. One female beach *fale* owner, for example, had a US$8000 loan that she had used to construct a large communal eating house. When I asked if she ever had a problem with repayments, she mentioned that her brother had a big plantation: 'If there's been no tourists, taro talks!'.

Local men and women have also gained considerable skills through involvement in beach *fale* tourism enterprises and participating in training schemes for beach *fale* owners. The types of topics they noted as being of particular worth included ideas on making tourists feel welcome, meeting tourist expectations regarding service and cleanliness of facilities, waste management, marketing and advertising. There have been more women than men attending beach *fale* owners' seminars to date, and it appears that the opportunity to run their own business has been empowering for many women:

> Samoan women have shown considerable initiative and used the opportunities available in the tourism industry to develop their entrepreneurial skills. In a society where there are very few income-generating avenues, tourism has provided opportunities for learning new skills and applying old skill in new fields'. (Fairburn-Dunlop, 1994: 122)

Beach *fale* tourism also fosters social development in rural communities. Several people interviewed commented that communities with successful beach *fale* ventures were now more vibrant and attractive places to live in, and that young people were moving back to the villages from Apia. For example, a pastor who had recently returned to Samoa after 24 years in the United States commented on the changes he had noticed in rural areas, many of them associated with beach *fale* development:

> Beach fale tourism has helped to boost the morale of communities and helped people to cater for their day to day needs . . . . It's also helped them to improve their surroundings, their gardens etc. (Middle-aged male, returning resident, June 2003)

On one occasion I spoke with three young men aged 17, 20 and 21, on the streets of a village where beach *fale* tourism had become popular, asking them where they would prefer to work, in Apia (Samoa's capital) or in their village. Given the large numbers of Samoans who have migrated to Apia or beyond to metropolitan countries, I was somewhat surprised when they unanimously replied that they preferred their village, because this meant they could be closer to their family, friends and church. Clearly it was now also easier for them to pick up casual work in the village, such as cleaning the beach or waiting on tables at a beach *fale* enterprise.

Owners reported a lot of support from other villagers for beach *fale* development because of the wider community benefits they received, which included support for community groups and projects. For example, the Women's Committee running Paradise Beach have donated money to build a new house for the pastor, while the *matai* (chiefs) running Matareva Beach have donated money to the local school. Another beach *fale* owner donated money to a school group in exchange for them putting on a cultural performance (*fiafia*) for tourists one night each week.

Many international tourists were very interested in learning about Samoan culture. Even a young surfer backpacking his way around the world, noted: 'I just sort of – read about all these countries, and [chose Samoa because it] balanced the culture and the surf' (Young British male tourist, July 2003). This interest in culture was noted by a number of beach *fale* owners, and there was a genuine sense of sharing ideas, stories and skills, between 'hosts' and 'guests', rather than a strictly commercial and/or one-way relationship of cultural learning which developed. For example, one European tourist relayed how at the end of a *fiafia* night, during which she had been encouraged to try Samoan-style dancing, she had stayed up late with some of the young female performers who asked her to teach them how to do some Western-style dancing. Many tourists expressed that they had experienced 'genuine Samoan hospitality' and some even suggested that because beach *fales* were generally run by an extended family, after a few days in one place they felt like 'part of the family'. Villagers in general felt proud about their villages and culture when visitors showed an interest in talking with them, visiting their churches and homes.

Beach *fales* can also benefit the local environment, or at least impact on it less than more up-market initiatives, in a number of ways. In the popular tourist region around Aleipata, for example, a Marine Protected Area has been established in order to help restore the coral and fish populations within the reef. Undoubtedly, the fact that tourist dollars contribute significantly to the local economy helped to influence local decision makers to support the idea of the Marine Protected Area. In addition, budget tourist facilities like beach *fales* are more environmentally benign than other forms of tourism as they put less pressure on the natural resource base. For example, cold showers instead of warm mean that showers are shorter, and no energy is required for heating, and beach *fale* tourists are happy to swim in the sea, rather than expecting a fresh water swimming pool. Similarly, there is no air conditioning or even fans in the *fales*, rather, tourists have to hope for a cool sea breeze. The fact that beach *fales* cannot offer every modern convenience is turned into a benefit. Some beach *fales*, for instance, promote themselves on the Internet under titles such as 'Your Own Grass Hut', where they note you will have peace and quiet when you come to stay with them because they are in a remote location with no telecommunications linkages. They trade on *not* being five-star resorts, yet say they will deliver five-star service and hospitality.

Beach *fales* also contribute to development in a political sense in that they are controlled by local families, and this means that prime beach sites remain under the management and ownership of local people. This challenges foreign domination of the tourism sector. Beach *fale* tourism is also overseen by the council of *matai* (chiefs) of each village, who set rules to ensure that village life is not adversely affected by beach *fale* operations, and that visitors feel welcome and safe. Thus for example, beach *fale* owners are expected to instruct their guests in cultural protocol with respect to how they must dress when entering a village, how they must wait quietly during evening prayer time rather than wandering around the village, and at what time noise from the beach *fales* should stop in the evenings. In terms of rules for local people living in popular beach *fale* areas, villagers not directly associated with beach *fale* enterprises are generally not permitted to be on the beach in the evening. This is a security measure deemed necessary to make Western visitors feel secure in the context of the relatively open sleeping arrangements of the beach *fale*. In the case of Paradise Beach on Upolu, the local pastor lobbied the council of *matai* to close the beach to all visitors on Sundays as he felt it disturbed the peace of the holy day unduly when there were large numbers of cars driving through the village, and also when some visitors got drunk and behaved inappropriately.

Finally, encouraging domestic tourism enables local people to benefit from government investment in tourism infrastructure, including national parks and reserves. This challenges the colonial mentality evident in many Third World countries whereby interests of foreigners are prioritised (Scheyvens, 2002b).

While this section has focused on ways in which beach *fale* tourism is contributing to local development in Samoa, there are still some concerns about beach *fale* development that will need to be addressed in the future. These include potential over-supply of beach *fales* and problems with maintenance of facilities (Pearce, 2000: 200), lack of sufficient business know-how and subsequent failure of some businesses (Terra Firma Associates, 2001), inadequate disposal of sewage and lack of safe drinking water (Twining-Ward & Butler, 2002), and the influence of *faaSamoa* on business success, particularly because of heavy expectations on small beach *fale* owners to contribute to communal activities (Twining-Ward & Twining-Ward, 1998). My fieldwork also revealed potential antagonism associated with restrictions placed on villagers' access to the beach in some popular beach *fale* areas. Overall, however, the feeling among beach *fale* owners and villagers in general was that beach *fale* development had been very positive for rural communities.

Lack of Recognition of the Value of the Beach *Fale* Sector

Despite the significant growth of the beach *fale* sector and the benefits this has brought to rural communities, it has been overlooked, disregarded and harshly criticised by some commentators. Thus estimates of the number of beds available for tourists in Samoa do not include beach *fale* accommodation (for example, Pearce (1999: 145) states that in 1996 there were 740 rooms in 36 establishments). Similarly, an Asian Development Bank report, *Samoa 2000* (ADB, 2000), which is purported to 'provide a comprehensive analysis of current economic and key sector developments in Samoa' does not even mention that beach *fales* exist, despite having an entire chapter devoted to tourism. Claims in this report that domestic tourism in Samoa is very small are not accurate because the beach *fale* sector has been overlooked. Others have overlooked the value of beach *fales* because they are more interested in development of high-class tourist facilities, which they feel will earn the country more foreign exchange (see ADB, 2000; Pearce, 2000). Such people are not happy to see beach *fales* occupying prime beachside locations:

> Since beach fales came up in Samoa we've had a sort of unchecked rash of huts [develop] all over the place. A perfect example is Aleipata: that whole strip used to be a beautiful place but now it's just littered with beach fales'. (Tour company owner, June 2003)

This business person went on to suggest that the rapid growth of beach *fales* was bad for the image of Samoa internationally as it was projecting itself as a backpacker destination: 'It shouldn't be [a backpacker destination] because it is such a beautiful place ... Having all these beach *fales* all over the coastline ... it's just giving that wrong impression' (Tour company owner, June 2003). There is certainly some jealousy of the success of beach *fales* from the owners of small, lower-class hotels, which now see many of their former clientele (e.g. staff of government agencies) preferring to stay in beach *fales,* and it is likely that this jealousy contributes to negative perceptions of what beach *fales* have to offer the tourism sector.

Of even greater concern, however, is the fact that the government is introducing changes that may eventually undermine beach *fale* tourism in some areas. First, an amendment bill was passed in parliament in on 26 June 2003, to encourage more foreign investment in higher-class resorts. This involves government playing a stronger role in assisting outsiders to lease land, and tax breaks being given to new hotel/resort developments, with the size of the tax relief being proportional to the size of the resorts. This may see more land moving out of community hands, at least temporarily, in the future, but it is unclear if this is also signalling less government support for the small-scale beach *fale* initiatives. Second, because of concerns from within the tourism industry about supposed sub-standard accommodation and facilities provided by some beach *fale* operations, staff of the Samoan Tourism Authority are formalising planning procedures regarding beach *fales* by developing minimum standards, which they must abide by if they want to be promoted/endorsed by the government. This will mean that poorer families will be even less likely than at present to be able to establish a beach *fale* venture, as greater resources will be required to meet the minimum standards. This is unfortunate as when there is a wide range of standards of beach *fales* available, they can meet the needs of different parts of the market. For example, very basic beach shelters are usually quite acceptable to domestic day visitors, while more sophisticated beach *fales,* which are partially walled and have light fittings, can provide well for the needs of international visitors.

Conclusion

The discussion above has provided an overview of the context of tourism in Samoa, stressing the cautious official approach to tourism which has been adopted, and respect for *faaSamoa,* as well as demonstrating the benefits that the budget beach *fale* sector is bringing to rural communities. A key concern about the future of budget tourism, however, is that formalisation of planning procedures and the idea of 'minimum standards' may force out some small businesses, and that the government is becoming more concerned with supporting large-scale resort style tourism. While this is a more glamorous side of the industry, it does not necessarily equate that this will bring more benefits for the Samoan people or be of 'high value'.

Rather than assuming that growth of the industry and attracting higher spending tourists should be key goals, the material herein suggests that it could be in Samoa's interests to stay with small- to medium-scale tourism development and cater for a diverse range of tourists, including domestic tourists and those travelling on a budget. Many international tourists who come to Samoa are attracted at least partly because of what a locally-controlled tourism industry can offer, namely, low–moderate prices, friendly service, basic accommodation in stunning locations, and a cultural experience. Interestingly, Twining-Ward and Twining-Ward (1998: 270) argue that commonly perceived constraints to the growth of tourism in Samoa (including land tenure arrangements, aspects of *faaSamoa*, air access and weak institutions), may have been to the overall benefit of the country and its people:

> *these* constraints ... have also resulted in a more socially equitable and ecologically sustainable tourism industry than is found in other Pacific island countries. Local participation in the tourism industry is high, and the kind of dependency on foreign investor and expatriate staff that has befallen larger destinations such as Fiji does not exist in Samoa. The critical indicator, visitor satisfaction, also shows that the country is on the right track. (Twining-Ward & Twining-Ward, 1998: 270)

From a community development perspective as well, which stresses reliance on local skills, knowledge and resources, and emphasises local ownership and control, improved standards of living for rural communities, respect for environmental and cultural assets, and local level empowerment, beach *fale* tourism in Samoa is also largely on the right track.

Acknowledgements

The author would like to acknowledge the valuable research assistance of Bronwyn Tavita Sesega during fieldwork in Samoa, and the ongoing, friendly and insightful help extended by Louise Twining-Ward. In addition, sincere thanks go to all of the beach *fale* owners, villagers, tourists and government officials who consented to interviews in the process of this research.

References

ADB (Asian Development Bank) (2000) *Samoa 2000*. Manila: Asian Development Bank.

Ashley, C., Boyd, C. and Goodwin, H. (2000) Pro-poor tourism: Putting poverty at the heart of the tourism agenda. *Natural Resource Perspectives* 51, 1–12.

Fairburn-Dunlop, P. (1994) Gender, culture and tourism development in Western Samoa In Kinnaird, V. and Hall, D. (eds) *Tourism: A Gender Analysis* (pp. 121–41). Chichester: Wiley.

Government of Samoa (2002) *Tourism Development Plan (2002–2006)*. Apia: Government of Samoa.

Hall, C.M. and Page, S.J. (1996) Australia's and New Zealand's role in Pacific tourism: Aid, trade and travel. In Hall, C.M. and Page, S.J. (eds) *Tourism in the Pacific: Issues and Cases* (pp. 161–89). London: International Thomson Business Press.

Meleisea, M. and Meleisea, P.S. (1980) 'The best kept secret': Tourism in Western Samoa. In *Pacific Tourism As Islanders See It* (pp. 35–46). Suva: Institute of Pacific Studies of the University of the South Pacific.

Page, S. and Lawton, G. (1996) The Pacific Islands: Markets, development and planning issues. In Hall, C.M. and Page, S.J. (eds) *Tourism in the Pacific: Issues and Cases* (pp. 273–302). London: International Thomson Business Press.

Pearce, D. (1999) Tourism development and national tourist organizations in small developing countries: The case of Samoa. In Pearce, D.G. and Butler, R.W. (eds) *Contemporary Issues in Tourism Development* (pp. 143–57). London: Routledge.

Pearce, D. (2000) Tourism plan reviews: Methodological considerations and issues from Samoa. *Tourism Management* 21, 191–203.

Peteru, C. (1998) Samoa's tourism future looks bleak. *Pacific Islands Monthly* April, 35–6.

Scheyvens, R. (2002a) *Tourism for Development: Empowering Communities*. Harlow: Prentice Hall.

Scheyvens, R. (2002b) Backpackers and local development in the Third World. *Annals of Tourism Research* 29 (1), 144–64.

Shah, K. and Gupta, V. (2000) *Tourism, the Poor and Other Stakeholders: Experience in Asia*. Ed. Boyd, C. London: Overseas Development Institute and Tourism Concern.

Stanley, D. (2000) *South Pacific Handbook*. Emeryville, CA: Moon Travel Handbooks.

Talbot, D. and Swaney, D. (1998) *Samoa*. Hawthorn, Victoria: Lonely Planet.

Terra Firma Associates (2001) *Review of the NZODA Samoa Tourism Development Programme 1995–2001 for the Ministry of Foreign Affairs and Trade, Wellington*. Wellington: Ministry of Foreign Affairs and Trade.

Theuns, L. (1994) Tourism in Western Samoa: Situation, impacts and constraints. *Tourism Recreation Research* 19 (1), 49–58.

Twining-Ward, L. and Butler, R. (2002) Implementing STD on a small island: Development and use of sustainable tourism development indicators in Samoa. *Journal of Sustainable Tourism* 10 (5), 363–87.

Twining-Ward, L. and Twining-Ward, T. (1998) Tourism development in Samoa: Context and constraints. *Pacific Tourism Review* 2, 261–71.

Chapter 13
Doing it Right the First Time?
Ecotourism on the Wild Coast
of South Africa

DOROTHY QUEIROS AND G.D.H. (DEON) WILSON

Introduction

The rugged Wild Coast of South Africa contains spectacular scenery and has remained fairly undeveloped. Its people are among the poorest in South Africa and desperate for development and social elevation. As this unique area opens up for tourism, it is vital that the right type of tourism takes place with due sensitivity to local communities and the natural environment.

With the Wild Coast as a blank canvas in terms of tourism development, the question is – can we do it right first time? To tackle this question, the chapter focuses on Mkambati Nature Reserve, which will form the hub of future development plans. The study involved taking postgraduate ecotourism students to Mkambati to research alternatives for its future development. Participants worked closely with local authorities, and ultimately submitted the proposals for their consideration.

The Ecotourism Tetrahedron Model forms the basis of the study. It sets out the four fundamentals of ecotourism – resource base, local community, tourist and ecotourism industry. Each of these was examined at the reserve, and proposals outlined for implementing ecotourism. If developed wisely, this keystone of the Wild Coast can benefit impoverished communities, create enlightening and interactive experiences for the ecotourist, conserve natural resources and be coordinated by an industry dedicated to sustainability.

The Wild Coast

The Wild Coast on the Indian Ocean falls within the Eastern Cape province of South Africa. Under the previous apartheid government's policy of separate development, this 254km coastline formed part of a homeland for the Xhosa people and was known as the Transkei. Shortly before South Africa's first democratic elections in 1994, it was reincorporated into the country as part of the Eastern Cape. Its isolation is one of the reasons why the area has remained relatively unspoiled by outsiders. Other reasons for this are that the tribal lifestyle was well integrated into the area's ecology and geographical constraints prevented major coastal development (Costello, 2001).

The Wild Coast has earned its name because it is truly wild – deep gorges, impenetrable forests, remote beaches, high cliffs, unusual stone sculptures and huge waves crashing on a rugged coastline. The latter have claimed numerous ships over the centuries, including the famous treasure ship, the *Grosvenor*, in 1782. The area contains numerous lagoon-like estuaries and rivers winding through deep valleys towards the sea, interrupted by many waterfalls. The highest of these, the Mfihlelo Falls, fall 160m directly into the ocean below and is the highest waterfall of this type in the world (Mayhew, 1985). At higher altitudes, the vegetation is predominantly tall grassland dotted with proteas, aloes, and patches of forest (Oakes, 1991). The coast is washed by the warm Agulhas current, making bathing possible almost all year round (Erasmus, 1995).

Along the coast there are important and environmentally sensitive areas, for example: nature and marine reserves; the Pondo Centre of Diversity along the Pondoland Coast, with high levels of endemism and biodiversity; indigenous coastal forests; muti/ethnobotanical plants; marine and estuarine resources; and a rich archaeological and cultural heritage (Taylor, 2000). Despite this, the Wild Coast region, together with the inland areas of the former Transkei, has less than 1% of land formally protected within nature reserves. This is in comparison to the 4% for South Africa, and the international norm of approximately 10%.

The original inhabitants of the area were the San and Khoi Khoi. Both groups were displaced in medieval times by the ancestors of the Xhosa people who occupy the area today (Mertens & Broster, 1987). They are divided into a number of clans, with rivers forming the natural boundaries between them. The Transkei is also home to former President Nelson Mandela who was born into the Thembu royal family in the village of Qunu near the city of Umtata.

The traditional Transkei homesteads of hardened mud huts with thatched roofs form an enchanting spectacle. Most huts are incompletely painted, but with good reason. The part facing the rising sun is often painted with a gloss paint or white to deflect heat, thus keeping the hut cool on hot summer days. As the sun continues west, by evening it shines on the unpainted mud, which absorbs the heat so that the hut is warm after dark (Mayhew, 1985; Oakes, 1991).

The people of the Transkei are probably the poorest in South Africa (Bristow, 2000), with the only people in permanent employment being those working for government. Against this backdrop, locals are desperate for development and social elevation (Bristow, 2000), which makes the tourism development earmarked for the region so vital.

Tourism on the Wild Coast

As this area of spectacular natural beauty, botanical diversity and endemism opens up to outsiders and is identified as a hotspot for tourism and strategic development, there is real concern that the wrong type of tourism development could occur. A few kilometres to the north-east lies the KwaZulu-Natal South Coast which is already littered with beach-front hotels and concrete jungles. With the pervading awareness of sustainability today – can the Wild Coast be prevented from becoming an extension of the Natal coastline? Is there sufficient commitment and know-how from the involved parties to ensure that this unique area is developed right the first time round? This section outlines the various initiatives impacting on the Wild Coast.

A Wild Coast Tourism Development Policy has been drawn up, which applies to all proposed developments and commercial activities whose prime actions relate to tourism. It provides guidelines on tourism development and management, environmental policy guidelines, institutional arrangements and procedures for development applications – right from the conceptualisation stage through to the operational stage (Taylor, 2000). The policy states that the relatively unspoilt environment will be the basis for tourism rather than traditional coastal recreation resorts (Prinsloo, 1999b). It has divided tourism development into different nodes, which allows for varying degrees of development. One of these is the ecotourism zones, which will make provision for low impact environmental and cultural tourism developments.

The Tourism Development Policy has determined that tourism on the Wild Coast must be sustainable, private sector driven, equitable, and provide a special quality experience to all visitors (Taylor, 2000). It needs its own distinct identity, and to be promoted in line with this. To ensure that development is environmentally sustainable, various funding bodies such as Nedbank's Green Trust, TOTAL, and the WWF South Africa, have supported initiatives that include and train local people in environmental and tourism projects, such as setting up information centres (Derwent, 1998). The European Union (EU) has also set aside R80 million for responsible community-driven tourism initiatives. It has appointed the Triple Trust Organisation to develop and build the capacity of local Small, Medium and Micro Enterprises (SMMEs) in the Wild Coast region to enable them to take advantage of tourism development initiatives. One of these is the Pondo Community Resource Optimisation Programme (Pondocrop), which has identified 300 small-scale, low impact projects for local communities.

Recognising the under-utilised yet inherent potential of the Wild Coast, the South African national government delineated it as a Spatial Development Initiative (SDI) in 1998 (Taylor, 2000). The SDI programmes are strategic initiatives aimed at unlocking the under-utilised economic development potential of certain areas in South Africa (Prinsloo, 1999a). For the Wild Coast, the SDI has determined that all other proposed developments must be measured in terms of their impact on tourism. The objectives of the SDI are to:

- generate sustainable economic growth and development in relatively underdeveloped areas;
- generate long-term and sustainable employment for locals; and
- enable locals to exploit spin-off opportunities arising from public and private sector investments. (Taylor, 2000)

Incorporated into the plans for the Wild Coast is the proposal to create Pondoland Park – a 50,000ha coastal biosphere reserve, stretching 80km along the coast (Costello, 2001). This designated area has been identified as one of South Africa's four unconserved biodiversity 'hotspots' (Gray, 2000). Population densities in the area are very low, thus making it viable to have a park where people live within its borders. The cultural landscape and people are seen as valuable resources, and the proposal has stated that there must be participation, beneficiation and acceptance by all interested and affected parties. Mkambati Nature Reserve will form the development core of the biosphere reserve (Costello, 2001), which will have significant repercussions on the reserve's future role within the Wild Coast.

In spite of government and policies that use the right wording, there is concern over the future of the Wild Coast. Gray (2000) reports that the SDI is being criticised for its slow delivery on providing impoverished communities with economic opportunities through tourism. A further criticism is that, in spite of the lip service to small-scale sustainable ventures, the SDI appears to favour glitzy, capital-intensive bids that are clearly unsuitable for a region which draws visitors due to its unique rural beauty (Gray, 2000). Another ongoing threat is the possibility of a highway being built closer to the coastline. Conservationists are highly concerned about the possible impact of this on the area (Costello, 2001). There seems to be a constant tension between fast-track 'mass tourism type' developments and making sure we do it right the first time round – slow but steady sustainable development capitilising on the unique scenery and culture of the region. A good working example of ecotourism in action on the Wild Coast is needed to prove that it can work. With Mkambati Nature Reserve as the hub of future development plans, it seems the obvious place to start.

Mkambati Nature Reserve

Mkambati Nature Reserve is situated between the Msikaba River and the Mtentu River on the north-eastern coast of the Eastern Cape, near the border with KwaZulu-Natal. It has fulfilled a variety of functions over the years such as a missionary base, leper colony, tuberculosis hospital and hunting preserve. Today it is the largest nature reserve in the Transkei (7720ha) and contains (among other species) eland, blue wildebeest, kudu, red hartebeest, impala, springbuck, gemsbok, blesbok, Burchells and Hartmans zebra and baboon (Prinsloo, 1999b). Being able to view wildlife against the backdrop of the ocean is just one aspect contributing to making Mkambati unique. As the keystone of a proposed biosphere reserve, Mkambati may be increased to 12,500ha. The introduction of white rhino and buffalo is also under consideration (Costello, 2001). At present, however, it is a little-known reserve with extraordinary natural beauty, including rock pools, numerous waterfalls, gorges and deserted beaches. It contains grasslands, indigenous forest and approximately 490ha of wetland (Prinsloo, 1999b). The reserve contains a variety of estuaries that are important for biodiversity conservation as they act as nursery areas for marine fish (Prinsloo, 1999b). Mkambati is also home to the rare and highly localised Pondo coconut palm or Mkambati palm (*Jubaeopsis caffra*), and is the only place in the world where this palm occurs naturally. Current visitors to the reserve are mainly nature-lovers and fishermen.

The mission of Mkambati is to:

- conserve biodiversity and sound environmental management in the terrestrial and marine environment as well as on communal land associated with the reserve;
- sustainably use the reserve for local and regional economic benefit by means of ecotourism and direct utilisation of natural resources; and
- have the participation, on an equal partnership basis, of the local community in the planning and management of the reserve. Regarding the latter, a legal framework and institutional arrangements will formalise the relationship between the community and nature conservation. Local culture will also be integrated into the planning, development, and management. (Prinsloo, 1999b)

At present, little is offered on an organised basis to the tourist besides horse riding; accommodation has been developed ad hoc; and facilities have deteriorated. The reserve's future is uncertain at present, with the strongest option being a partnership between Eastern Cape Nature Conservation (which will run the conservation side) and a private sector body (which will focus on the tourism side). Nature Conservation is currently running both the conservation and tourism sides at the reserve and face:

- restricted budgets;
- conservation of fauna and flora in a large area;
- poaching;
- poor access, decayed facilities and bureaucratic maintenance procedures;
- barriers to privatisation, in that outsource companies require profitability and long-term guarantees;
- tense and complex community and political issues;
- unrealistic benefit expectations by local communities; and
- unresolved tourism policies and withdrawal of state funding for research.

The Fundamentals of Ecotourism

For the purposes of this study, the following definition for ecotourism applies:

> Ecotourism is an enlightening, interactive, participatory travel experience to environments, both natural and cultural, that ensures the sustainable use at an appropriate level of environmental resources, while producing viable economic opportunities for the ecotourism industry and local communities, which make the sound environmental management of the resources beneficial to all tourism role players. (adapted from Hattingh, 1996)

It can be subdivided into the following elements:

- An enlightening, interactive, participatory travel experience.
- Natural and cultural environments.
- Sustainable use of resources.
- Economic opportunities for industry and local communities.
- Sound environmental management beneficial to all role-players.

This definition of ecotourism contains measurable fundamentals, which are clearly set out in the ecotourism tetrahedron (Figure 13.1). It comprises the ecotourism industry, tourists, local community and resource base (natural and cultural environments). In any ecotourism operation, there will be considerable overlap between the fundamentals as is illustrated by the proposals made. This model was used as a departure point for the planning guidelines for Mkambati Nature Reserve.

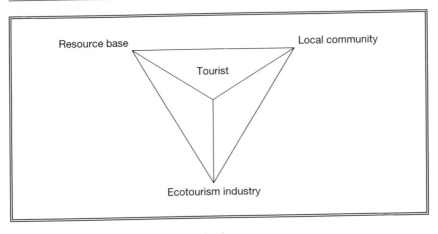

Figure 13.1 The ecotourism tetrahedron

Source: adapted from Bewsher and Hattingh (2000)

Proposals for Ecotourism at Mkambati

The proposals were made from the viewpoint that the tourism side of Mkambati would be outsourced in the future. This would mean that funding would be available to implement the more expensive proposals. However, numerous smaller scale suggestions were made which can be implemented with few resources at hand. At all times, the constraints faced at Mkambati were taken into consideration, so that the proposals would be practicable and implementable. It was also ensured that proposals comply with instructions set out in the Wild Coast Tourism Development Policy and with the carrying capacity determined for the reserve through previous studies. Equally vital is that they are appropriate to the 'sense of place' of the reserve and the wider Wild Coast. Some of the proposals made, aiming to apply the fundamentals of ecotourism, are now highlighted.

Implementing ecotourism: Accommodation and facilities

The following proposals dealt with the fundamental of the *ecotourism industry*, the enlightenment of the *tourist* and the incorporation of *local community* input and culture into accommodation and facilities.

Accommodation should be restored according to its 1920s colonial and sandstone theme, and incorporate a mix of self-catering and full and half board. Buildings, which have been constructed between the sandstone houses over the years, could ultimately be demolished and replaced with similar style buildings. Indigenous vegetation such as coast silver oak, wild blue plumbago and cape honeysuckle should be planted between the cottages to add privacy and shade. Interpretation (the activity of making places understandable and meaningful to tourists (Prentice *et al.*, 1998)) could take place in the various accommodation units by placing notices in rooms explaining Mkambati's past and cultural heritage, and the history of that specific accommodation unit. For guests staying in the sandstone Lodge, the significance of the Mkambati palm planted next to the Lodge would provide interesting reading. These notices should be brief, enticing guests to visit other parts of the reserve and to read up more detail in the comprehensive Mkambati Guide Booklet, which should be given to guests prior to arriving as part of pre-contact interpretation (Forestell, 1993 cited in Fennell, 1999).

Gwe Gwe is a tranquil spot right on the coast consisting of seven huts that are currently very run down, but still in active use by tourists, especially fishermen. With the law prohibiting any new permanent structures being built within one kilometre of the coastline, management is reluctant to demolish the existing structures, since they cannot be replaced on the same site. It is therefore essential that an Environmental Impact Assessment be done to determine how the negative effects of Gwe Gwe can be mitigated. Gwe Gwe could become a Xhosa cultural village to cater for tourists interested in indigenous culture, and to provide employment and involvement for members of the local community. The huts could be restored as accommodation units and painted in the traditional two-tone colour scheme, with its highly effective thermal function communicated to guests via a leaflet posted in the rooms. The traditional colour scheme of blue, turquoise and white can be used within the huts and, once again, explained to tourists. A cattle fold (*kraal*) should be erected and used for storytelling, traditional dances and stick fighting. The relationship between the Xhosa people and their environment needs to come forth in these activities. Traditional food could also be served here on designated evenings, when other guests from around the reserve could also visit. The development and management of this village can be outsourced to the local community. This initiative could be 'sold' as a flagship project to the private sector body awarded the tender for Mkambati. Financing, training and mentoring are vital to its success. A treetop walk and bird hide are also suggested for the forest near Gwe Gwe. Selected trees can be marked with nametags at the level of the walkway. The structure can be built from the bluegum trees, which the reserve is in the process of eradicating.

The reserve can currently accommodate 90 people, but the Natal Parks Board have recommended a carrying capacity of 200. This is supported by conservationists working with Mkambati. To provide for the extra numbers, an 'Mkambati Gates Lodge' was proposed on the side of a steep gorge, which forms two 'gates'. Whereas Gwe Gwe forms the cultural hub, this Lodge will focus on the natural environment and its sustainable use. It is suggested that five luxury chalets be built, incorporating features such as trees and rocks where possible. The structures will be raised on stilts to minimise disturbance to vegetation and placed on different levels of the slope to ensure privacy. Chalets will be joined by walking paths. As with all suggestions made, these would need to be approved by the local community and the opportunity afforded them for their input. Use will be made of local labour in every case. This Lodge would cater to the upmarket guest and those who enjoy experiencing the sustainable use of natural resources. Various proposals regarding the implementation of energy conservation and waste management techniques were also made, such as: solar energy sources; photovoltaic/wind generation and storage of electricity; 'enviroloos'; and composting and recycling facilities.

A small camping site is also proposed to ensure that Mkambati is accessible to a variety of income groups. This will be screened off from other accommodation units through a line of bluegum trees. It is suggested that indigenous trees be planted soon, to replace the bluegums once they are eradicated. A small overnight rustic bushcamp with very basic facilities has been suggested for a remote corner of Mkambati for guests on the longer hiking or horseriding trails. This will be a low maintenance site as vehicles cannot access it – providing basic outdoor cooking facilities and one 'enviroloo'. An unused education centre is situated at the entrance to the reserve. This could become a Learning Centre, which can be used as a teaching hub for the locals to learn skills such as craftwork; to learn about conservation; and where guides, room attendants and waiters could be trained. Through suggestions such as these, accommodation becomes a window to the natural and cultural environment (Andersen, 1993), drawing on its character and providing the tourist with a unique and enlightening experience.

Implementing ecotourism: Culture and community

Part of Mkambati's mission statement is to achieve participation, on an equal-partnership basis, from the local community in planning and managing the reserve. The statement also mentions the integration of local culture into operations. The challenge here was to see how ecotourism could be applied in the realm of culture and community at Mkambati. The fundamental of the *local community* forms the focus, but the *ecotourism industry* and *tourists* also have a role to play in utilising culture as a resource and fostering community involvement.

The complex and contentious community and political issues at the reserve have already been mentioned, with much tension and disagreement about who comprises the local community. It was a difficult task to formulate realistic proposals while taking these extensive constraints into consideration. One proposal was to implement a two-tier benefit system, where local community members living nearby would benefit more from the reserve than those further afield.

Although attempts are being made within the Wild Coast to create a strong 'sense of place', there is currently very limited information on, and use of, the Xhosa people and their history and culture at Mkambati. The reserve has an opportunity to carve a unique niche for itself by linking its cultural ventures to the natural environment.

The importance of promoting an ecotourism ethos and culture among the local community was recognised as a starting point. This could be achieved through workshops and education programmes. Mkambati can play a role in identifying opportunities for local SMMEs to benefit financially from the development of the reserve, for example, arts and crafts (with accompanying interpretive information), the management of an indigenous nursery inside the reserve, and the provision of accommodation within the community. The indigenous nursery could supply trees to the reserve as well as for guests and locals to purchase. It is suggested that this nursery be on Mkambati property but owned and managed by locals. SMMEs could also be used as far as is possible, in the production of information materials, for example, recycled unbleached paper. To aid this process, Mkambati management can work in close partnership with the Triple Trust Organisation that has been appointed by the EU to develop SMMEs on the Wild Coast. The indigenous knowledge system of the locals should be acknowledged and incorporated into the interpretation of the reserve to guests. In whatever way local community members are involved, it is important that this should supplement income and not replace other livelihood sources due to the seasonal nature of tourism.

It was proposed that sites of cultural–historical interest within the reserve should be pointed out to guests. These include two old churches, buildings over 100 years old, and a shipwreck. These could be linked with the history of the reserve to form a cultural–historical ramble. A further proposal was to interpret fauna and flora to the visitor from a cultural perspective. For example, an information board can be placed on the mahogany tree explaining its cultural significance (medicinal) to the indigenous Xhosa people of the area. In addition, if local people have contributed to natural resource management using indigenous methods, these practices could be interpreted to tourists. Young people from surrounding communities can be trained to guide these walks and information sessions.

Traditional Xhosa household items could be displayed in accommodation units, with information boards explaining how these items are used. Some items can be available for sale at reception. Useful Xhosa translations could be posted up at reception since many tourists are keen to learn phrases of the local language. The code of conduct issued to all tourists should include guidelines on interacting with, and supporting the local community. In all tourism activities, local produce and services should be used as much as possible. Even the laundry and maintenance services could be outsourced to locals. However, locals would need training and initial support in establishing these ventures.

Implementing ecotourism: Activities

The activities that could be offered at Mkambati are now examined, describing how these can involve local communities and provide an enlightening and interactive experience for tourists. Activities and particularly multi-activities, are essential for the 'new tourist' (Ayala, 1995, cited in Wight, 1996), of which the tourist engaging in ecotourism is an example. In providing activities, the local repertoire in terms of knowledge, interpretation and skills should not be overlooked. The local community can add much to the activities offered. These proposals therefore dealt with the fundamentals of the *ecotourism industry* as the instigators of activities, the *local community* as contributors, and the *tourists* as recipients. The *resource base* is also important, as activities must be sustainable.

To begin, the importance of training the locals involved in activities was highlighted. Formal qualifications would be difficult for rural people to achieve, and thorough 'on-the-job' training was suggested as a substitute. The reserve has much to offer in terms of activities, but this is currently not packaged and promoted properly. Different attractions can be packaged according to the themes of the natural and cultural environment. A rock pool theme and a waterfall theme were just two of those suggested. Numerous trails were mapped out throughout the reserve, using existing routes wherever possible. These were divided into horseriding, mountain biking and hiking routes and were classified according to difficulty using a colour scheme – hardcore (red), enthusiastic (blue) and novice (green). They pointed out the importance of monitoring the trails to ascertain environmental damage; and using natural signage such as wood or a flat rock to indicate the route type, difficulty and direction. It was advised that the reserve make use of polytechnic/college students to carry out environmental impact assessments (EIAs) on the trails as part of their practical. The importance of using established principles of trail design was also acknowledged. For each activity, guidelines were set out which followed the soft management technique of explaining the reasons for restrictions and making use of 'friendly' wording. The proposals gave detailed descriptions of the routes and ensured that most practicalities had been dealt with, such as the need for a horse enclosure to be built at the overnight camp. Another proposal was that local people could hire their horses out to the reserve during the busy season.

Other activities (not yet offered within the reserve) were suggested such as abseiling, cliff jumping and canoeing. For each of these, possible sites were proposed and some guidelines given. For canoeing, it was suggested that sites of interest viewed from the rivers could be pointed out to guests in the Mkambati Guide Booklet. Other activities were proposed that need not be expensive, but would certainly enhance the tourist experience, such as:

- stargazing – identifying the southern hemisphere clusters in the Guide Booklet; erecting a telescope which functions once money has been placed into it;
- whale and dolphin watching – identifying local marine resources and interesting facts relating to them in the Mkambati Guide Booklet;
- canyoning;
- spotlighting – wildlife viewing at night accompanied by a ranger – on foot or by vehicle; and
- helicopter flights offered by helicopter owners outside the reserve.

Attention was also given to children's activities. An unused large loft area near reception could be converted into an Environmental Education Centre, which could contain board games relating to nature or those played by local African children, traditional musical instruments and simple durable games such as darts and table tennis. Other suggestions included traditional storytelling (even via video); drawing competitions of anything the children saw or participated in that day; information displays on the walls; and simple colourful maps of the reserve. Children would only have access to the Centre at certain times of day and under supervision of an environmental education officer.

Implementing ecotourism: Fauna and flora

The following proposals deal mainly with the fundamentals of the *natural resource base*, although the *ecotourism industry*, *local community* and *tourist* are also involved due to the influence thereof on the resource base.

To date, ten different invasive plant species have been identified at Mkambati (Prinsloo, 1999b). The problem is serious and conservation officials are already working at eradicating these. A management plan needs to be devised whereby new infestations, particularly in and around watercourses, can be quickly detected and removed. The reserve could begin an aggressive replanting of indigenous and endemic plant communities around the disturbed areas. These will only be fully established in 10 to 15 years time. Pioneer grasses on the roads, propagating due to continual disturbance, should be monitored on an annual basis. It provides an excellent opportunity for a community arrangement – the removal of pioneer grasses in exchange for the thatch, which the locals require for their huts.

Hunting at Mkambati was very successful in the past. Although the reserve is small, hunting has the potential to be a major income generator, also involving local communities as wildlife custodians. Sport hunters are often prepared to spend large sums of money and travel long distances for the opportunity to shoot a highly valued animal. If the proposed expansion of the reserve occurs, hunting will become even more viable. At Mkambati, animals currently overstocking the reserve should be hunted first, which would create initial funds for further planning and development. This is also important to prevent further overgrazing, which is particularly noticeable close to the coastline. If hunting quotas are a fraction of natural population growth rates, controlled hunting will have a negligible impact on overall population sizes. In order to attract trophy hunters to Mkambati Nature Reserve, there must be a sufficient choice of wildlife. The introduction of cape buffalo should be considered since trophy hunters pay between US$5300 and US$5500 for buffalo. To keep large and valuable animals within the reserve, fences would have to be upgraded. The airstrip will also need repairing, so that hunters can be flown in.

Social considerations include the surrounding community and the impacts of sport hunting on them. By allowing locals to benefit economically from hunting, a positive attitude towards conservation can be fostered. All conservation, permit and trophy handling fees can be divided and deposited in a fund for the administration of Mkambati and other conservation activities, and into community funds. Communities can decide whether to divide the proceeds equally among village heads of households, or to finance community projects such as schools and clinics.

Non-hunting tourists must also be considered. Visitors currently enjoy a wide variety of activities all over the reserve, including hiking, mountain biking, swimming and fishing. However, there is insufficient space for simultaneous sport hunting and tourism; there is a risk element; and the shots fired would be annoying to other tourists. It is therefore suggested that hunting only be allowed during part of the hunting season, which extends from May to September. During the designated period, no tourists other than hunters should be allowed in the reserve, unless they are willing to accept restricted activities and range of territory.

Conclusion

The Wild Coast, with its reputation for being wild, rugged, and inhospitable is now also vulnerable and defenceless. Unless action is taken to preserve it, its very special character will disappear ... We standing by and allowing this to happen unchecked, will be guilty of handing on to future generations far less than that which we inherited. (Costello, 2001: 76)

Faced with the blank canvas that the Wild Coast currently is, it appears that it could go either way. Although terms such as sustainable tourism and ecotourism are churned out by all parties, it remains to be seen whether the commitment and know-how required to realise these, actually exists. As the focus falls on Mkambati as the keystone of this region, it becomes even more vital that the reserve be a flagship project – an example to the rest of the Wild Coast. The reserve has abundant potential for ecotourism and it is hoped that the proposals made are one step in the direction of doing it right the first time.

Moves like this, along with the many other people who have a passion and dedication to the Wild Coast, can hopefully contribute to the region going the right way – and being developed in a manner that is appropriate to the 'sense of place' of this spectacular coast while simultaneously benefiting impoverished communities, creating enlightening experiences for the visitor and sustainably utilising the natural resource base.

'[We are] rapidly . . . losing and destroying what would in any other part of the planet be declared a World Heritage Site' (Costello, 2001: 76). The sense of urgency is real. Actions in the right direction need to take place now, rather than looking back in years to come and asking how we can fix the mess we have made – if that is possible.

References

Andersen, D.L. (1993) A window to the natural world: The design of ecotourism facilities. In Lindberg, K. and Hawkins, D.E. (eds) *Ecotourism: A Guide for Planners and Managers* (pp. 116–133). North Bennington: The Ecotourism Society.

Bewsher, P.K. and Hattingh, P.S. (2000) Eco-auditing and performance management. Paper presented at the Twelfth PATA Adventure Travel and Ecotourism Conference, 28–31 January, Pokhara, Nepal.

Bristow, D. (2000) From the editor. *Getaway*, November, 5.

Costello, J. (2001) The Wild Coast: Unnatural developments. *Africa Geographic* November, 70–76.

Derwent, S. (1998) The Wild Coast: Wreck or renaissance? *Africa – Environment and Wildlife* 6 (3), 69–74.

Erasmus, B.P.J. (1995) *On Route in South Africa*. Johannesburg: Jonathan Ball Publishers.

Fennell, D.A. (1999) *Ecotourism: An Introduction*. London: Routledge.

Gray, M. (2000) Bush notes: What's happening to our Wild Coast? *Getaway* November, 35–39.

Hattingh, P.S. (1996) Guidelines for the development of cultural resources for tourism. Unpublished paper. Pretoria: University of Pretoria.

Mayhew, V. (ed.) (1985) *Illustrated Guide to Southern Africa*. Cape Town: The Reader's Digest Association South Africa (Pty) Limited.

Mertens, A. and Broster, J. (1987) *African Elegance*. Cape Town: Struik Publishers.

Oakes, D. (ed.) (1991) *Southern Africa from the Highway*. Cape Town: AA The Motorist Publications.

Prentice, R., Guerin, S. and McGugan, S. (1998) Visitor learning at a heritage attraction: A case study of Discovery as a media product. *Tourism Management* 19 (1), 5–23.

Prinsloo, D. (1999a) Environmental conflict and public policy. Unpublished document. Bloemfontein: University of the Free State.

Prinsloo, D. (1999b) *Discussion Document: Management Planning Framework for Mkambati Nature Reserve*. Draft document. Province of the Eastern Cape: Department of Economic Affairs, Environment and Tourism.

Taylor, G. (2000) *Wild Coast Tourism Development Policy*. Province of the Eastern Cape: Department of Economic Affairs, Environment and Tourism.

Wight, P. (1996) North American ecotourism markets: Motivations, preferences, and destinations. *Journal of Travel Research* Summer, 3–9.

Chapter 14
Penguins as Sights, Penguins as Site: The Problematics of Contestation

ERIC J. SHELTON AND HILDEGARD LÜBCKE

Introduction: The Contestants in Context

This is the story of a contested environment. Sandfly Bay, on Otago Peninsula, New Zealand is home to the world's rarest, and oldest, species of penguin, *Hoiho*, the Yellow-eyed Penguin (*Megadyptes antipodes*). The species is estimated to comprise about 3000 breeding pairs (McKinlay, 2001) and is the one most closely related to early forms of penguin, being the least adapted of the current penguin species (Peat & Patrick, 2002). Approximately 300 breeding pairs live along the southeast coast of New Zealand (McKinlay, 2001), mainly from Oamaru through to Fiordland, and on Stewart Island and its surrounding islands. The remainder of the birds live on the Auckland Islands, a sub-Antarctic group about 700km roughly south of New Zealand, and on Campbell Island, so much further south and exposed to the wild weather of the 'Furious Fifties' that no trees grow, but where there are extensive alpine meadows of megaherbs (Fell, 2002). Otago Peninsula, then, provides an opportunity to view essentially sub-Antarctic 'charismatic megafauna' within the relative comfort of temperate zone climatic conditions, and within 15 minutes' drive of Dunedin, a university city of about 150,000 people. Dunedin is close to the southern hemisphere forty-fifth parallel while Bordeaux, France is situated at a similar northern hemisphere latitude. There is no similarity of weather, though. Dunedin experiences a maritime climate marked by changeability and Otago Peninsula can experience extremes of weather at virtually any time of year. Sandfly Bay, so named for its flying sand, enjoys not infrequent gale force winds (sometimes to the point where standing is difficult) and horizontal sleety snow, seemingly (but not actually) direct from the South Pole. Nevertheless, Dunedin people are philosophical that this 'Costa Antarctica' is meat and drink to the fauna that engender the nature-based tourism industry that complements education and high-tech industry as the economic backbone of the city. Along with Yellow-eyed and Little Blue Penguins (*Eudyptula minor*) are New Zealand Fur Seals (*Arctocephalus fosteri*), New Zealand Sea Lions (*Phocarctos hookeri*), breeding Northern Royal Albatross (*Diomedea sanfordi*) and visiting Elephant Seals (*Mirounga leonina*), all able to be viewed from the relative comfort of various commercial operations. This year, for the first time ever recorded, an Elephant Seal pup was born on the peninsula (Vallance, 2003). The popularity of the peninsula with visitors, especially over the five-month high season, November through March, leads inevitably to sometimes-conflicting demands among a range of uses of the space available. Although these issues of multiple use and crowding are of an order of magnitude different from those experienced in some other parts of the world, locally ten people on a kilometre-long isolated beach are viewed as nine people too many, still the core expectation of individual close contact with wildlife in natural settings can fail to be fulfilled. Sandfly Bay well illustrates the contested nature of such issues as how close is 'close', how natural is 'natural' and can a site advertised internationally for its wildlife legitimately support other uses?

Sites and Sights

Sandfly Bay, situated at the end of Seal Point Road hosts about 30 Yellow-eyed Penguins, one of the larger colonies on the peninsula. The Bay itself was formed by the drowning of one of the steep river valleys that ran down the sides of the peninsula, which is a volcanic caldera that erupted 12 million years ago. Otago Harbour, which benefits from the protection of the peninsula, is another such drowned river valley. Over the past 20,000 years the area has experienced spectacular changes in sea level, to the point where the previous coastline that the penguins would have inhabited is now submerged around 30km offshore and is deep enough to accommodate the birds' 150m dives. These changes have had important implications for the Yellow-eyed Penguin in that, as a bottom-feeding species, individuals must travel to this deeper water to locate their preferred diet of mackerel (*Trachurus novazelandiae*), Yellow-eyed Mullet (*Aldrichetta fosteri*) and squid. As an aside, these daily forays of 60-plus kilometres can be contrasted with the 4,000km round trip that the Emperor Penguin (*Aptenodytes fosteri*) undertakes between the Antarctic and the Southern Convergence, a rich feeding ground in the southern ocean where nutrient-rich currents mix.

The typically daily travel patterns of the Yellow-eyed Penguins mean that human viewing of the species, for most of the year, is best done at dawn and dusk. There is wide variability to this rule but certainly the two commercial operators providing penguin viewing alter their time of arrival at the site according to sunrise and sunset. During December and January Nature Guides Otago, who hold the morning concession, depart Dunedin at 4.30 a.m., and Back to Nature Tours, who operate an afternoon concession, can still be on the beach at 9.30 p.m. By mid-winter the morning departure time has crept forward to 6.30 a.m., and the afternoon visit can be as early as 3 p.m. Penguins are present every day of the year although numbers vary. When the Bay is on the receiving end of a fierce southerly storm, complete with pounding waves and the horizontal sleet or snow, morning birds can be observed to survey the ocean and then retreat back into the flax (*Phormium tenax*) bushes where they have spent the night. This behaviour may reflect the definite risk of being killed or injured attempting to time an entry off the rocks. When not feeding chicks, birds already at sea may not come ashore for up to seven days if good fishing or bad weather make deeper water appealing. The annual cycle of activity involves, roughly, courting in August, mating in September, egg-laying in October, hatching of the two eggs 40 and 42 days later, guarding for four weeks, followed by fledging through to late March, and then adult moulting. The adults take it in turns day-about to remain on the nest during incubation and guarding, and then the chicks are left on their own while both parents gather food until, sometimes strongly parentally encouraged, fledging occurs. The other colony dynamic that potentially interacts with human presence is the recruitment and retention of juveniles. Fledglings spend at least the first year of their lives away from their home colony and some of them, and juveniles from other colonies, must return to replenish the breeding stock and thus ensure the continuation of that particular colony. Establishing the parameters of colony population dynamics requires long-term time series analysis. Short-term recording of breeding success and fledgling weights must be set against long-term sinusoidal variations in food supply caused by the Southern Oscillation, a major, centuries-old weather generator with its attendant *la nina* and *el nino* coastal water temperatures. Contributing to this system is the surface temperature of the Indian Ocean, several thousand kilometres distant. The Southern Oscillation and the related Pacific Oscillation are the subject of significant research relevant to wildlife conservation (e.g. Renwick *et al.*, 2003).

It is clear, then, that even before humans ever set eyes on a Yellow-eyed Penguin the species experienced fluctuating sea level, retreating coastline and variable food supply. Recent evidence from Antarctica suggests that penguins have the ability to evolve much more rapidly than previously thought (Lambert *et al.*, 2002). Nonetheless, the fossil record indicates that the Yellow-eyed Penguin has coped with three million years' worth of changes in the non-human environment, itself unchanged. A useful way to introduce *Homo sapiens* into the picture is by considering predation. Prior to Polynesian migration, perhaps one thousand years ago, there were no land mammals in New Zealand. Penguin predation most likely occurred in the water, and involved various species of shark, Orca (*Orcinus orca*) and Leopard Seals (*Hydrunga leptonyx*), while on land chicks could have fallen prey to the now-extinct Giant Sea-eagle (*Harpagornis moorei*). New Zealand Fur Seals, although abundant on penguin breeding beaches, appear never to have been a major predator. With the arrival of Polynesians, not only were rats (*Rattus exulans*) introduced, but both the Yellow-eyed Penguin and the New Zealand Sea Lion were hunted, with the result that, on Otago Peninsula, New Zealand Sea Lions were locally extinct for the most recent 400 years (Peat, 2002). During this period individuals visited from their main breeding area on Enderby Island, in the Auckland Islands, but not until 1993 did breeding recommence locally. At Sandfly Bay, a group of about ten animals of mixed age and sex spend from May until October, though it is possible to come across individuals throughout the summer. Some young males have been reported engaging in 'kill' events with penguins, usually chasing and killing the bird on the beach, but only one local female has developed a taste for penguins in 'prey' events, where the bird is eaten (Lalas, 2003). Obtaining and analysing the contents of Sea Lions' stomachs to obtain such information is not a task for persons with weak stomachs. The New Zealand Sea Lion has been completely protected since 1885 and has a total population of only 15,000. There are no conservation management strategies available to prevent this recovering marine mammal preying on its less numerous companion.

Of more immediate concern is the impact of the stoat (*Mustela erminia*), a mustelid introduced by 19th-century Europeans to control a plague of then recently introduced rabbits. This attempt was unsuccessful. The stoat has since devastated a wide variety of bird species, penguins included. Stoats have characteristics that make them both a particular threat to birdlife and particularly hard to study. The female stoat is impregnated at birth and has the ability to delay implantation until new juveniles are required to replenish or expand the population. If this demand does not eventuate then the fertilized but unimplanted egg is reabsorbed. A trigger for completing the pregnancy seems to be the adult male discovering, through detecting stale urine spotting, that the male of the adjoining home range (typically huge for such a tiny animal) is no longer there. Once this availability of extra territory is communicated to the already-pregnant female implantation occurs and the result is a plague of juveniles. Each stoat operates on a 45-minute activity cycle and, upon waking, kills all available prey, the majority of which is not eaten. Forty-five minutes later the killing spree is repeated (Gillies, 2000). Thus it is not sensible to trap the occasional adult male since this will lead to intense replacement by juveniles. Where traps are used to capture stoats, as at Sandfly Bay, many traps are set over a large area in an attempt to temporarily eliminate all the stoats and provide a 'window of opportunity' for nesting and a delay in reinfestation while the chicks are small. Sporadic trapping is avoided. Trapping manuals are available (e.g. Yellow-eyed Penguin Trust, 2002), although techniques are constantly being evaluated and revised. Stoats have, until recently, been hard to study in captivity since they have proved to be difficult to breed. An ongoing programme of research into better ways of controlling this introduced predator is underway (e.g. Bryom *et al.*, 2001; Gillies, 2001).

Three further groups associated with the Bay deserve mention also. One group is the surfers who capitalize on the waves at the south end of the beach during certain weather conditions. Surfing has been a feature of Sandfly Bay for decades and coincident with increased use of the south end for this and other public access has been a decrease in the number of penguin nests in this area, to the point where there is now only one, high up the cliff. Few people with a professional involvement with the penguins would dispute the notion that the birds have been displaced from their previous nesting sites by human activity.

The second user group worth noting comprises local people who struggle with the idea that their access to certain parts of the coast, and behaviour while there, should be modified to help cope with problems caused, as they see it, entirely by 'tourists'. This debate about local access to traditional attractions without charge and with minimal restriction currently echoes throughout New Zealand society and reflects the rapid and relatively recent growth and recognition of tourism as a major export industry. Both the management of national parks and wider conservation management are the subjects of discussion documents, with public submissions closing in December this year (*Otago Daily Times*, 2003). It is distressingly easy to anticipate the likely areas of conflicting opinion. Guaranteed free access by locals to sites popular with tourists will undoubtedly be high up the list of topics that various outdoor pursuits groups will demand be considered. The tourism industry will stress the need to extract revenue from what are essentially 'free goods', and will emphasize the transfer of costs involved when this is not done.

The third group intimately concerned with Sandfly Bay, its flora and its fauna, are those people who are members of environmental lobby groups. In particular the Yellow-eyed Penguin Trust and the Royal New Zealand Forest and Bird Protection Society are two organizations dedicated to the preservation of endemic and native plants and animals. Although both organizations actively encourage public enjoyment of the species they strive to protect, both have struggled to formulate policy specifically addressed to the rapidly expanding tourism industry. One difficulty has been the sheer speed of expansion of numbers of tourists, many of whom visit environmentally sensitive areas. This rapidity of growth has highlighted weaknesses in the consultation, lobbying and feedback mechanisms traditionally used during policy development by national and local government. Also, normally occurring delays between the development of protective policy and its implementation have begun to seem unacceptable as perceived negative impacts develop much more rapidly. The penguins at Sandfly Bay are well served by the Yellow-eyed Penguin Consultative Group, a forum that allows region-wide concerns to be aired informally and that is attended by representatives of the Derpartment of Conservation, territorial authorities, conservation biologists, university researchers, environmental organizations, commercial operators and individuals involved in the rehabilitation of injured and sick penguins. Even with this forum available, the rapid pace of tourism development has meant that most issues are dealt with reactively rather than proactively.

The Contest

In order to appreciate the nature of what occurs at Sandfly Bay it is pertinent to consider the concepts of *sight* and *site*. There is a rewarding literature on the constructed notion of *sight*, as in *sightseeing* (e.g. Adler, 1989), and a provocative literature around the notion of *site*, as in *contested site*. These constructs inform any attempted interpretation of the multiple roles Yellow-eyed Penguins play in the construction of the *place*, Sandfly Bay, within a broader context of the production of *space* (e.g. Lefebvre, 1974, 1991). In one sense the Bay is well defined in that it is fenced as a designated part of the Conservation Estate, administered by the Department of Conservation (almost always referred to as 'DoC'). This simple act of classification, though, using a fence to produce spatial division, is in itself problematic in that transgression of the boundary is inherent within the process of constructing the boundary (see Murdoch & Lowe, 2003 for an historical context to this issue). On one side of the fence is farmland, and on the other, wildlife reserve. The paddock adjacent to the fence is closely grazed. Over the fence is 20 years' worth of regenerating coastal forest. This contrast ensures that sheep will take rapid advantage of any occasion when a visitor leaves the gate open. The commercial operators, their clients, and unregulated free and independent travellers (FITs) must all walk about 500m over the farmland from the road-end parking space to this perimeter fence and gate. This access is by grace and favour of the neighbouring farmer, whose co-operation has extended to allowing DoC to construct a metre-wide well-formed pathway between the two points. The road-end and adjacent road reserve is the responsibility of the territorial authority, in this case the Dunedin City Council (DCC). The first of several DoC interpretive panels is situated here on the road reserve, again by grace and favour, this time of the DCC, and interestingly acknowledges an alternative use of the Bay by specifically requesting that 'sand sledders' take their sleds home with them. This request refers to the popularity, particularly with local students, of sliding down the large sand dune that needs to be negotiated to gain access to the beach and the wildlife. Hence, the site is constructed both spatially and socially.

The Dunedin City Council has two further roles with respect to Sandfly Bay. Firstly, the council is responsible for discharging partially treated effluent from Dunedin city out to sea from a pipeline a few kilometres down the coast. Under certain weather conditions there is a possibility that the faecal coliform bacteria count in the Bay, measured every fortnight, will exceed acceptable levels. In response to this possible danger to public health the DCC has erected signs along the seaward side of the peninsula warning visitors not to collect shellfish in these areas since they could be contaminated. The Sandfly Bay sign indicating the existence of a sewage outfall is sufficiently close to the DoC interpretive panel indicating a wildlife reserve that a single photograph can include both signs and a visitor posing between them. Visitors, to the ongoing embarrassment of their guides, take just such photographs and remark upon the irony of this situation. Environmental concerns have prompted the DCC to plan to extend the length of the pipeline, citing the burden to ratepayers as the reason for rejecting the more expensive alternative of completing tertiary effluent treatment ashore.

The council-funded Regional Tourism Organisation (RTO) Tourism Dunedin is charged with the task of promoting Dunedin as a tourist destination, both domestically and internationally. Until 2003, the visitor most sought after for the region was the backpacker since, through staying in the country longer than those of any other group, individuals in this sector produced the biggest 'spend' (Norris, 2002). Since Sandfly Bay is part of the Conservation Estate, and thus available to be visited free of charge, and since the availability of free penguin watching at this location has in recent years been noted in the *Lonely Planet* guidebook, popular with backpackers, there has been a rapid increase in unregulated visitors. Recent estimates (Seddon *et al.*, 2004) indicate that 20,000 visitors per year may be a realistic figure. Of course this raises issues of visitor satisfaction for those who pay for a guided tour in that only one small hide is available and this is either shared between paying and non-paying visitors, thus making the guides' commentary available to both groups, or the hide is full of non-paying visitors before the paying visitors arrive. In this case the paying visitors must content themselves with sitting on a nearby sandy bank, despite the fact that the operators' concessions specifically state that all paying visitors' viewing must be done from inside the hide. In response to this state of affairs the two tour operators have been given permission to erect a private locked hide, and plans are afoot to reconfigure and enlarge the public hide. These developments have been contemporaneous with planning on how to influence how visitors navigate the area. Currently, the most used route along the beach is the one that gets people as close to the penguins as possible, as quickly as possible. Interpretive panels are being designed that tell multiple stories of the Bay, and thus lead visitors gently towards the hide and away from the point on the rocks where the penguins emerge from the sea. This focus on encouraging visitors to keep their distance is an important yet difficult aspect of the developing site-based 'statement of management intent' that is expected to inform visitor operations policy and practice. These statements will take into account tourism, a relatively recent phenomenon of significance, and will complement previous species recovery plans (e.g. Lalas, 1985; Department of Conservation, 1991; McKinlay, 2001) that focused on more immediate threats to penguin survival. This broadened focus is important in that, although penguins appear relatively phlegmatic when exposed to humans in close proximity, they experience species-specific elevated heart rates of unknown, but almost certainly detrimental, effect (Ellenberg *et al.*, 2003). Ensuring visitors keep their distance is difficult in that the photographer's maxim of 'get close, and then get closer' rarely results in the birds fleeing. This behaviour is more prevalent at Sandfly Bay than at some other colonies and may reflect a degree of habituation (Shelton *et al.*, 2004). However, penguins who observe people on the beach awaiting their arrival, routinely will stay out at sea until the coast is clear, disrupting the changeover of adults during incubation or delaying the daily feeding of chicks after hatching. Again, the results of these disturbances are unknown, but are unlikely to be beneficial. Certainly there is general agreement among the local 'penguin community' that the current measures, of breeding success and fledgling weight, are likely to be inadequate indicators of impact.

Specific acknowledgement of tourism as a major focus of conservation planning is producing an informative but as yet rather uncoordinated and disparate literature. This year there has been a change in the kind of visitor being targeted to travel to New Zealand. The 'interactive' traveller is now the focus of international marketing (Tourism New Zealand, 2003). How successful this campaign will be and what effect it will have on demand for close encounters of the penguin kind remains to be seen. Some attempts have been made to gauge the effects of ecotourism on penguins and sea lions on Otago Peninsula (e.g. Wright, 1998) and on marine mammals nationally (Constantine, 1999). One of the issues to be considered is that of human–sea lion interaction. Sea lions at Sandfly Bay often are perceived to be acting aggressively in that they propel themselves, barking and snorting towards humans. For the first three metres from rest these animals can outrun most people and, when sea lions are present, most days on the beach witness numerous short chases. Visitors regularly report having been 'attacked' by sea lions and having 'escaped' by running away. In fact, the sea lion has a dark- and depth-adapted eye (Peat, 2002) and they probably do not rely primarily on their vision when ashore, which is approximately 50% of their time. The motivation for sea lions' approach behaviour is to attempt to exchange breath with the visitor and by analysing the breath establish, among other things, availability for mating. In the company of an experienced guide this exchange can be accomplished without violating the ten-metre avoidance zone set by DoC, since the animal approaches the visitor and not the other way around. Nevertheless, some skill is required to 'know when to walk away . . . know when to run' (Schlitz, 1978) and this guiding party piece should not be attempted at home. The conservation biologist locally most skilled in working with sea lions, and whose breath they may by now be most familiar with, Chris Lalas, has been bitten seriously only twice (Lalas, 2003). Sea lions, as resident charismatic megafauna stumbled across at this site as a by-product of visiting the penguins, are thus themselves available for more or less well-informed interpretation.

The Contested Nature of the Sandfly Bay Penguins

The protagonists have been identified. Penguins are central to any consideration of site management since the area was designated a nature reserve specifically to protect them. The previous, already heavily modified, farming landscape would not, in its own right, have warranted protection. The non-human contest is of two kinds: competition between equally protected species, and competition between protected species and introduced predators. With respect to the former, as the population of sea lions grows, and in particular as an increasing number of females become resident rather than migratory, the number of penguins taken for food will increase. The only management approach acceptable within DoC's charter is to work towards increasing penguin numbers, and not in acting to limit sea lion activity. This approach places extra emphasis on the latter contest, the challenge of non-protected predators. Stoats, weasels (*Mustela fenata*), ferrets (*Mustela furo*), dogs, cats, brushtail possums (*Trichosurus vulpecula*) and hedgehogs (*Erinaceus europaeus*) all pose a threat to eggs and/or chicks and/or adult birds. Hares (*Lepus europaeus*) disrupt penguins sitting on nests during both incubation and chick raising and have been observed by Shelton to work as a pair, much like sheepdogs, to herd penguins heading for the sea back towards their nests. Although hares' effects on vegetation have been studied (Wong & Hickling, 1999), the effects of their behavioural disturbance on penguins are yet to be examined. Similarly, Black-Backed Gulls (*Larus dominicanus*) and Australasian Harriers (*Circus approximans*) hover over nesting penguins in order to take advantage of any unguarded eggs or chicks, spilled regurgitated fish or discarded dead chicks. Penguin as prey, or target of disturbance, then, are two aspects of the nature of Yellow-eyed Penguins individuals' life experiences at Sandfly Bay.

Human perceptions of the penguins and their environment are more complex. For visitors who hold deep green values penguins often are treated as if they are sacred and, alternatively, treated by other visitors as profane. Penguin watching on Otago Peninsula can be an emotionally rewarding experience (Schänzel & McIntosh, 2000). For other visitors penguin watching can be quite simply something novel to do. For these visitors, the birds' style of walking invokes laughter, and anthropomorphic comparisons with Charlie Chaplin. In 2002, one of the halls of residence of Otago University offered a pre-dawn visit to Sandfly Bay as part of their orientation week activities with the result that the four visitors on the guided tour that morning got to share the experience with 35 students. The guides' policy on occasions like these is to try to engage the larger group in some way and to try to impart at least the basics of an appropriate code of behaviour. This approach was adopted after discussions with visiting staff from Tourism Tasmania who manage similar issues at their wildlife sites where there are both guided and independent visitors. In most cases this technique works reasonably well, and certainly better than when different groups of unguided visitors with values of varying hues of green attempt to regulate one another's behaviour. The local policeman reports that he is informed of about ten assaults each year involving disagreements following a request or demand by one visitor that another visitor move back from the penguins.

The contrasting behavioural codes emanating from these differing views of penguins as sacred biodiversity icon and penguins as entertainment cannot easily be reconciled. Historically, until the mid-19th century, the birds were viewed by local Maori as a food source; then by farmers as irrelevant remnants of the pre-European world, sometimes set on fire during the clearing of rabbit habitats (Richdale, 1944); as failures to adapt in the struggle of the 'survival of the fittest'. Richdale's efforts as an ornithologist to protect the penguins are the modern source locally of the penguin-as-sacred ethos. Tisdell (1988a, 1988b), in suggesting that the birds could provide the nucleus of wildlife tourism and at the same time increased the feasibility of funding the rescue of the species *and* established the phenomenon of penguin-as-entertainment. Any 'statement of management intent' for Sandfly Bay must acknowledge this tension and attempt to provide visitor operations strategies that ameliorate its behavioural consequences. Although subject to differing visitor motivations, the penguin is central to both the sacred and entertainment interpretations of its role. Thus, again, penguins provide a sight and also a site, in this case a site of contested intergroup values.

What about activities at Sandfly Bay to which the penguins are not central? Certainly other, non-penguin-related management decisions and implementation of policy are contentious. In late summer 2002 one of the New Zealand Fur Seals from the colony on the rocks at the eastern end of the Bay moved onto the beach, obviously unwell. Within a day Black-Backed Gulls had pecked out the seal's eyes and every day for more than a week this seal responded to human presence by turning its head towards visitors in a way that emphasized the empty and bloodied sockets where its eyes had been. DoC policy is, as far as is possible, to 'let nature take its course', and this precluded 'putting the seal out of its misery', an option proposed as humane by many visitors. This intervention decision, not to intervene, chafes against the growing demand, often articulated by visitors to wildlife sites, that human-designed ethical systems should be applied to non-human organisms. Similarly, when sheep fall off while grazing the cliffs at the south end of the Bay, a fate of many sheep at many bays throughout New Zealand, no attempt is made to remove the carcass. The consequent process of evisceration by gulls and putrefaction could be labelled either fascinating or repulsive depending on visitors' interests. The transformation from fresh carcass to bare bones takes about three months and is observed by visitors at close quarters. This 'failure to intervene' sparks discussion among visitors about European versus Antipodean stock management practices, the latter often being perceived as being commercially focused to the point of being neglectful of the animals. Such perceptions can be formulated as being informed by visitors' romantic notions of landscape and farmed animals' place within it. A dead sheep in a farm paddock is not worthy of comment. A dead sheep in a nature reserve becomes the focus of the tourist gaze and a touchstone for tourists' values and consequently is a contested site.

Conclusion

How visitors view Sandfly Bay, its history, wildlife, adjacent farms, species management and visitor operations depends on the value system each of them brings with them on the visit. These values are not necessarily specific to the Yellow-eyed Penguins who are the tourist drawcard of the area, but reflect deeper beliefs about the world. In order effectively to formulate either a comprehensive 'species management plan' or a site-based 'statement of management intent' managers must make value judgements about other aspects of local life. How central to ethical wildlife tourism business practice is tertiary sewage treatment for a nearby city? Should a territorial authority promote an area as an attraction system while feeling obliged to warn visitors of possible habitat contamination of the focal species? Should visitors have unregulated access to sites containing threatened or endangered species, or should all visitors be guided (as happens at the albatross colony) and if so how should this guiding be funded? Should visitors be warned that if they hold certain core values (e.g. green or Romantic) they might find some local practices offensive? Should these practices be changed in order not to offend the sensibilities of visitors, even though they are a longstanding part of local 'culture'?

At the centre of these considerations sits *Hoiho*, the Yellow-eyed Penguin (*Megadyptes antipodes*), survivor of three million years of changing habitat, climate, sources of food and predation. The species' newfound popularity with tourists ironically has brought with it a whole new set of challenges. Whether being the focus of ecotourism attention will be a long-term state or a short-term phase of the product life cycle remains to be seen. What is certain is that, when located at the margins of human settlement as is the case at Sandfly Bay, the Yellow-eyed Penguin will require ongoing human intervention in order to thrive.

References

Adler, J. (1989) Origins of sightseeing. *Annals of Tourism Research* 16, 7–29.

Byrom, A., Spurr, E. and O'Connor, C. (2001) Making predator control more cost effective: Capturing natural prey odours as lures for stoats. *Conservation Science* 42, 10–12.

Constantine, R. (1999) *Effects of Tourism on Marine Mammals in New Zealand*. Science for Conservation: 106. Wellington: Department of Conservation.

Department of Conservation (1991) *Yellow-eyed Penguin Species Conservation Strategy: Revised November 1991*. Dunedin: Department of Conservation.

Ellenberg, U., Mattern, T. and Luna-Jorquera, G. (2003) The most timorous of all? Impact of human disturbance on Humboldt penguins. *New Zealand Journal of Zoology* (in press).

Gillies, C. (2000) Stoats in New Zealand: A challenge for pest managers. Presentation to Yellow-eyed Penguin Trust Mustelid Workshop, 18–20 August, Pukehiki, Otago Peninsula.

Gillies, C. (2001) *What's Happening with Stoat Research? Third Report on the Five-Year Stoat Research Programme*. Wellington: Department of Conservation.

Fell, D. (2002) *Campbell Island, Land of the Blue Sunflower*. Auckland: David Bateman.

Lambert, D., Ritchie, P., Millar, C., Holland, B., Drummond, A. *et al.* (2002) Rates of evolution in ancient DNA from Adelie penguins. *Science* 295, 2270–2273.

Lalas, C. (1985) *Management Strategy for the Conservation of Yellow-eyed Penguins in Otago Reserves: Draft Report*. Dunedin: Department of Lands and Survey.

Lalas, C. (2003) Personal communication.

Lefebvre, H. (1974, 1991) *The Production of Space*. Oxford: Blackwell.

McKinlay, B. (2001) *Hoiho (Megadyptes antipodes) Recovery Plan*. Threatened Species Recovery Plan 35. Wellington: Department of Conservation.

Otago Daily Times (2003) Views sought on conservation policy, 23–24 August, A31.

Murdoch, J. and Lowe, P. (2003) The preservationist paradox: Modernism, environmentalism and the politics of spatial division. *Transactions of the Institute of British Geographers* 28, 318–332.

Norris, J. (2002) Backpackers to be targeted by tourism body. *Otago Daily Times*, 14 February.

Peat, N. (2002) Sea lions are back. *Otago Daily Times*, 7–8 September, B5.

Peat, N and Patrick, B. (2002) *Wild Dunedin: Enjoying the Natural History of New Zealand's Wildlife Capital*. Dunedin: University of Otago Press.

Renwick, J., Salinger, J., Mullan, A. Folland, C. and Gosai, A. (2003) *Relative Influences of the Interdecadal Pacific Oscillation and ENSO on the South Pacific Convergence Zone*. National Institute of Weather and Atmospheric Research (NIWA). Available at: http://www.niwa.co.nz/ncc/icu/2002–10/article (accessed 3 October 2003).

Richdale, L. (1944) *Camera Studies of New Zealand Birds*, Series B, No. 6. Dunedin: Otago Daily Times.

Schänzel, H. and McIntosh, A. (2000) An insight into the personal and emotive context of wildlife viewing at the Penguin Place, Otago Peninsula, New Zealand. *Journal of Sustainable Tourism* 8 (1), 36–52.

Schlitz, D. (1978) *The Gambler*. (Words and music), United Artists.

Seddon, P., Smith, P., Dunlop, E. and Mathieu, R. (2004) Tourist visitor attitudes, activities and impacts at a yellow-eyed penguin breeding site on the Otago Peninsula, Dunedin, New Zealand. *New Zealand Journal of Zoology* 31, 119.

Shelton, E., Higham, J. and Seddon, P. (2004) Habituation, penguin research and ecotourism: Some thoughts from left field. *New Zealand Journal of Zoology* 31, 119.

Tisdell, C. (1988a) *Economic Potential of Wildlife on the Otago Peninsula, Especially the Yellow-eyed Penguin*. University of Otago Economic Discussion Paper 8818.

Tisdell, C. (1988b) *Conserving Our Biological Resources: Economics, Ecology and Ethics*. University of Otago Economic Discussion Paper 8811.

Tourism New Zealand (2003) *Profile*. Wellington: Tourism New Zealand.

Vallance, N. (2003) Naturally Otago. *Otago Daily Times*, 11–12 October, 51.

Wong, V. and Hickling, G. (1999) *Assessment and Management of Hare Impact on High-altitude Vegetation*. Science for Conservation: 116. Wellington: Department of Conservation.

Wright, M. (1998) *Ecotourism on Otago Peninsula: Preliminary Studies of Yellow-eyed Penguin* (Megadyptes antipodes) *and Hooker's Sea Lion* (Phocartos [sic] hookeri). Science for Conservation: 68. Wellington: Department of Conservation.

Yellow-eyed Penguin Trust (2002) *Field Guide to Mustelid Trapping* (Compiled by D. Blair). Dunedin: Yellow-eyed Penguin Trust.

Chapter 15

Dolphins, Whales and Ecotourism in New Zealand: What Are the Impacts and How Should the Industry Be Managed?

MARK ORAMS

Introduction

The rapid growth of whale- and dolphin-based tourism (including 'watching' and 'swim with' programmes) over the past decade has been widely reported in the literature (for example, Beach & Weinrich, 1989; Baxter, 1993; Duffus & Dearden, 1993; International Fund for Animal Welfare, 1995; Duffus, 1996; Orams, 1997a). Whale and dolphin watching now takes place throughout the world and in countries as diverse as Italy, Canada, Brazil, South Africa, Japan, Norway, New Zealand and the Cook Islands. Hoyt's (2000) review of the industry illustrates its spectacular growth. He estimated that the worldwide economic impact derived from whale and dolphin watching activities in 1998 was more than US$1 billion. He also pointed out that in 1983 whale and dolphin watching occurred in only 12 countries, but by 1995 it had expanded to 295 communities and 65 countries and that by 1998 almost 100 countries or territories and nearly 500 communities were involved in dolphin- and whale-based tourism. As a consequence there appears to be widespread optimism about the future potential of this industry and predictions are that it will continue this rapid growth rate (Hoyt, 2000).

Many view whale and dolphin watching as viable, sustainable 'ecotourism' and a more desirable 'use' of these animals than the harvesting of them for products (International Fund for Animal Welfare, 1995). However, there is widespread concern about the impacts that tourism activities have on whales and dolphins (Beach & Weinrich, 1989; Forestell & Kaufman, 1990; Jeffery, 1993; Phillips & Baird, 1993; International Fund for Animal Welfare, 1995). Many of the species of whales and dolphins that are popular for tourism are classified as endangered and the potential for disturbance of their natural behavioural patterns has attracted much research effort in recent times. Examples include Baker and Herman (1989), Briggs (1991), Corkeron (1995), DeNardo (1996) and Gordon *et al.* (1992). Some of this research has suggested that close approach by tourist boats for watching and, in some cases, swimming with dolphins and whales, has altered the behaviour of the animals and it has been suggested that this could be detrimental (Beach & Weinrich, 1989). One view is that the 'use' of whales and dolphins as a tourist attraction can be seen as another form of harmful exploitation of these marine mammals (Orams, 1999).

The growth of cetacean-based tourism in New Zealand has been relatively recent. For example, watching sperm whales in Kaikoura (the only location where exclusively whale-based tourism operations exist in New Zealand) did not start until 1987 (Donoghue, 1996) and dolphin-based tourism really only appeared by the beginning of the 1990s. However, a decade later there were 75 cetacean-based marine mammal tourism permits issued in New Zealand – almost all of them for dolphin watching and/or swimming (Neumann, 2001). By end of the decade it was clear that dolphins and whales had become an important 'selling point' used by Tourism New Zealand to attract visitors to the country and that a significant number of the estimated two million annual international visitors to New Zealand were participating in dolphin watching and swimming activities (Orams, 2003). There are also, of course significant (but not quantified) numbers of domestic tourists who also patronise the industry. In addition, there are growing numbers of private recreational boats in New Zealand that watch and interact with dolphins in the wild (personal observation). Thus, in New Zealand, there is a so-called 'ecotourism' industry that has grown rapidly and that potentially can cause significant impacts on the natural attraction. More significantly as Constantine in her review of the marine mammal tourism industry in New Zealand (1999a: 8) points out:

> We know little about the long-term, or even short-term, effects of humans interacting with marine mammals in the wild. More specifically, issues such as the impacts of noise produced by vessels, boat handling practices, numbers and proximity of boats and humans, effects of swimmers in the water, continual disturbance versus sporadic disturbance, differences in responses of different species, age classes, sexes, individuals, or seasonal changes are not known. Research, therefore, has an important role in the future management of this industry.

Unfortunately, as is often the case in the development of ecotourism, research on impacts has only been undertaken after the industry has become established. Recently, however, there have been a number of important studies completed that examine the impacts of this industry on the targeted animals. This chapter provides a brief review of this research and considers the implications for management. This review is preceded by a consideration of the challenges inherent in the study of small cetaceans. This is necessary in order to understand the context of the findings of the impact studies reviewed and has important implications for the suggestions posed later in the considering management challenges.

Research on Impacts

Challenges in studying cetaceans

To conclude that studying wide ranging marine mammals that spend the great majority of their lives under water is 'challenging' is understating the situation marine mammal researchers face. Cetacean societies are complex and dynamic, individuals are difficult to recognise, behaviour is often subtle, always multi-faceted and contextual (Mann, 2000). An accurate analogy is that cetacean behavioural ecologists are attempting to create or visualise a complete picture from only a few small pieces of the puzzle. When you add the considerable challenges provided by weather, waves, working from small boats (often far from shore) it is little wonder that many aspiring marine mammal biology students are discouraged by academics who know from experience how difficult a task it is.

Fortunately there have been many determined individuals who have persisted despite these challenges and who have contributed to a growing understanding of accepted research protocols and methods that are rendering useful results (Mann *et al.*, 2000). However, while methods have advanced significantly over the past three decades and understanding of the behavioural ecology of a variety of species has increased (Perrin *et al.*, 2002), difficulties in interpreting what is observed remains. With regard to assessing the impacts of tourism, one of the greatest problems is determining cause and effect.

Cause and effect issues

Because cetacean behaviour is complex and dynamic, and also because observation of behaviour is difficult, determining the causal factors that drive observed behaviour is often impossible. Most often researchers infer or make an estimate of the probable cause on the basis of experience with the species (both their own and others reported in literature), and on the basis of context and repetition. Thus, for example, if repeated and co-ordinated movement away from a vessel that is attempting to approach dolphins closely is observed, it is inferred that dolphins are attempting to flee from the vessel and that the vessel is the cause of this behaviour. However, most observable behaviour is not so obvious or uniform. Movement, for example, is not always co-ordinated among a group. Within a group of dolphins, some individuals may flee an approaching boat, others may be attracted to it to 'bow-ride' for a period, while others may appear unaffected. In another circumstance co-ordinated movement away from an area where a boat is present could be due to the presence of a predator (such as a large shark) or some other factor undetected by researchers and not due to the presence of a vessel at all. Thus, it is difficult for researchers to draw conclusions about causes of behaviour with absolute confidence.

The behaviour of cetaceans has, however, been shown (to varying extents) to be affected by boat traffic by a number of researchers overseas (e.g. Acevedo, 1991; Kruse, 1991; Corkeron, 1995; Nowacek, 1999). This, of course, presents additional challenges for researchers because field-work (or, more accurately, 'sea-work') on small cetaceans is often carried out from onboard a boat – and thus, the researchers themselves through the presence and activity of their boat may influence behaviour. While some studies have been successful in conducting land-based observations (e.g. Janik & Thompson, 1996; Bejder *et al.*, 1999), this has not been possible for the majority of cetacean tourism research situations. Despite these difficulties, boat-based studies can still provide valid information on dolphin behaviour. By adhering to established approach and follow-protocols, which are intended to minimise disturbance, researchers can gather valid and reliable data (Mann, 2000). For example, Würsig and Würsig (1979) found no apparent impact on the activity or direction of movement of bottlenose dolphins, during boat-based follows by researchers. What appears to be important is that vessels are piloted in a slow and predictable manner off to one side of the cetaceans being observed and that gradual and careful approaches help to minimise a research vessel's impact. In her review of observational methods for cetacean research Mann (2000: 53) recommends that 'experienced observers avoid sudden turns, accelerations, and decelerations, approaching the animals head-on, or zooming up from behind'. She also argues that 'maintaining a steady speed so as to keep pace with the animals helps to maximize their visibility and minimize disrupting their behaviour'. Thus, researchers, by following accepted research protocols and with careful research design, can assess tourism impacts in terms of quantifying changes in cetacean behaviour as a result of tourism activities.

Is impact always detrimental?

In his overview of issues surrounding whale watching Findlay (2001) draws the important distinction between a 'response' – when an animal shows a reaction to the presence of vessels or swimmers, an 'impact' –

the resultant effect of the response, and a 'disturbance' – an assessment that the impact is detrimental. This classification is helpful because it counters the common conclusion that any observed response from targeted animals to tourism activities is a detrimental impact. This is often not the case. Dolphins and whales have been exposed to human activities for centuries (but at no time more so than at present). They are extremely adaptable organisms as evidenced by the wide variety of habitats and situations where they survive in close proximity to human activities. Thus, in many situations cetaceans have become 'habituated' to human activities – that is they have adapted to and become tolerant of human influences. Therefore, responses observed to tourism activities may be adaptive but not necessarily detrimental.

A Brief Review of Impact Studies in New Zealand

Despite the significant challenges (outlined above) in conducting cetacean-based research and in assessing the impact of cetacean-based tourism, a number of recent studies have been completed in New Zealand. This research provides valuable insights into the potential impacts of tourism (particularly on dolphins) and it represents an important first step in improving our understanding and will contribute to more enlightened management of this growing industry. The following is a brief overview of the findings of some of these studies.

Bottlenose dolphins (*Tursiops truncatus*)

Bottlenose dolphins are the most well studied and understood cetacean (Connor *et al.*, 2000). They are also the most frequently studied cetacean with regard to tourism – over half of published studies focus on this species (Richter, 2002). They are present in New Zealand in what appears to be several discrete areas – the northeast coast of the North Island (Constantine, 2002), the northern and northwestern coasts of the South Island (including the Marlborough Sounds) (Brager & Schneider, 1998) and Fiordland (southwest of the South Island) (Schneider, 1999).

Constantine's work from the Bay of Islands (1995, 1999b, 2001, 2002) has a number of important findings with regard to the impacts of tourism. First, she found that the method of placement of swimmers into the water had a significant influence on dolphin responses. When swimmers were placed in the water directly in the path of the dolphins travel, or directly within the dolphin group while 'milling' – significantly higher rates of 'avoidance' were observed than when swimmers were placed 'line-abreast' (adjacent to the dolphins' path of travel). Another important finding has been that Bay of Islands' bottlenose dolphins appear to have become 'sensitised' to swimmers in the water. That is, they have shown increasing levels of avoidance behaviour as tourism levels have increased over time (Constantine, 2001).

Lusseau's recent work (Lusseau, 2003; Lusseau & Higham, 2004; Chapter 16, this volume) on bottlenose dolphins in Doubtful Sound (Fiordland) also revealed some disturbance as a result of tourism operations. In particular, he found that the dolphins resident in the Sound were sensitive to disturbance from vessels when the dolphins were resting or socialising.

Dusky dolphins (*Lagenorhynchus obscurus*)

In New Zealand, dusky dolphins are typically found in large aggregations close to shore off the northeastern coast of the South Island (Würsig *et al.*, 1997). They are most reliably sighted off the town of Kaikoura where the continental shelf is found close to the coast (Orams, 2002).

Yin (1999) found that dusky dolphins' 'whistle rate' (underwater vocalisations) off Kaikoura increased when swimmers entered the water close by. In addition, she reported that dusky dolphins were more active and travelled more when boats were present during the early afternoon – a time period usually used for resting. Barr (1997) also carried out research on dusky dolphins' reaction to tourism activities at Kaikoura. She found that they were accompanied by vessels during 72% of her observations (daylight hours, summer seasons). She also found an increase in aerial activity when vessels were present and also noted that the dolphins formed 'tighter' groups when boats were present during the early afternoon time period when dusky dolphins often 'rested'.

Hector's dolphins (*Cephalorhyncus hectori*)

Hector's dolphins are endemic to New Zealand and are distributed in several discrete areas, primarily around the coast of the South Island at Porpoise Bay, Southland, around the Banks Peninsula in Canterbury, and in a number of places off the West Coast. Because Hector's are a small, near-shore dwelling dolphin they do not appear to move great distances (Bejder *et al.*, 2002). As a consequence, there appears to be little genetic inter-change between these geographically separated populations (Pichler *et al.*, 2001). Recent research has revealed that the small (<100 individuals) population found off the West Coast of the central North Island are genetically distinct from all others and they have been designated as a separate species which is vulnerable to extinction (Dawson *et al.*, 2001; Pichler, 2002).

Lars Bejder's (1997) research on Hector's dolphins at Porpoise Bay, Southland found that the dolphins used a preferred area less frequently when swimmers were present. He also found that the presence of vessels and swimmers increased the probability of the dolphins being observed in 'tighter' groups – that is swimming in closer proximity to one another. However, dolphins were not displaced from the area due to the presence of boats. In fact, initially they were attracted to boats (for bow-riding) but after 50–70 minutes they behaved unequivocally towards the presence of vessels.

Nichols *et al.* (2001) found that Hector's dolphins increased their active swimming behaviour with increasing numbers of boats in the Akaroa Harbour area. In the same location, Stone (1999) observed short-term changes from interacting with conspecifics (one another) to interacting with boats. Stone and Yoshinaga (2000) also reported on a potential increase in boat strike on calves that could be correlated with increasing tourism and interest in Hector's dolphins in this area.

Common dolphins (*Delphinus delphis*)

Common dolphins are typically a pelagic species found in large aggregations far from shore (Gaskin, 1992). However, in New Zealand they can be found relatively close to shore off the northeastern and central eastern coasts of the North Island (Neumann, 2001) and off Kaikoura in the northeast of the South Island (Würsig *et al.*, 1997).

Common dolphins have been examined from a tourism impact perspective for the Bay of Islands (Constantine, 1995), for the Hauraki Gulf (Leitenberger, 2001) and for the east coast of the Coromandel Peninsula and Bay of Plenty (Neumann, 2001). Common dolphins typically showed patterns of initial attraction to vessels (for bow-riding) for around 10 minutes, followed by around an hour of 'neutral' response (neither attracted or avoided) then avoidance. Smaller groups of dolphins exhibited avoidance behaviour earlier than larger groups. Interaction with swimmers was in all cases brief (around two minutes) and dolphins maintained a 'safety distance' (greater than three metres). Larger groups (more than 50 dolphins) were more likely to interact with swimmers than smaller groups.

Sperm whales (*Physeter macrocephalus*)

In New Zealand, sperm whales are only reliably sighted off Kaikoura (northeast coast of the South Island). At this location the continental shelf is close to shore and a bathymetric feature known as the 'Kaikoura canyon' is a favoured foraging location for the species (Jacquet *et al.*, 2000). Sperm whales at Kaikoura are almost exclusively males, there is little social interaction and a reasonable predictable surfacing, re-oxygenation and diving pattern exists for the whales (Richter, 2002). This predictability and near-shore location has formed the basis of a considerable whale watching industry in the area (Orams, 2002).

MacGibbon (1991) found that sperm whales responded to the presence of whale watching boats by having shorter respiratory intervals (less time between blows) and by spending less time at the surface. He also noted that sudden changes in boat speed, high-speed approaches and proximity to whales all produced responses from the whales – usually by submerging without 'fluking' (conducting a short shallow dive, presumably to avoid the boat). Gordon *et al.* (1992) showed that individual whales responded differently to the presence of whale watching vessels, some were tolerant, others not. Richter (2002) showed that 'resident' sperm whales (those that were regular visitors to Kaikoura) were more tolerant of vessels than 'transients' (whales not recorded more than once at Kaikoura). He also found that respiratory intervals were decreased in the presence of vessels, and an increase in the frequency and amount of heading changes (direction the whale was swimming) in the presence of boats. There was also a decrease in time to 'first click' (first echolocation signal) after the whale had dived.

Other species

While the above species of cetaceans are those explicitly targeted for tourism in New Zealand, there are a number of other species that are encountered opportunistically or, in some cases periodically, that form part of the 'tourism attraction' on a variety of marine tours (including those specifically focused on marine mammals but also including other more general marine tours). There are no currently completed studies that assess the impacts of tourism on these species. There are, however, a number of studies that have addressed more fundamental questions surrounding the species distribution, abundance, biology and behavioural ecology of these species in New Zealand waters. Species and studies include: humpback whales (Gibbs & Childerhouse, 2000), killer whales (Visser, 2000), southern right whales (Patanaude, 2000), North Island Maui's (Hector's) dolphins (Russell, 1999), Brydes whales (O'Callaghan & Baker, 2002) and a variety of species of beaked whales (Dalebout, 2002). Species that are sometimes encountered but for which no studies have been currently completed include minke whales and pilot whales (see Childerhouse & Donoghue, 2002 for a summary of cetacean research in New Zealand).

While the findings of all the above (briefly) reviewed impact studies identify some impact from tourism activities, in many cases (but not all) the behavioural changes reported are not statistically significant. While scientists dwell excessively on this issue (statistical significance), the issue of greater relevance here, as Richter (2002) quite rightly points out, is whether such behavioural changes are *biologically* significant. This is extremely difficult to assess given the wide-ranging behaviour, habitat and situationally specific issues that exist in cetacean-based tourism scenarios. What appears logical is that recorded responses and impacts are considered in terms of the known biological parameters of a species at a certain location. Thus, a fundamental understanding of the biology and behavioral ecology of a species is essential in making judgements regarding 'disturbance' resulting from tourism activities.

There are, therefore, significant challenges in quantifying impacts of tourism activities on cetaceans. As a consequence, there is a need for a management regime that recognises this potential and provides opportunities for managers to take a conservative approach in managing the industry. New Zealand's legal framework for protecting marine mammals is considered one of the strongest in the world, nevertheless, challenges remain in implementing the protective intent of the legislation. It is worthwhile reviewing the management regime utilised in New Zealand because it is often held up as a 'model' for the industry worldwide (Baxter, 1993) and because the variety of completed studies reviewed above allows for a consideration of the 'model's' effectiveness in managing the industry.

Management of Marine Mammal Tourism in New Zealand

Marine mammals in New Zealand waters are afforded complete protection under the *Marine Mammals Protection Act* (New Zealand Government, 1978). Marine mammal tourism is regulated under the *Marine Mammals Protection Regulations* (New Zealand Government, 1992). Responsibility for administering these laws and regulations falls to the Department of Conservation (DoC). DoC's primary mechanism for doing this is via the issuing of marine mammal tourism permits. A permit is required for any commercial enterprise wishing to offer and promote interaction opportunities (observing, swimming, snorkelling and so on) with marine mammals. Permits can have a variety of conditions attached to them, however, all permits require the operator to have no significant adverse effect on the species targeted, be in the interests of conservation, management or protection of marine mammals and have sufficient educational value. Operators are also required to have experience with marine mammals and the local area.

In a number of situations DoC has set conditions of a permit to require an operator to provide support for research, both in terms of a direct financial contribution or, in some cases, by providing a 'platform' (i.e. passage onboard a boat) for research activities. The flexibility provided in the permitting and related permit condition procedures has allowed DoC to 'tailor make' management regimes to suit particular locations, species and, in some cases, vessel types. A variety of conditions have been utilised including restrictions on species targeted, animal status (such a no approaches for mothers with calves), locations, minimum depths, minimum approach distances, maximum number of vessels within a specified range, vessel types, vessel speed, vessel propulsion types, time spent with animals, maximum number of trips and so on.

A real advantage has been the ability to require operators to provide support for research. The majority of marine mammal tourism impact studies conducted in New Zealand to date have received support via this mechanism and many have been published in DoC's 'Science for Conservation' series (see http://www.doc.govt.nz/Publications/ 004~Science-and-Research/index.asp). Furthermore, the permit renewal procedures have allowed DoC to update permit conditions when research has revealed the need for differing approaches to reduce potential impacts.

The system is not without criticism, however. From personal observation it is apparent that many marine mammal tourism permit applicants find the application procedure frustrating and too long and some operators find the conditions arduous. Probably of greater significance is that DoC has, at times, found it difficult to enforce permit conditions as a result of innocuous wording in the regulations (for example, what is 'sufficient educational value') or when transgressions of regulations or permit conditions are difficult to prove (for example, in assessing minimum approach distances). Also of relevance is the large number of permits that have been issued in New Zealand while the long-term impacts of such operations is not known. Of particular concern must be the potential issue of stress and its long-term implications for endangered species such as the Hector's dolphin – an endemic species that currently supports significant tourism activity.

Conclusions

In New Zealand, there has been a rapid and widespread growth of cetacean-based tourism (particularly based on dolphins). There is also a framework that attempts to provide a mechanism for the careful and sustainable management of the industry. However, a number of studies have identified that tourism activity is having a variety of impacts on the targeted cetacean populations. What is frustrating (but not unusual) is that 'despite the obvious need, no New Zealand cetacean population has received detailed study before being targeted by commercial whale or dolphin-watching operations' (Bejder & Dawson, 1998: 2) and thus, 'before and after' comparisons have not been possible.

It is also important to remember that all of the completed studies have been relatively short-term with regard to their assessment of impacts. It is entirely possible (even likely) that many of the most significant impacts and disturbance that may have biological significance may not be detected for many years (even decades). From a scientific point of view it is simply too early to reach conclusions regarding the long-term effects of tourism on dolphins and whales in New Zealand. It is, therefore, premature to hold up the New Zealand marine mammal tourism industry as a 'showcase' for enlightened ecotourism. It is possible that, on balance, tourism could be a contributor to the health and viability of marine mammals in New Zealand. Perhaps through experiencing marine mammals in the wild – and by learning about them – tourists can be changed to become more environmentally responsible citizens (Orams, 1997b). The marine mammal tourism industry certainly provides an economic value to these animals that add an incentive to ensure that healthy and abundant populations exist into the future. However, because significant uncertainty remains regarding impacts, a careful and precautionary approach is still essential. What is certain is that research has a critical role to play in the long-term sustainability of the marine mammal tourism industry.

Acknowledgements

The author wishes to acknowledge the work of students, scientists and managers in the field of marine mammal science in New Zealand, particularly (but not limited to), C. Scott Baker, Kirsty Barr, Andrew Baxter, Lars Bejder, Stefan Brager, Simon Childerhouse, Rochelle Constantine, Merel Dalebout, Steve Dawson, Aaron Donaldson, Mike Donoghue, Padraig Duignan, Nadine Gibbs, David Lusseau, Dirk Neumann, Franz Pichler, Cristof Richter, Kirsty Russell, Aline Schaffar-Delaney, Karsten Schneider, Liz Slooten, Karen Stockin, Greg Stone, Rob Suisted, Ingrid Visser, Bernd Würsig and Suzanne Yin. The author would also like to acknowledge the work of marine mammal tour operators in New Zealand, the great majority of whom are very supportive of research and who are doing their best to do the 'right thing' by the animals that form the basis of their industry.

References

Acevedo, A. (1991) Interactions between boats and bottlenose dolphins, *Tursiops truncatus*, in the entrance to Ensenada de la Paz, Mexico. *Aquatic Mammals* 17, 120–4.

Baker, C.S. and Herman, L.M. (1989) Behavioral responses of summering humpback whales to vessel traffic: Experimental and opportunistic observations. Report to the National Parks Service, United States Department of the Interior, NPS-NR-TRS-89–01, 50pp.

Barr, K. (1997) The impacts of marine tourism on the behaviour and movement patterns of dusky dolphins (Lagenorhynchus obscurus), *at Kaikoura, New Zealand*. Master's thesis, University of Otago, Dunedin, New Zealand.

Baxter, A.S. (1993) The management of whale and dolphin watching in Kaikoura, NZ. In Postle, D. and Simmons, M. (eds) *Encounters With Whales '93* (pp. 108–20). Townsville, Queensland, Australia: Great Barrier Reef Marine Park Authority.

Beach, D.W. and Weinrich, M.T. (1989) Watching the whales: Is an educational adventure for humans turning out to be another threat for an endangered species? *Oceanus* 32, 84–8.

Bejder, L. (1997) Behaviour, ecology, and impact of tourism on Hector's dolphins (*Cephalorhynchus hectori*) in Porpoise Bay, New Zealand. Master's thesis, University of Otago, Dunedin, New Zealand.

Bejder, L. and Dawson, S.M. (1998) Responses by Hector's dolphins to boats and swimmers in Porpoise Bay, New Zealand. Report SC/50/WW11. International Whaling Commission Scientific Committee.

Bejder, L., Dawson, S.M. and Harraway, J.A. (1999) Responses by Hector's dolphins to boats and swimmers in Porpoise Bay, New Zealand. *Marine Mammal Science* 15, 738–50.

Bejder, L., Dawson, S., Slooten, L., Smith, S., Stone, G.S. *et al.* (2002) Site fidelity and along-shore range in Hector's dolphin, an endangered marine dolphin from New Zealand. *Biological Conservation* 108 (3), 281–7.

Brager, S. and Schneider, K. (1998) Near-shore distribution and abundance of dolphins along the west coast of the South Island, New Zealand. *Journal of Marine and Freshwater Research* 32, 105–12.

Briggs, D. (1991) Impact of human activities on killer whales at the Rubbing Beaches in the Robson Bight Ecological Reserve and adjacent waters during the summers of 1987 and 1989. Unpublished report to the Ministry of Parks, Victoria, British Columbia, Canada.

Broom, D.M. and Johnson, K.G. (1993) *Stress and Animal Welfare*. London: Chapman and Hall.

Childerhouse, S. and Donoghue, M. (2002) *Cetacean Research in New Zealand 1997–2000*. DoC Science Internal Series 46. Wellington: Department of Conservation.

Connor, R.C., Wells, R.S., Mann, J. and Read, A.J. (2000) The bottlenose dolphin. Social relationships in a fission-fusion society. In Mann, J., Connor, R.C., Tyack, P.L. and Whitehead, H. (eds) *Cetacean Societies – Field Studies of Dolphins and Whales* (pp. 91–126). Chicago: University of Chicago Press.

Constantine, R.L. (1995) Monitoring the commercial swim-with-dolphin operations with the bottlenose (*Tursiops truncatus*) and common dolphins (*Delphinus delphis*) in the Bay of Islands, New Zealand. Master's Thesis, University of Auckland, New Zealand.

Constantine, R.L. (1999a) *Effects of Tourism on Marine Mammals in New Zealand.* Science for Conservation 106, Department of Conservation, New Zealand.

Constantine, R.L. (1999b) Increased avoidance of swimmers by bottlenose dolphins in the Bay of Islands, New Zealand. *Abstracts of the 13th Biennial Conference on the Biology of Marine Mammals. 28 Nov.–3 Dec. 1999, Wailea, Maui, Hawaii.*

Constantine, R.L. (2001) Increased avoidance of swimmers by wild bottlenose dolphins (*Tursiops truncatus*) due to long-term exposure to swim-with-dolphins tourism. *Marine Mammal Science* 17 (4), 689–702.

Constantine, R.L. (2002) The behavioural ecology of bottlenose dolphins (*Tursiops truncatus*) of northeastern New Zealand: A population exposed to tourism. Ph.D. thesis, University of Auckland, New Zealand.

Corkeron, P.J. (1995) Humpback whales (*Megaptera novaeangliae*) in Hervey Bay, Queensland: Behaviour and responses to whale-watching vessels. *Canadian Journal of Zoology* 73, 1290–9.

Dalebout, M.L. (2002) Species identity, genetic diversity and molecular systematic relationships among the *Ziphiidae* (beaked whales). Ph.D. thesis, University of Auckland, New Zealand.

Dawson, S., Pichler, F.B., Slooten, L., Russell, K. and Baker, C.S. (2001) The North Island Hector's dolphin is vulnerable to extinction. *Marine Mammal Science* 17 (2), 366–71.

DeNardo, C. (1996) A behavioural study: The potential effects of boat tourist traffic on killer whale (*Orcinus orca*) group behaviour in Tysfjord, northern Norway. Unpublished report to the Whale and Dolphin Conservation Society, United Kingdom.

Donoghue, M. (1996) The New Zealand experience – one country's response to cetacean conservation. In Simmonds, M.P. and Hutchinson, J.D. (eds) *The Conservation of Whales and Dolphins: Science and Practice* (pp. 423–45). New York: John Wiley and Sons

Duffus, D.A. (1996) The recreational use of grey whales in southern Clayoqout Sound, Canada. *Applied Geography* 16 (3), 179–90.

Duffus, D.A. and Dearden, P. (1993) Recreational valuaion and management of killer whales (*Orcinus orca*) on Canada's Pacific coast. *Environmental Conservation* 20 (2), 149–56.

Findlay, K. (2001) Can we watch whales and not disturb them? *Abstracts of the Southern Hemisphere Marine Mammal Conference 2001 29 May–1 June, Philip Island Conference Centre, Cowes, Philip Island, Victoria, Australia.* Philip Island Nature Park.

Forestell, P.H. and Kaufman, G.D. (1990) The history of whale watching in Hawaii and its role in enhancing visitor appreciation for endangered species. In Miller, M.L. and Auyong, J. (eds) *Proceedings of the 1990 Congress on Coastal and Marine Tourism* (Vol. 2) (pp. 399–407). Corvallis, OR: National Coastal Resources Research Institute.

Gaskin, D.E. (1992) Status of the common dolphin, *Delphinus delphis*, in Canada. *Canadian Field Naturalist* 106, 55–63.

Gibbs, N. and Childerhouse, S. (2000) *Humpback Whales Around New Zealand.* Conservation Advisory Science Notes 287. Wellington: Department of Conservation.

Gordon, J., Leaper, R., Hartley, F.G. and Chappell, O. (1992) *Effects of Whale-watching Vessels on the Surface and Underwater Acoustic Behaviour of Sperm Whales off Kaikoura, New Zealand.* Science and Research Series 52. Wellington: Department of Conservation.

Hoyt, E. (2000) Whale watching 2000: Worldwide tourism numbers, expenditures and expanding socioeconomic benefits. Report to the International Fund for Animal Welfare. 157pp.

International Fund for Animal Welfare (1995) (and Tethys European Conservation) *Report of the Workshop on the Scientific Aspects of Managing Whale Watching.* International Fund for Animal Welfare, Tethys European Conservation, Montecastello di Vibio, Italy.

Jacquet, N., Dawson, S. and Slooten, L. (2000) Seasonal distribution and diving behaviour of male sperm whales off Kaikoura: Foraging implications. *Canadian Journal of Zoology* 78, 407–19.

Janik, V.M. and Thompson, P.M. (1996) Changes in surfacing patterns of bottlenose dolphins in response to boat traffic. *Marine Mammal Science* 12, 597–602.

Jeffery, A. (1993) Beyond the breach – managing for whale conservation and whale watching in Hervey Bay Marine Park, Qld. In Postle, D. and Simmons,

M. (eds) *Encounters With Whales '93* (pp. 91–107). Workshop Series No. 20. Townsville, Queensland, Australia: Great Barrier Reef Marine Park Authority.

Kruse, S. (1991) The interaction between killer whales and boats in Johnstone Strait, B.C. In Mann, J., Connor, R.C., Tyack, P.L. and Whitehead, H. (eds) *Cetacean Societies – Field Studies of Dolphins and Whales* (pp. 335–46). Chicago: University of Chicago Press.

Leitenberger, A. (2001) The influence of ecotourism on the behaviour and ecology of the common dolphin (*Delphinus delphis*), in the Hauraki Gulf, New Zealand. Master's thesis, University of Vienna, Austria.

Lusseau, D. (2003) Male and female bottlenose dolphins *Tursiops spp.* have different strategies to avoid interactions with tour boats in Doubtful Sound, New Zealand. *Marine Ecology Progress Series* 257, 267–74.

Lusseau, D. and Higham, J. (2004) Managing the impacts of dolphin-based tourism through the definition of critical habitats: The case of Doubtful Sound, New Zealand. *Tourism Management* 25 (6), 657–67.

MacGibbon, J. (1991) Responses of sperm whales (*Physeter macrocephalus*) to commercial whale watch boats off the coast of Kaikoura. Unpublished report to the Department of Conservation, Wellington.

Mann, J. (2000) Unraveling the dynamics of social life – long-term studies and observational methods. In Mann, J., Connor, R.C., Tyack, P.L. and Whitehead, H. (eds) *Cetacean Societies – Field Studies of Dolphins and Whales* (pp. 45–64). Chicago: University of Chicago Press.

Mann, J., Connor, P.L., Tyack, P.L. and Whitehead, H. (eds) (2000) *Cetacean Societies – Field Studies of Dolphins and Whales.* Chicago: University of Chicago Press.

Neumann, D.R. (2001) The Behaviour and Ecology of Short-Beaked Common Dolphins (*Delphinus delphis*) Along the East Coast of Coromandel Peninsula, North Island, New Zealand. Ph.D. thesis, Massey University, New Zealand.

New Zealand Government (1978) *New Zealand Marine Mammal Protection Act.* Wellington: New Zealand Government Printer.

New Zealand Government (1992) *New Zealand Marine Mammal Protection Regulations.* Wellington: New Zealand Government Printer.

Nichols, C., Stone, G.S., Hutt, A., Brown, J. and Yoshinaga, A. (2001) *Observations of Interactions Between Hector's Dolphin* (Cephalorhynchus hectori*), Boats and People at Akaroa Harbour.* Department of Conservation Research Investigation No. 2531. Wellington: Department of Conservation.

Nowacek, S.M. (1999) The effects of boat traffic on bottlenose dolphins, *Tursiops truncatus*, in Sarasota Bay, Florida. M.Sc. thesis, University of California, Santa Cruz.

O'Callaghan, T.M. and Baker, C.S. (2002) *Summer Cetacean Community, with Particular Reference to Bryde's Whales, in the Hauraki Gulf, New Zealand.* DoC Science Internal Series 55. Wellington: Department of Conservation.

Orams, M.B. (1997a) Historical accounts of human – dolphin interaction and recent developments in wild dolphin based tourism in Australasia. *Tourism Management* 18 (5), 317–26.

Orams, M.B. (1997b) The effectiveness of environmental education: Can we turn tourists into 'greenies'? *Progress in Tourism and Hospitality Management* 3 (4), 295–306.

Orams, M.B. (1999) *Marine Tourism. Development, Impacts and Management.* London: Routledge.

Orams, M.B. (2002) Marine ecotourism as a potential agent for sustainable development in Kaikoura, New Zealand. *International Journal of Sustainable Development* 5 (3/4), 338–52.

Orams, M.B. (2003) Marine ecotourism in New Zealand: An overview of the industry and its management. In Garrod, B. and Wilson, J.C. (eds) *Marine Ecotourism: Issues and Experiences* (pp. 233–48). London: Channel View Publications.

Patanaude, N.J. (2000) *Southern Right Whales Wintering in the Auckland Islands.* Conservation Advisory Science Notes 321. Wellington: Department of Conservation.

Perrin, W.F., Würsig, B. and Thewissen, J.G.M. (eds) (2002) *Encyclopedia of Marine Mammals.* San Diego: Academic Press.

Phillips, N.E. and Baird, R.W. (1993) Are killer whales harassed by boats? *The Victorian Naturalist* 50 (3), 10–11.

Pichler, F.B. (2002) Population structure and genetic variation in Hector's dolphin (*Cephalorynchus hectori*). Ph.D. thesis, School of Biological Sciences, University of Auckland, Auckland, New Zealand.

Pichler, F.B., Robineau, D., Goodall, R.N.P., Meyer, M.A., Olavarria, C. *et al.* (2001) Origin and radiation of southern hemisphere coastal dolphins (genus *Cephalorynchus*). *Molecular Ecology* 10, 2215–23.

Richter, C. F. (2002) Sperm whales at kaikoura and the effects of whale-watching on their surface and vocal behaviour. Ph.D. thesis, University of Otago, Duendin, New Zealand.

Russell, K. (1999) Hector's dolphins in the North Island, New Zealand. M.Sc. Thesis, University of Auckland, New Zealand.

Schneider, K. (1999) Behaviour and ecology of bottlenose dolphins in Doubtful Sound, Fiordland, New Zealand. Ph.D. thesis, University of Otago, New Zealand.

Stone, G.S. (1999) Conservation and management strategies for Hector's dolphins in the coastal zone. Ph.D. thesis, University of the South Pacific, Fiji.

Stone, G.S. and Yoshinaga, A. (2000) Hector's dolphin (*Cephalorhyncus hectori*) calf mortalities may indicate new risks from boat traffic and habituation. *Pacific Conservation Biology* 6 (2), 162–71.

Visser, I.N. (2000) Orca (*Orcinus orca*) in New Zealand Waters. Ph. D. thesis, University of Auckland, New Zealand.

Würsig, B. and Würsig, M. (1979) Behaviour and ecology of the bottlenose dolphin, *Tursiops truncatus*, in the South Atlantic. *Fishery Bulletin* 77, 399–413.

Würsig, B., Cipriano, F., Slooten, E., Constantine, R., Barr, K. *et al.* (1997) Dusky dolphins (*Lagenorhynchus obscurus*) off New Zealand: Status of present knowledge. Paper SC/48/SM32 of the *47th Annual Report of the International Whaling Commission*, Cambridge, England.

Yin, S.E. (1999) Movement patterns, behaviors, and whistle sounds of dolphin groups off Kaikoura, New Zealand. M.Sc. thesis, Texas A & M University, Galveston, Texas.

Chapter 16

The State of the Scenic Cruise Industry in Doubtful Sound in Relation to a Key Natural Resource: Bottlenose Dolphins

DAVID LUSSEAU

Introduction

Fiordland has long been one of New Zealand's key tourist attractions. A recent study (Higham *et al.*, 2001) shows that Fiordland was the most visited location/attraction by ecotourists coming to New Zealand. Moreover 20% of these visitors came to New Zealand primarily to view wildlife (Higham *et al.*, 2001). Doubtful Sound is one of the 14 fjords that comprise Fiordland (Figure 16.1). It is more difficult to access than Milford Sound, yet easier than Dusky Sound. No roads lead to Doubtful Sound, but companies operate regular ferries to cross Lake Manapouri and a bus service to access the fjord. A small resident population of bottlenose dolphins lives in this fjord (Lusseau *et al.*, 2003). These dolphins seldom leave the fjord and therefore can be observed on a daily basis by tour operating companies.

Doubtful Sound can be experienced in many different ways. The tourism industry in this fjord offers a diverse array of tours from half-day cruises to multi-day kayak trips. Activities started in the late 1950s and remained undeveloped until the early 1990s. Since then the industry went through two stages of development from 1992 to 1995, passing from 1 to 6 operating vessels, and more recently from 2000 to 2002 when the fleet size increased from 6 to 15. The assets on which the industry is based are natural resources. Companies using Doubtful Sound advertise the scenery, wilderness experience, and wildlife such as seals, penguins and bottlenose dolphins. All companies advertise offering, to some level, ecotours as defined in Weaver (2001), where ecotourism is a form of tourism that is understood to be (1) based primarily on nature-based attractions; (2) learning-centred; and (3) conducted in a way that makes every reasonable attempt to be environmentally, socio-culturally

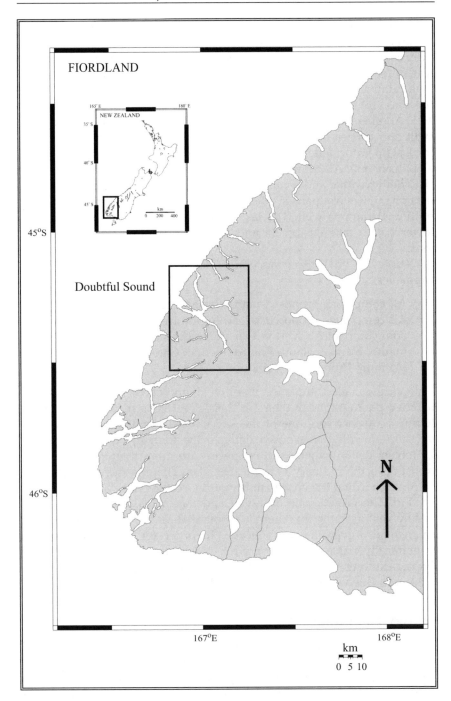

Figure 16.1 Location of Doubtful Sound

and economically sustainable. A definition deemed to apply to the New Zealand context by Higham *et al.* (2001).

Six companies operate in the Sound, but only three companies operate year-round. One of these three companies offers daily tours aboard a large catamaran (180 passengers) and overnight cruises aboard a vessel that was upgraded from 8 passengers to 72 passengers in November 2001. Another proposes multi-day cruises for eight passengers aboard a yacht and carries out cruises in Doubtful Sound and the other fjords. The last operator undertakes daily cruises aboard a semi-inflatable vessel (12 passengers). All companies operating only in summer offer kayaking trips. Both weather and water temperature prevent the viability of winter kayaking. Two companies offer overnight trips, one of them offering multi-day tours as well. The last operator proposes day trips using a powerboat to take customers and kayaks to different locations in the fjord.

A survey of advertising materials showed that out of five surveyed companies:

• All companies proposed nature-based attractions.
• All companies proposed a learning-centred experience.
• Four companies advertised an attempt to sustainability by adhering to the New Zealand Environmental Care Code or the Marine Mammal Protection Regulations.

In addition, all companies mentioned bottlenose dolphins, and/or included photographs of them, in their advertising material. Bottlenose dolphins are therefore one of the key natural resource of the industry and subsequently are exposed daily to the tourism industry (Lusseau & Slooten, 2002). Other wildlife species are more migratory and their exposure to the industry is more irregular. There is therefore growing concern regarding the sustainability of the scenic cruise industry in this location. The growth rate observed and the increase in interest in the area by visitors show that there is a potential for the industry to expand exponentially over the next decade. In order for the industry to be economically viable it is necessary for its activities to be sustainable. The chapter explores the sustainability of the industry in Doubtful Sound in relation to this wildlife asset, namely, bottlenose dolphins.

Industry Characteristics

Two types of vessels are operating scenic cruises in Doubtful Sound and approach bottlenose dolphins. The Department of Conservation (DoC) granted a dolphin-watching permit to three companies; while, as of 2002, three other companies are operating without dolphin-watching permit. The non-permit holders are required not to seek interaction with dolphins and if they do encounter a group of dolphins to avoid lengthy interactions. Therefore, the nature of the interactions between non-permit holders and dolphins should be very similar to the interactions observed between dolphins and other boats using Doubtful Sound but not targeting bottlenose dolphins. The number of both types of scenic cruise operations increased over the past decade. In addition to scenic cruises, private vessels and fishing charters can also be encountered in the fjord. The nature of their interactions with bottlenose dolphins should be similar to the ones of non-permit holders.

The number of scenic trips offered in Doubtful Sound varies seasonally (Figure 16.2). Summer and autumn are peak seasons corresponding to the peak in tourism activities in Fiordland. In addition, the number of trips is on a steady increase with approximately 40% more trips in summer 2002 than during summer 2000. This growth may in part be a consequence of two new companies starting to operate during the study period, one offering daily trips year-round since November 2000 and the other offering daily kayak trips since November 2001.

Pre-existing companies also increased the intensity of their activities. One kayak company extended from one overnight trip to four during the study period. The two remaining companies did not increase their fleet. However, one company upgraded its overnight boat to increase its capacity and the other company, offering multi-day trips, increased the

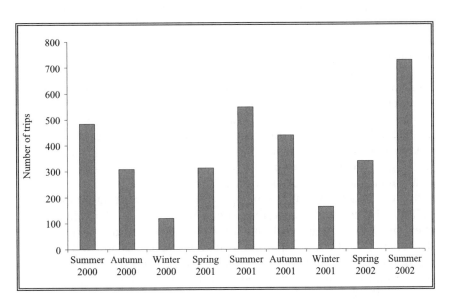

Figure 16.2 Number of boat trips offered in Doubtful Sound each season between December 1999 and February 2002

frequency of its cruises. Overall, the boat traffic in Doubtful Sound reflects the increase in interest in the location, with companies expanding their ventures in order to accommodate for the growing number of tourists coming in the fjord.

Interactions Between Boats and Dolphins

Defining the interactions

Boat–dolphin interactions in Doubtful Sound were observed from December 1999 to February 2002. Every time a vessel interacted with the dolphins the following were recorded:

(1) the time it spent with them;
(2) the type of vessel it was (private, tour operator with or without watching permit, and fishing charter);
(3) the minimum distance between the vessel and the dolphins during the interaction; and
(4) whether the skipper breached the Marine Mammal Protection Regulations (MMPR).

Dolphins spent 10.8% of the time that the author spent observing them interacting with other vessels. Following the variation in boat traffic, dolphins spent more time with vessels during summer and autumn (Figure 16.3). The time spent with boats varied from 16% during peak months to 4% during winter. Most of the interactions took place from 10 a.m. to 5 p.m. (New Zealand summer time, on average 0.5 to 0.65 interactions per hour) with three distinct peaks at 10–11 a.m., 12–1 p.m. and 3–4 p.m. These peaks correspond to the peaks in scenic cruise activities. After 5 p.m., the intensity of interactions decreased steadily to reach 0.1 interactions per hour at 7 p.m.

Interestingly, tour operators without dolphin-watching permit, spent a substantial amount of time with dolphins coming second to permit holders (23% of all interactions vs. 64%). The time they spent interacting was higher than the time private and fishing charter vessels spent (8% of all interactions, and 5% respectively).

It could be expected that tour operators might spend more time with dolphins by chance because they spend more time on the water. However, the length of interactions from each boat category explains the discrepancy. Both tour operator categories spent as much time with the dolphins when interacting, which was significantly more time than private and fishing charter vessels did (Kruskal–Wallis $H = 100.79$, $df = 3$, $p < 0.001$) (Figure 16.4).

During these interactions, vessels most commonly came within 50m of the group of dolphins (77% of interactions), while they rarely stayed more

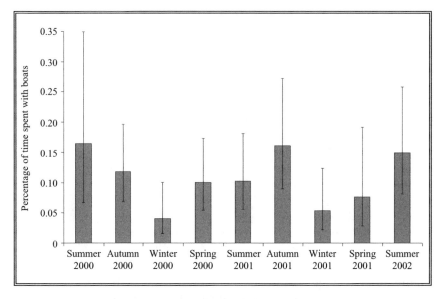

Figure 16.3 Percentage of time dolphins spent with boats each season in Doubtful Sound. Error bars are 95% confidence limits

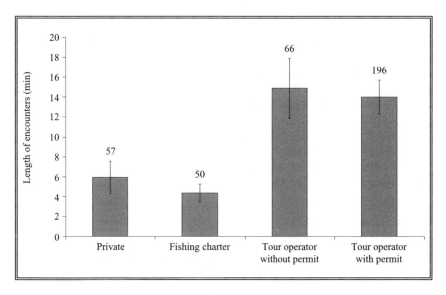

Figure 16.4 Average length of encounters (min.) with each boat category in Doubtful Sound. Error bars are 95% confidence intervals; numbers above each bar are number of interactions

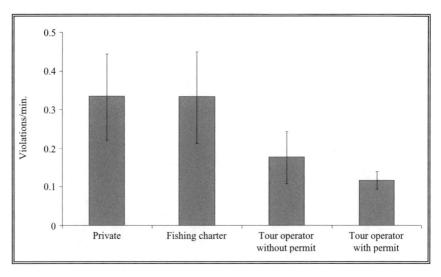

Figure 16.5 Average number of violations of the MMPR per minute
of interaction for each boat category in Doubtful Sound.
Error bars are 95% confidence intervals; sample sizes
are the same as for Figure 16.4

than 200m away (8%). Only 34% of the interactions did not breach the
MMPR. In 32% of cases there was more than one violation during the
interaction. Non-permit holders had slightly less interaction without any
violations (29.7% of 66 interactions) compared to permit holders (35% of
196 interactions), private vessels (40.4% of 57 interactions) and fishing
charters (42% of 50 interactions). There was an average of 1.0 violation
per interaction and all boat categories had similar number of violations
(Kruskal–Wallis $H = 4.16$, $df = 3$, $p = 0.245$). However when considering
the number of violations per minute of interaction, private and fishing
charter vessels had more aggressive interactions than the tour operators
did (Kruskal–Wallis $H = 9.68$, $df = 3$, $p = 0.022$) (Figure 16.5).

Violations of the MMPR

The Marine Mammal Protection Regulations (New Zealand Government, 1992) provide operation requirements that skippers must follow
when interacting with marine mammals. Specifically when a vessel interacts (when within 300m) with a group of dolphins, the skipper must:

(1) Not proceed through the pod of dolphins.
(2) Approach from a direction that is parallel to the dolphin and slightly
    to the rear of the dolphin.

(3) Not cut off the path of a marine mammal.
(4) Remain at a constant slow speed no faster than the slowest marine mammal in the vicinity, or at idle speed.
(5) Not make sudden or repeated change in the speed or direction of the vessel except in the case of emergency.

Following these requirements, the author recorded every time a vessel would:

(1) Not proceed at the speed of the group of dolphins when within 300m or at idle speed.
(2) Proceed through the pod.
(3) Cut the path of the pod.
(4) Approach the pod head-on.
(5) Circle the pod.
(6) Proceed astern (in reverse gear) when within 50m of the pod.

The author observed 461 violations of the MMPR during the 373 interactions. Most commonly boats did not respect the speed limit when interacting with dolphins (Figure 16.6). This speeding behaviour was not

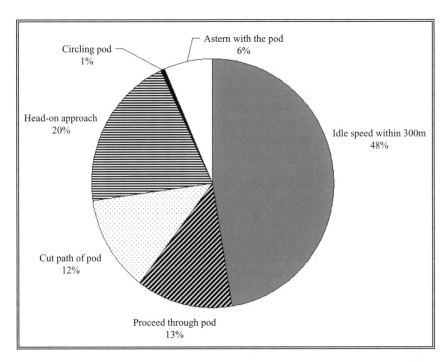

Figure 16.6 Types of violations of the MMPR observed during the study period (*n* = 461 violations) in Doubtful Sound

due to vessels passing at close range of the dolphins without noticing their presence. In almost all cases the vessel had already interacted with the animals for a while before accelerating in order to either make the dolphins jump or have them bow ride. Impairing the dolphin's movement came second (cutting the path of the pod, proceeding through the pod and circling the pod) with 26% of cases. These four behaviours, collectively represented 74% of the violations observed, indicate aggressive boat behaviour with the skipper trying to actively interact with the dolphins.

Social Issues

During casual interviews with eight skippers, several social issues were raised. These issues represent a current stress on the local community and therefore affect the sustainability of the scenic cruise industry in the area. Because they are related to dolphin–boat interactions it is valuable to address them here.

Misbehaviour

All skippers raised concern about the behaviour of tour boats around the dolphins. They all 'knew what they were doing', but tended to express concern about the behaviour of other skippers. These skippers represented all boat types described earlier and therefore were really concerned about the behaviour of one another. Observations described above show that all operators have similar responsibilities when it comes to misbehaviour.

Value of dolphin-watching permits

Another problem relates to dolphin-watching permits. It would appear that tension is rising between permit holders and non-permit holders. The benefit of holding a permit has been lost. Because tour operators without dolphin-watching permit can spend as much time with dolphins as they do, the other operators only see the policing side of the permit. In other words by having a permit they have everything to lose because they are legally bound to the requirements of the MMPR. Their permit can be revoked if they breach the regulations, while other non-permitted operators can always state that they did not intend to interact with dolphins. However, permit holders do not have the benefit to be able to solely target the dolphins during their tours, because non-permit holders can do so without running any legal risk.

Mitigation: Establishment of a Reserve Network

Environmental needs

A longitudinal study shows that boat interactions in Doubtful Sound affect the behavioural budget of bottlenose dolphins (Lusseau, 2003a). Interactions severely disrupt resting and to a lesser extent socialising bouts. They also decrease the chance to instigate a resting bout. This study also shows that violations of the MMPR increase the impact of boat interactions (Lusseau, 2003b), especially for female dolphins. Therefore, there seems to be four levels of interaction.

(1) Low impact interactions when dolphins are not socialising or resting and when the boat is not breaking the regulations.
(2) Medium impact interactions when dolphins are socialising and when boats are respecting the MMPA.
(3) High impact interactions when dolphins are resting and when boats are not breaking the law.
(4) Extreme impact interactions when vessels are breaching the regulations and dolphins are socialising or resting.

The high impact interactions can be avoided by impeding boat interactions in these situations. Locations where dolphins are known to rest and socialise can be restricted to boat traffic (Lusseau & Higham, 2003).

Benchmarking the activities

In all cases there is an immediate need to increase the quality of dolphin–boat interactions by decreasing the number of violations of the MMPR. There is especially a pressing need to decrease the occurrence of aggressive active interactions where the skipper attempts to obtain a response to his/her presence from the dolphins. In other studies of the impact of tourism activities on cetaceans, violations of the MMPR are usually given as case studies because of their rarity (Herrington, 2000). In a pilot study that assessed the risks of habituated dolphins to human interactions, a habituated dolphin was found at risk once per 12 minutes of interaction. The researchers concluded that 'the risks to habituated dolphin in Panama City Waters are so blatant and so dire, that immediate action could be justified without further study' (Samuels & Bejder, 2004). If MMPR violations are considered as a direct measure of the risk that dolphins encounter during boat interactions in Doubtful Sound, dolphins are at risk once per seven minutes when interacting with tour operators and once per three minutes when interacting with the other user group (see Figure 16.6). Interactions in Doubtful Sound are well below standard and justify immediate action.

Education

In the light of the reported observations, previous operator education attempts have obviously failed in Doubtful Sound. Moreover non-permit holders, that did not receive any education on how to behave around marine mammals, have a slightly worse behaviour than permit holders. The author therefore proposes to establish a roadshow to educate tour operators about the responsibilities they have when interacting with dolphins. The educational material will both explain in details the rationale behind the regulations already in place and present the problems observed in Fiordland. All tour operators will be targeted regardless of whether they have a watching permit or not. At the end of the presentation of the educational material, tour operators will be asked to sign a document explaining that they attended the roadshow and understood the problems at hand. Such a document will therefore be available in the future if enforcement is necessary. In addition, it is important that operators understand that by violating the MMPR they do not deliver to their customers what they advertised. The third most common concern of ecotourists visiting New Zealand is adverse visitor impacts (16.3% of respondents, Higham *et al.*, 2001). In other words ecovisitors want to make sure that they do not participate in activities that have an adverse effect on the location they are experiencing. This issue will also be raised during the roadshow and it will be explained how tour operators can raise the satisfaction level of their customers just by letting them know that they adhere to regulations. By explaining the rationale behind the regulations to their customers, and therefore explaining why skippers behave the way they do around dolphins, tourists will not have a high expectation level of dolphin display (refer also to Amante-Helweg, 1996). Therefore the skipper will not be pressured to aggressively interact with the dolphins, 'to make them jump', and tourists will value more the company because it shows genuine care for the location (Higham *et al.*, 2001). Similar techniques have been successfully applied in Hawaii with humpback whales (Forestell, 1993). In this location pre-contact briefing and post-contact debriefing are used to adjust the expectation of visitors and increase their awareness of problems faced in the area by the whales (Forestell, 1993).

As a footnote it is also worth noting that non-commercial vessels and fishing charters had short, yet intensively aggressive interactions. There is a lack of education here that needs to be addressed as well. All vessels that operate in Doubtful Sound have a high likelihood to encounter dolphins. It would be worth advertising the MMPR guidelines at the pier and the boat ramp in order to increase the awareness of this user group.

Restoring equal legal risks

It is necessary to re-establish the benefits of having a dolphin-watching permit. Doubtful Sound is a very difficult location to police. The fjord can only be accessed by ferry across Lake Manapouri by one of the tour operators or a related boat. Undercover activities are difficult to carry out. The community is small and therefore the likelihood that the tour operator will be warned of the arrival of an undercover officer is high. Therefore, it would be almost impossible to successfully prosecute a tour operator for targeting bottlenose dolphins as part of their tour regardless of the clauses of their Resource Consent. Moreover, it is difficult to prosecute a person under the Marine Mammal Protection Regulations (New Zealand Government, 1992). It is a problem faced in all countries that have MMPR because of the difficulty to demonstrate intent.

It is therefore necessary to concentrate on the re-establishment of the benefits of possessing a dolphin-watching permit. The establishment of a network of protected areas could help to solve this issue. As previously described there are currently four levels of interactions depending on their impact. Cases with the highest impact factor (dolphins resting) could be completely closed off to interactions. Areas where dolphins are known to socialise could be open only to tour operators that possess a dolphin-watching permit. Other areas would be open to general boat traffic, tour operators without a watching permit could still interact with dolphins (as long as the interaction is not sought by the skipper but random) and permit holders could interact as well. In all cases, the vessels should strictly follow the regulations of the MMPA during interactions. This 'segregation' could also apply to periods of the day when dolphins are known to socialise and rest.

The former solution may increase the intensity of boat interactions during a state that is still sensitive for the dolphins. Another solution would be to close to interactions locations where animals socialise and rest and restrict to permit holders the use of locations with high density of dolphin sightings where dolphins are known not to socialise and rest. Both solutions need to be explored to achieve a balanced cost–benefit approach for both tour operators and dolphins. Policing would still be a problem. It would be easier to prosecute any breach in the protected areas because the sole presence of the vessel in these areas will be sufficient to demonstrate non-compliance. To detect vessels remote cameras, coupled with solar power units, could be mounted to survey the area. A similar technique has been successfully used against poaching in Poor Knights Island Marine Reserve in 2001–2 (*New Zealand Herald*, 2002). This system would be cheaper and more effective than staffed undercover operations.

Intrinsic economic value of Doubtful Sound

A by-product of the creation of this network of protected areas is an increase in the intrinsic economic value of the location (Davis & Tisdell, 1996). Like their terrestrial counterpart, marine reserves and protected areas help to promote the location and can be used as advertisement tools (Davis & Tisdell, 1996). In addition, by preventing interactions with dolphins during sensitive behavioural states, the protected areas will permit to maximise the use of dolphins as a resource and minimise its 'consumption', hence allowing for sustainable development of the industry. It will therefore help meet the increasing demand, depicted by the increase in visitor numbers, without depleting the resource.

Stepping Towards Sustainability

The International Institute for Sustainable Development and the European Union suggest the protection of areas as part of their indicator guidelines for the sustainable management of tourism (Welford *et al.*, 1999). On a long-term basis, bottlenose dolphins cannot sustain the types of activities undertaken by the scenic cruise industry in Doubtful Sound. The tourism sector is currently at a crossroad in this fjord, a crossroad that has been reported in many other situations (Duffus & Dearden, 1990). Sustainability can still be achieved if the results of this study are incorporating in a management framework. If the current development scheme is left unaltered the industry will impact upon both the local natural resources and the local community beyond repair. Moreover, the activities offered in the fjord will not match the expectation of visitors, which will irrevocably compromise the economic sustainability of the tourism operations. The current management framework needs to be urgently reviewed in collaboration with all parties involved on this issue.

Acknowledgements

The author has received continuous support from many people during the three years of this study. I would like to thank all the volunteers who have helped me in the field. Many thanks go to Oliver J. Boisseau and Susan Mærsk Lusseau for their continuous support and help in the field and during the writing phase. Christoph Richter has also been a great source of constructive comments. James E.S. Higham, Elisabeth Slooten and Steve M. Dawson have been a tremendous source of support, inspiration and constructive comments throughout this study. Many of the ideas presented here emerged from discussions with them. This project was funded by the New Zealand Department of Conservation, Southland Conservancy, with thanks to Alan Munn, Helen Kettles,

Lindsay Chadderton and the staff from the Te Anau DoC office for their help and support. The author would also like to thank Fiordland Travel (Real Journeys) and Fiordland Ecology Holidays for providing information on boat traffic; Paul Stewart, from Deep Cove Outdoor Educational Trust, for his help and support and for making life easier in Deep Cove; and, finally, Fiordland Travel's Manapouri office staff, especially Paul Norris and Frank Wells, for their continuous support, help and keen interest.

References

Amante-Helweg, V. (1996) Ecotourists' beliefs and knowledge about dolphins and the development of cetacean ecotourism. *Aquatic Mammals* 22 (2), 131–40.

Davis, D. and Tisdell, C. (1996) Economic management of recreational scuba diving and the environment. *Journal of Environmental Management* 48, 229–48.

Duffus, D.A. and Dearden, P. (1990) Non-consumptive wildlife-oriented recreation: A conceptual framework. *Biological Conservation* 53, 213–31.

Forestell, P.H. (1993) If Leviathan has a face, does Gaia have a soul?: Incorporating environment education in marine eco-tourism programs. *Ocean and Coastal Management* 20, 267–82.

Herrington, K.L. (2000) Adherence to the Marine Mammal Protection Act by dolphin-watching companies in Pinellas County, Florida. Unpublished undergraduate thesis, Eckerd College, Saint Petersburg, FL. 82pp.

Higham, J.E.S., Carr, A. and Gale, S. (2001) *Ecotourism in New Zealand: Profiling visitors to New Zealand Ecotourism Operations*. Research Paper Number Ten. Dunedin: Department of Tourism, University of Otago.

Lusseau, D. (2003a) The effects of tour boats on the behavior of bottlenose dolphins: Using Markov chains to model anthropogenic impacts. *Conservation Biology* 17, 1785–93.

Lusseau, D. (2003b) Male and female bottlenose dolphins (*Tursiops spp.*) have different strategies to avoid interactions with tour boats in Doubtful Sound, New Zealand. *Marine Ecology Progress Series* 257, 267–74.

Lusseau, D. and Slooten, E. (2002) Cetacean sightings off the Fiordland coastline: Analysis of commercial marine mammal viewing data 1996–99. *Science for Conservation* 187. 42pp.

Lusseau, D. and Higham, J.E.S. (2004) Managing the impacts of dolphin-based tourism through the definition of critical habitats: The case of Doubtful Sound, New Zealand. *Tourism Management* 25 (6), 657–67.

Lusseau, D., Schneider, K., Boisseau, O.J., Haase, P., Slooten, E. *et al.* (2003) The bottlenose dolphin community of Doubtful Sound features a large proportion of long-lasting associations. Can geographic isolation explain this unique trait? *Behavioral Ecology and Sociobiology* DOI 10.1007/s00265–003–0651-y.

New Zealand Government (1992) *Marine Mammal Protection Regulations 1992 (S.R. 1992/322)*. Wellington: New Zealand Government Printer.

New Zealand Herald (2002) Navy joins war on marine poachers. *New Zealand Herald*, 15 May.

Samuels, A. and Bejder, L. (2003) Chronic interactions between humans and wild bottlenose dolphins (*Tursiops truncatus*) near Panama City Beach, FL. *Journal of Cetacean Research and Management* 6 (1), 69–77.

Weaver, D.B. (ed.) (2001) *The Encyclopedia of Ecotourism*. Wallingford: CABI
    Publishing.
Welford, R., Ytterhus, B. and Eligh, J. (1999) Tourism and sustainable develop-
    ment: An analysis of policy and guidelines for managing provision and
    consumption. *Sustainable Development* 7, 165–77.

Part 4: Nature-based Tourism in Peripheral Areas: A Tool for Regional Development?

Chapter 17
Ecotourism/Egotourism and Development

BRIAN WHEELLER

As early as 1990, Pigram cogently argued that without the effective means of translating ideas into action, sustainable tourism 'runs the risk of remaining irrelevant and inert as a feasible policy option for the real world of tourism development' (Pigram, 1990: 20). Authors such as Butler (1990), in his visionary article 'Pious Hope or Trojan Horse', and Cazes (1989) were similarly sceptical. So too, my own writings around that time were scathing of the 'new' forms of tourism – and of the fawning plaudits and laurels being garlanded on them (Wheeller, 1991, 1993). One of my main criticisms was that while ecotourism (or, indeed, sustainable tourism in its many, many guises) may, as a planning 'control', be fine in theory, it is useless in practice – primarily because it does not, and cannot, confront the unfortunate harsh realities of human behaviour. Although actually acknowledging these traits as part of the problem it, I argued, completely failed to address or incorporate them in the so-called solutions. A decade later, the concerns of the dissenting voices are as valid now as they were then, if not more so. But, just as before, it comes as no surprise that they are still being ignored.

For ecotourism to have real, practical credibility we must exit fantasyland and contextualise the ecosustainability debate within the wider arena of power, economics, greed, racism and hypocrisy – a 'whole-istic' not 'hole-istic' approach. That is, one where all the relevant issues are tackled and addressed head on, rather than a partial, selective, cherry-picking attitude in which the difficult issues are conveniently dispatched into a black hole and quietly forgotten. It is this biting realism that is totally lacking in most writing on ecotourism and sustainability. What we have instead is the continued preaching, the perpetual goody-two-shoes mantra of sustainability ('Green is Good/God') being peddled by the tourism industry, planners, politicians and many academics. When will we ever learn? Well, probably never. Unfortunately, it is extremely difficult to achieve 'the truth' . . . or even get an inkling of it . . . when the powerful, dominant forces of society dictate otherwise – namely, obfuscation, duplicity and deception. Forget the genteel 'being economical with the truth': here, in a welter of cases, we are talking downright lies.

We need to ask ourselves some difficult – and I suggest unpalatable – questions. Are we ready to wholeheartedly embrace the fundamentals of sustainability? Are we, for example, really prepared to put long-term interests before short-term immediacy: to adopt a philanthropic, rather than vested interest, approach to life: to really 'care'? I doubt it very much. While sustainability is supposed to be concerned with the long term, just about everything else in our society and our lives (certainly in the West) is geared to the short term: to the immediate, quick returns. Perhaps even more disturbing, this proclivity appears to be increasingly accompanied by an overriding selfishness, to getting our licks in now. The obvious connotations of the 'Come to Bangladesh before the Tourists get here' campaign reveal, and illuminate further, the true motivations of the supposedly selfless 'traveller'. In the wider arena, two quotes from the movies spring to mind that perhaps best reflect this. In *Pirates of the Caribbean* (Sparrow, 2003), (Captain) Jack Sparrow's counsel to 'Take as much as you can. Put nothing back' mirrors the earlier advice given by Dennis Hope, the band's manager to his touring acolytes, Lightwater, in *Almost Famous* (Hope, 2000) 'You've got to take what you can, when you can, and you've got to take it now'.

Now compare these examples with the (too) oft-quoted Brundtland Report's (1987) sins of compromising the interests of future generations and the concomitant eulogy to our children's children. And ask yourself which most accurately reflects actual contemporary behaviour and lifestyle, be it your own, or society's in general. Then ponder whether there is anything whatsoever in the eco/sustainable tourism package that is really going to radically alter and reverse this situation? Or anything that will, in reality, come remotely close to being a solution, other than in terms of palliative empty words, easy platitudes. Surely, any tourism planning that chooses to ignore contemporary trends and fails to incorporate them in its underlying philosophy must be fundamentally flawed. And, in practical terms, have a built-in obsolescence. This, it seems to me, is a charge that can, and should, be laid at eco/sustainable tourism.

To most liberal minds, sustainability conjures up images of gentleness, of care, compassion and of preservation. However, a statement from the US military gives a more disturbing, but nevertheless revealing, slant on sustainability. In introducing a new computerised, digital helmet, the spokesman revealed 'This one is more lethal, more sustainable' (CNN, 1994 quoted in Wheeller, 1998: 53). Those of us of a delicate disposition who had previously foolishly considered sustainability more in the realms of preserving rather than destroying might be affronted by this.

However, the logic of the military makes chillingly effective sense. If you want to sustain/preserve something, kill anything and everything that threatens it. Simple. Anyway, in many facets of our 'environmental' behaviour, we do just that.

We should (but choose not to) be aware of our vagaries when it comes to just what precisely we mean by 'sustainability'. We are, of course, flexible in our interpretation of 'sustainability'. When it suits us we are pragmatic and selective, particularly when it comes to sustaining flora and fauna. On holiday, be it mass package or a custom designed eco-itinerary, there is no crisis of conscience when it comes to killing mosquitoes. And back home, in the garden, aphids are eradicated with similar relish and unwelcome weeds unceremoniously dispatched off. Even at the environmental/sustainable paradigm, The Eden Project – 'the Living Theatre of Plants and People'– there are no apparent qualms at how best to deal with this potential dilemma. Keen to attract the tourist but deter the unwanted visitors (plant pests), an on-site information sign reads:

> Within our biomes we use many techniques to control plant pests. One example is the UV-light trap which produces light at night, attracting moths and mosquitoes. Many moth caterpillars damage plants and mosquitoes damage humans. They are trapped on sticky board in the traps, then we can identify and count the captured creatures.

Is not this simply a reassuring, marketing euphemism, echoing the military dictate?

While on a trip to Amazonia, staying at the Ariau Jungle Tower, I witnessed animals from the surrounding forest coming down each evening, onto the terrace to feed ... so providing pleasure and entertainment to the tourist cosily ensconced in the luxury ecolodge. Should the mood have taken me, any attempt to stamp on a monkeys head, or throttle a macaw would have been considered, let us say, inappropriate. However, crushing a cockroach underfoot in the dining room was de rigueur. Similarly, one suspects, any unsightly spider, or potentially dangerous snake slithering in the vicinity, would have been dispatched of with equal alacrity.

Alarming inconsistency is apparent too when fish, caught for sport, are strung up and displayed as trophies – always accompanied in suitable triumphant pose by the conquering hero/heroine. Why no universal outrage at this appalling spectacle? I guess because most see nothing wrong with this conduct. But take a closer look at a page from *The Times* Travel Section on holidays in the Seychelles: 'Hooked on Big Game Fishing in the Sun' (Herbert, 1996). The lead photo shows the proud tourist and bloodied sail fish, the latter prone, vanquished on the boat deck. A smaller picture, top left, depicts Esmerelda, the world's heaviest tortoise, weighing in at 600lbs, being admired, tenderly and lovingly. All perfectly civilised and acceptable. Now imagine the situation reversed, the fish swimming happily, unhindered and at peace, and the tortoise upturned, skewered, tangled up with hook and tackle, at death's door. Wild animal as trophy. Outrage. Similarly, if it were a lion or, taking examples from further afield, say a polar bear or a tiger or, heaven forbid, a panda that had been strung up then, undoubtedly, there would have been an almighty outcry. But a fish? Well no, after all is said and done, it's only a fish.

A further dimension to this irrationality is reflected by a seemingly throwaway, yet succinct, line from the Director General of the Wildlife Trust who, in response to the 'cult of the cuddly' sardonically mused: 'We get lots of sponsorship for otters and red squirrels but none for the narrow-headed ant' (Lyster, 1998: 4). Beauty may indeed only be skin deep but in our society many creatures are in this respect, unfortunately, 'thick skinned'.

But it is not only with animals and plants where the superficial seems to suffice. If the one of the pillars of the new forms of tourism is to respect the wishes and customs of the locals, what happens when their customs fail to meet the existing, prevailing moral and/or political agenda of the outside, eco/sustainable tourists? Some say tourism should only change the indigenous culture for the better – but are rather circumspect as to delineating what precisely constitutes 'better'. Others argue that tourism should not change local customs, that it shouldn't impinge on, or undermine, traditional ways of life. Yet, as has been well documented in the broader ramifications of the enclave tourist debate, we are perfectly happy to museumise another society while we continue to reap the benefits of our own continued growth. More fundamentally, in addition to problems inherent in such fossilisation, there is a disturbing lack of consistency and logic in approach. If, as frequently purported, tourism shouldn't change an indigenous society then when, or indeed why, is it acceptable to use tourism as an economic/political weapon to discourage tourists to go to places considered unethical or politically incorrect – for example Myanmar? And therefore, by default, undermine and attempt to alter the (perceived unsavoury) status quo at the destination?

Undoubtedly tourists bring (some) money, which will inevitably influence/change a vulnerable recipient society. So by introducing, or denying, tourism we are automatically using our 'outside' power to influence an internal situation economically. By discouraging tourists, the economic viability of the region is undermined: surely an overt attempt to change the political structure of a country using tourism as an integral part of that strategy. The point here is not one of passing moral judgement on such sensitive issues as the rights or wrongs of democracy/dictatorship in, say, Myanmar. Rather it is on the flexible, I would argue dubiously inconsistent, interpretation of when exactly it is considered acceptable, or conversely, unacceptable for tourism to influence local (or national) communities. And then there is the question of who should be the arbitrator, the judge and jury of that extremely complex set of decisions . . . tour operators, tourists, human rights groups? When it suits us (as academics/members of politically correct pressure groups) to affirm that tourism should not alter an indigenous culture we will follow that line of 'logic'. Yet, when it appears apposite to argue that tourism should be used (by boycott/default) to alter an indigenous culture, we will just as readily do this too.

As always, it is a selective, manipulative process. While tourists are discouraged by some organisations to go to Myanmar on socio/political grounds, they are encouraged to go to other destinations, for example, say to Tibet on more or less the same socio/political grounds, the argument appearing to be that, in the latter case, tourists should go, see for themselves the political situation and spread the (negative) word on their return home.

The political arena is a dangerously contentious theatre. But not one that should be shied away from if so-called sustainable tourism is to have credence in its supposed holistic approach to the physical, social, cultural, economic and political environment. The fact is that the actual development of tourism – the necessary wheeling and dealing – takes place in the real world, warts and all. Whereas elaborate academic tourism planning discussions, and discourse on sustainability, still remain essentially confined to, and cocooned in, the protected dream world of textbook theory . . . immune to the pressures and vicissitudes of actuality. The question of corruption and the levels of intensity to which it is practised are conveniently ignored in the supposedly 'holistic', yet somewhat arbitrary, sustainable tourism vacuum. The assertion that 'the world has the worry that corruption is now spreading throughout politics. One can almost say that corruption has now become the global norm' (Rees-Mogg, 1999: 18) must be continually borne in mind – but, of course, it is not. With only a few notable exceptions (see, for example, Hall, 1994; Brown, 1997) much of tourism's literature on planning chooses to ignore the uncomfortable reality, seemingly oblivious to the fact that the best intended plans may not be carried out in practice simply because they are waylaid by corrupt officials. Even case study material, often one assumes on grounds of expediency, tends to omit mention to this very real consideration, as do many Ph.D.'s presented by students studying abroad but empirically based on their own countries, who for very pragmatic, prudent reasons feel it judicious not to draw attention to corruption of their own governments, prior to their return home.

There are contradictory signals and policies, on the part of various governments in the emerging world, which, on the one hand expound green rhetoric while simultaneously pursuing policies that would seem to be resource destructive. Similar ambiguity is reflected in advanced economies with our reluctance, or refusal, to curb excessive consumption, while giving lip service to green lifestyles.

Another point on corruption: In the days of Marcos, the sensitive traveller was counselled not to visit the Philippines, which, because of the political situation, was deemed an inappropriate destination. However, did anyone contemplate that the boycott should (logically) also encompass America – the prime supporter of the Marcos regime? That consequently we should be discouraged from going to the United States for our holidays in order to undermine the democracy that supported the corrupt dictatorial regime?

The degree to which we are prepared to take our principles is a moot point. Usually just so far as to not have to give up anything we really want. Witness the sham of going ethnic, to act as the locals do. But here, as elsewhere, we are selective, superimposing our own values as and when it suits. 'Going ethnic' is merely a sop to our consciences as, indeed, is ecosustainability in general. While we are ostensibly keen to be 'at one' with the locals, to behave as they do, we as egotourists nevertheless take the precautions afforded to us by prophylactic medicine – vaccinations, tablets, whatever. We are only 'at one' on our own terms. So, for example, at the ecolodge, the jungle adventure is experienced from the safety of the environmental bubble:

> Even at the edge, as tourist/travellers in the most 'authentic' ecolodge we don't experience the 'true' experience of the wild. We are protected, cocooned. We have the safety (and mosquito) net of Mosiguaud and malaria tablets. We have our tampons and suntan lotion. And our indefatigable illusion/delusion of being at one with nature. (Wheeller, forthcoming)

And, if there is air-conditioning, then so much the better. Furthermore, those espousing immersion into the social fabric of destinations by experiencing the use of local transport, consuming indigenous food and meeting the 'locals' while on their travels are reluctant to practise what they preach at home. I would suggest they are the least likely to be seen on buses or in a corner fish and chip shop. Living the local, ordinary lifestyle seems to be a trait evident only when they themselves are 'abroad'.

McKercher, in a first-class article advocating a Chaos Theory approach to tourism, justifiably claims that: 'If the traditional models explained tourism fully, then they should also offer insights into controlling tourism. But none does. The reason is that tourism is simply too complex to be captured effectively in a deterministic model' (McKercher, 1999: 426). Similarly, it is an illusion to see sustainability, which begs for a cross-cultural, interdisciplinary approach, in isolation (see Mowfort & Munt, 2003). Or restrict it with nomenclature such as sustainable transport or sustainable tourism, thereby suggesting that it can somehow be ring-fenced (for academic study). Sustainability is also far too complex to separate and isolate. Like tourism planning, it too must be contextualised in the chaos of contemporary culture and behaviour. If this is indeed a fair reflection of reality, then to automatically assume that there is a solution (or indeed, a phalanx of palliatives that combined would constitute the 'solution') to the negative aspects of tourism seems overtly optimistic. Especially when it does not even appear too clear precisely what it is that we are actually trying to sustain in the first place? And over what time frame: the hardly definitive 'long term'?

Assuming here (for brevity and convenience, those expeditious 'catchalls') that ecotourism actually exists, and that we can define, 'isolate' and identify ecotourists, then continuing with the awkward questions, we might well ask how do ecotourists actually get to those destinations where they can indulge ecotourism? Rightly or wrongly, most academic writing on eco/sustainable tourism infers an international dimension and a concomitant use of transport. To reach those 'off the beaten track' destinations (oh so appealing to the discerning ecotourist) invariably necessitates air travel, 'a car to the airport and a jumbo jet hardly paradigms of virtue in the environmentally friendly stakes' (Wheeller, 1993: 125). So does not this raise the question as to whether international eco/ sustainable tourism is, by its very nature, an oxymoron in itself? This question is generally dismissed – unanswered, of course – as 'old hat' and 'boring' by believers.

True, some do respond, tangentially, by reasoning that it is better to believe in something (ecotourism) than have faith in nothing at all, retorting that ecotourism is at least a step in the right direction. But is it? For every 'good' ecotourism project there may be as many as say 30 'bad' projects created under the auspices and patronage of sustainability, and masquerading beneath the ecotourism banner. Maybe it is worth once again reminding everyone here that the eco in ecotourism is the eco in economics, not the eco in ecology and, as the song says, money makes the world go round.

If, as we are led to believe, tourism is the world's largest industry (and personally I do not believe for a moment it is . . . what, for example, about the food industry?) then it can only be so if its interlinkages with other industries are taken into consideration. When it comes to justifying more tourism development, this angle is always staunchly pointed to by the pro-tourism lobby. So, in the realms of the tourism multiplier we have the familiar direct, indirect and induced effects of tourism. But this type of analysis is often restricted to an interpretation of positive tourism impacts. The same must apply to the negative impacts too, and not just the economic. If the claim is made that tourism can be sustainable then, surely, this can only be valid if all the industries that tourism is linked to are also 'sustainable'. Is this really feasible? (See Buhalis & Fletcher, 1995; Wheeller, 1998.)

In similar vein, while it may be accepted here that the immediate, more tangible, major problems that accompany tourism growth can be identified – whether they can be measured is another matter. Whether all the more subtle, and longer term, ramifications of tourism development have as yet been recognised is also debatable. And just how these might manifest remains a mystery.

Or maybe I'm wrong and things have changed. And for the better. Certainly, the editors of the *Journal of Sustainable Tourism* see the last ten years or so in a far more positive light. With justification, they point to the Journal's undoubted success as a publication: 'it goes from strength to strength'. (*Channel Views*, 2002). While this may well adhere to the Journal itself, is it true for ecosustainability? Well, yes, and no. Where you stand on the issue very much depends on where your perspective. And on one's interpretation of 'success'. Those with a positive, jaunty outlook see ecosustainability as a 'success' – with far more to offer, while those of us detractors, with a somewhat more jaundiced outlook see it from a somewhat different perspective. It is here that the divergent views are most apparent. So when we look to 'judge' ecotourism's success then, even assuming we are looking at the same thing – which, given the nature of the multi-faceted beast is doubtful – hardly surprisingly, we see things differently.

In terms of status, eco/sustainable tourism has, appropriately enough, become elevated to dizzy heights. And in tourism, as elsewhere in our contemporary lifestyles, status is so important – for eco read ego (Wheeller, 1993). In academia there have been a plethora of articles, books, modules, programmes and dissertations dedicated to it. The tourism industry warmly embraces it. Professional bodies extol its virtues and approve codes of practice. There are prestigious industry awards for politically correct, sustainable ecotourism projects. A similar positive response gushes from tourist boards and planning departments. And, for what it was worth, 2002 was the United Nations International Year of Ecotourism. So, status wise ecosustainability has arrived. Big time. In this sense then, it has been an undoubted success.

But, if we take stock, and look for substance rather than image, what, precisely, has eco/sustainable tourism achieved in practice? Very little, I suggest. Even after all these years the emphasis is still on 'potential'. What do we actually have? A cosy symbiotic alliance ... on the one hand our own pretentious, egocentric foibles and on the other ecosustainability, pandering perfectly to them. A dangerously diversionary tactic, it is little more than an elaborate confidence trick – and one we are all party to. Somewhat perversely, ecosustainability owes its 'success' and durability to its actual in-built ineffectiveness in dealing with the real issues of tourism impact. Years ago I argued, with regard to behaviour and lifestyle, that it endorsed, even encouraged, the main stakeholders in tourism development to continue much as before (Wheeller, 1991). I went on to suggest that the central issues, those at the crux of tourism impact, were not being addressed. Has anything changed? According to some, 'Ten years on the worst predictions of the pessimists have been proved wrong' (*Channel Views*, 2002: 4). I do not think so. My interpretation of subsequent events leads me to quite the opposite conclusion.

To most tourists (living for the 'now'), sustainability continues to be of little import – far more pressing are matters of price, value for money and fun, fun, fun. For the 'believers', I again contend that though they might not be aware of it, the ineffectiveness of sustainable tourism is its strength and remains core to their acceptance of it. The continuing canard – one that allows them, the industry, politicians and tourism developers to carry on very much as before, cosseted in their green, Emperor's clothes. This, I fear, may sound arrogant on my part. I sincerely hope not, arrogance being a characteristic I despise. But it is, unfortunately, what I believe.

I really do not see ecotourism, or sustainability as the, or indeed an, answer. To me there is not an answer, nor a cure, to tourism impact problems. Primarily, I believe this is because tourism impacts are just one more symptom of the incurable cancerous greed endemic in society. Focusing in on this bleak view is depressing. And, to the vast majority (of privileged commentators), accepting it, impossible. Coming to terms with our hypocrisy might at least be a start, perhaps the best we can hope for. We are, I contend, driven (riven?) by short-term, selfish self-interest, any vestiges of genuine philanthropy subsumed, and consumed, by vested, material, immediate concerns.

Nothing necessarily wrong with this in itself. However, what seems unacceptable to me is, when advocating solutions, to blindly ignore these traits in our behaviour, this materialistic avarice. To continue to trumpet idealistic notions of ecosustainability, which are so obviously diametrically opposed to the culture of the dominant West is absurd. Yet the charade continues. Questions remain conveniently unanswered, ignored. And the gaping chasm between rhetoric and reality grows ever wider, the void to avoid at all costs. And the reason? Despite over a decade of practising, in practice it cannot be bridged.

References

Brown, F. (1997) *Tourism Reassessed. Blight or Blessing.* Oxford: Butterworth Heineman.

Brundtland Report (1987) *The World Commission on Environment and Development. Our Common Future.* Oxford: Oxford University Press.

Buhalis, D. and Fletcher, J. (1995) Environmental impacts on tourist destinations. In Coccossis, H. and Nijkamp, P. (eds) *Sustainable Tourism Development* (pp. 3–25). Aldershot: Avebury.

Butler, R.W. (1990) Alternative tourism: Pious hope or Trojan horse? *Journal of Travel Research* Winter, 40–45.

CNN (1994) *CNN TV News*, 14 December.

Cazes, G. (1989) Alternative tourism: Reflections on an ambitious concept. In Singh, T., Theuns, L. and Go, F. (eds) *Towards Appropriate Tourism* (pp. 117–126). Frankfurt: Lang.

Channel Views (2002) Ten years at the cutting edge. *Channel Views Newsletter* 1, p. 4.

Hall, C.M. (1994) *Tourism and Politics: Policy, Power and Place.* Chichester: John Wiley and Son.

Hope, D. (2000) *Almost Famous.* Dreamwork Pictures.

Herbert, M. (1996) Hooked on big game fishing in the sun. *The Times Weekend*, 30 November, p. 17.

Lyster, S. (1998) Independent Comment, 26 September, pp. 4, 14.

McKercher, B. (1999) A chaos approach to tourism. *Tourism Management* 20 (4), 425–434.

Mowforth, M. and Munt, I. (2003) *Tourism and Sustainability.* London: Routledge.

Pigram, J. (1990) Sustainable tourism, policy considerations. *Journal of Tourism Studies*, 2 (November), 2–9.

Rees-Mogg, W. (1999) A culture of corruption. *The Times*, 15 February, p. 18.

Sparrow, J. (2003) *Pirates of the Caribbean.* Buena Vista Home Entertainment, Inc.

Wheeller, B. (1991) Tourism's troubled times, *Tourism Management* June, 91–96.

Wheeller, B. (1993) Sustaining the ego. *Journal of Sustainable Tourism* 1 (2), 121–129.

Wheeller, B. (1998) The complete confidence trick. In Michel, F. (ed.) *Tourismes, Touristes, Sociétés.* Paris: L'Harmattan.

Wheeller, B. (forthcoming) Elvis, authenticity, sustainability and TALC. In Butler, R. (ed.) *The Tourism Area Life Cycle.* Clevedon: Channel View.

Chapter 18

Nature-based Tourism in Peripheral Areas: Making Peripheral Destinations Competitive

STEPHEN BOYD AND C. MICHAEL HALL

Introduction

Tourism has come of age: maturing as a discipline with a developed body of theory; taught and researched from many schools of thought; has an expanding list of journals devoted to tourism research; and has evolved beyond being viewed as an undifferentiated phenomenon to developing a number of distinct types and subtypes of tourism. Nature-based tourism has emerged as one of these main types of tourism, based on the reality that many tourism experiences are dominantly reliant on the natural capital that regions possess, along with the acceptance that in most cases tourists' experience of places has passive tendencies where casual viewing of natural surroundings is most common. Nature-based tourism exists in diverse environments, to include alpine and sub-Arctic regions, areas formally set aside with protected or national park status, islands, coastal and marine spaces, and has emerged as a type or umbrella label for more specific subtypes like ecotourism, wildlife tourism and peripheral areas tourism. As a definite 'type', nature-based tourism within locales can have a long history, developed as the first tourism opportunity based on the already present attraction of nature itself and the limited infrastructure needed to enjoy it. In other cases, nature-based tourism is relatively new, often linked to the regional development of peripheral areas that have little to offer other than tourism.

Regardless what part of the spectrum nature-based tourism is found to exist in and at what scale, what is somewhat surprising is the paucity of research and attention that has been devoted to this type of tourism (see Hall & Boyd, Chapter 1, this volume), compared to the volume of work that has been focused on a subtype of nature-based tourism, namely ecotourism. This book represents an effort to better understand the broad area of nature-based tourism, accepting that to many what is being

referred to is often researched under the label of ecotourism, acknowledging that in many contexts tourism that is nature-based is often tourism
present within peripheral regions. The objective, therefore of this
concluding chapter is to pull out those issues for further debate as well
as address the many challenges, areas often peripheral in character, that
offer a nature-based tourism experience, what issues they face and what
strategies they adopt to meet them. The issues and challenges that have
emerged from the chapters in this book include:

- A better understanding and knowledge of nature-based tourism.
- The importance of establishing community support for tourism
  development in peripheral areas.
- The need for investment to develop nature-based tourism.
- The need to develop a product that is different and unique but that
  remains true to the natural characteristics of areas.
- Ensuring ensure good management practices are in place.

Each of these are taken in turn and discussed in the remainder of this
chapter in terms of how peripheral regions can remain competitive.

Understanding Nature-based Tourism

Many tourism writers have written about the challenges of defining
terms within tourism (see Hall & Page, 2002), and there is no attempt
here to cover familiar ground other than to make a few observations,
one based on personal observation and the other based on comments
made within a number of chapters within this volume. First, a personal
comment. The academic community is guilty of over-assigning labels
and giving the same product and/or experience more than one label.
This fascination with labels has led to developing typologies that describe
the type of tourist, the type of tourism product or experience, and further
to typologies that segment both the type of tourist interested in individual types of tourism. In contrast, the tourism industry assigns labels
to areas based on the experiences that a region can offer visitors, be that
nature, recreation, wilderness, cultural, family or adventure, using labels
as a mode to place market and sell places. While there is merit in assign-
ing labels, it is important to realize that in most cases, apart from those
visitors who classify themselves as special-interest travellers, tourists do
not see themselves within a rigid classification that qualifies them as a
nature-based tourist, or an ecotourist, or a wildlife tourist. In many situations, the tourism experience is comprised of many sub-experiences,
which can be nature, eco, cultural, adventure and resort related.

Second, understanding nature-based tourism requires a holistic knowledge of the context in which tourism is said to take place. While virtually
all authors described the context in which nature-based tourism occurred,

offering in some cases a brief history of tourism as it pertained to a specific locale, the chapter by Saarinen (Chapter 3, this volume) also raised the need to be aware that meaning behind labels is linked to the culture of place. In his discussion he points to different 'discourses' of wilderness within Northern Finland and how a nature-based tourism product has varied over time within the Northern Wilderness Region based on shifting demands, new ways of thinking about wilderness, as well as having to compete within a global as opposed to local market-place. The concept of 'wilderness' in a Finnish context is very different to thinking about wilderness as defined and valued by early colonizers of New World countries.

A third point that may be raised, and which is alluded to by several authors in the volume, is that a nature-based tourism product is often offered to combat the challenge of seasonality, and that in many situations is not 'sold' as the main tourism product or attraction of a region. This point was well noted by Russell, Thomas and Fredline (Chapter 6, this volume) in their research of mountains parks and resorts in the state of Victoria, Australia, and the image that these destinations offer summer visitors. They stated that although nature-based tourism was a developing product for that time of year, shaped by an image of nature, scenery, passive enjoyment and uniqueness, the region remained a pre-dominantly winter destination catering to winter activities such as skiing. While nature-based tourism offers the opportunity to create a year-round destination, albeit based on a secondary product as compared to winter activities, uncertainty associated with climatic change may force some regions to promote forms of tourism, namely nature-based, that are more deliverable to visitors.

Community Support

A theme that was common in many of the chapters was the role that communities played in the development of nature-based tourism in peripheral regions. Given the scale on which most tourism research is undertaken, communities are by far the most used within a case study scenario. Communities have been studied from a geographical–ecological (see Murphy, 1985), a socio-anthropological (see Pearce *et al.*, 1996) or an interdisciplinary perspective (see Singh *et al.*, 2003), and this has resulted in the accumulation of knowledge of the role that the community plays in tourism development, control and the extent to which they directly benefit from tourism. Communities are rarely universally behind tourism development, often containing diverse viewpoints and levels of support (see Boyd & Singh, 2003). However, it may be argued that communities found in peripheral areas are often simple in their structure, hence more homogenous, and where tourism development is concerned, are more often favourable to that form of development and change for their community than opposed to it. Support can often be garnered on the belief that the type of tourism being developed is less exploitative of the natural capital of regions, less impact prone as a passive relationship with local surroundings is being encouraged, can directly benefit in monetary terms local communities and is in many cases the only real option open to them. Thinking along these lines is reflected in the discussion of several of the chapters contained within this volume.

Johnston and Payne (Chapter 2, this volume) in writing about the role of resource-based tourism within Northwestern Ontario, Canada, commented on the role of the need for cooperation in the development of tourism opportunity across the region, involving resource-based industries (timber and fisheries), those affected communities along with existing tourism operators. In the cases studies they presented, the extent to which local people were consulted and had some degree of involvement in the development of tourism initiatives had strong influence in the level of support they gave to projects, with local community workshops helping to allay community concerns being received better than one workshop for an entire project where a consortium of consultants set out the process which in essence excluded local opinion and expertise. The extent to which local people are tied to tourism projects also emerged in the chapter by Querios and Wilson (Chapter 13, this volume), which presented proposals for Mkambati Nature Reserve within the Wild Coast (northeast coastline, South Africa), that addressed setting, accommodation and facilities, culture and community. While Querios and Wilson's chapter presents proposals of potential tourism development, the contribution made by Tokalau (Chapter 11, this volume) was to illustrate the economic and tangible benefits an individual ecotourism tour of a single village (Namuamua) on the island of Vitu Levu, Fiji, can offer its residents. In this case, these include an additional source of income and employment, ongoing investment in community facilities, accommodation and lodgings, entrepreneurial development and new projects. The work by Scheyvens (Chapter 12, this volume) further illustrates the importance of ensuring that tourism benefits return and remain within the local community. In the case of the budget beach accommodation sector, Scheyvens points to the position of *fale* tourism as a form of high value tourism for community development that culturally educates guests, retains economic benefits in the local region, supports the conservation of resources, and ensures opportunity exists for local involvement and control of tourism. In contrast to the above works, Lovelock and Robinson (Chapter 10, this volume) report on the limited economic benefit that tourism, in this case in the form of deer hunting, offers the local community on Stewart Island, New Zealand, as much of the hunter expenditure takes place off the island, and the peripheral nature of this location and its limited infrastructure, commercial and retail establishments restricts opportunity to spend money locally. However, overall, most of the discussion in relevant chapters is supportive of ensuring community support for tourism and that nature-based tourism can bring benefits that are retained locally.

Need for Investment

Another theme that emerges in many of the chapters is the need for further investment within nature-based tourism. This point was raised by Hall and Boyd (Chapter 1, this volume) who stated that despite much of nature-based tourism being reliant on the presence of the natural capital of regions, tourism in peripheral regions also requires the necessary infrastructure (man-made capital), personnel (human capital) and freedom of choice and control (social capital) to turn many natural settings into a tourism resource. Developing the necessary support infrastructure to deliver tourism in peripheral areas was commented on in chapters by Frost; Russell, Thomas and Fredline; Müller; Lovelock and Robinson; and Tokalau; Querios and Wilson, Scheyvens, and Johnston and Payne also commented on the need for greater developments in human and social capital for nature-related tourism in peripheral areas to be a reality as opposed to a desirable option. The challenge for many peripheral regions will be to encourage reinvestment in tourism plant that originates locally as opposed to outside of region in order to limit the extent of leakage occurring. There is often, however, some reticence for local communities to make a financial commitment to develop the needed infrastructure and support systems especially if the product is more likely to be consumed by the international market as opposed to a local one. The reality is often however, that peripheral regions that offer little other choice than tourism have to take the financial gamble to invest in order to survive.

Second homes represent a different form of investment in peripheral regions (see Hall & Müller, 2004). These are important for they provide additional accommodation stock, but also create a new tourism market for regions. Müller (Chapter 9, this volume), in examining second home tourism in the Swedish mountain range however, sends a note of caution, for while second homes often are found within amenity-rich landscapes, at the same time this form of investment can change peripheral areas to places of temporary residence where the local population can no longer afford to live. The desire to own a second home in areas of high natural capital is indeed a growing global phenomenon but in many peripheral regions, caution is needed to ensure the local characteristics of the place remain in tact and that a local resident population is not replaced with a transitory, external one. The desire to bring about economic change through second home development may bring to many peripheral regions significant social and unwanted change, and therefore structures are needed to control the amount of change taking place in peripheral regions.

Development of the 'Unique'

Peripheral regions possess unique natural capital and a number of chapters in this volume position their discussion around creating attractions that play to an area's strength. Frost in his discussion of canopy walk developments in Australian rainforests points to the fact of erecting the structure to facilitate such walks differentiates them from other ecotourism and nature-based operations that make use of the rainforest as an attraction but do so at the ground level. In a similar way, the work of Westwood and Boyd in South Island, New Zealand, (Chapter 4, this volume) illustrates how traditional ideas about nature-based tourism activities can be expanded to include activities like scenic flights given their passive interaction with the natural environment and their potential to be a low impact form of tourism.

Need for Further Research

Any concluding chapter would not be complete if it did not make a call for the need for further research to be undertaken, and in this case, on the interaction of visitors within nature-based activities taking place in peripheral and often vulnerable environments. This call is heeded by a number of authors. Orams provides any excellent review and critique of impact assessment research that has been undertaken within a New Zealand context on the interaction between tourists and marine animals. However, although the author is clearly cognizant that further research is needed on how to assess impact, he believes New Zealand is positioned as a leader in marine mammal tourism management and a potential benchmark for other destinations to use (Chapter 15, this volume). One element of this area of research was presented in the case study of Doubtful Sound (Lusseau, Chapter 16, this volume) where boat interaction with bottlenose dolphins as part of the scenic cruise industry of the area warrants closer monitoring. While research that focuses on the nature of interaction is valuable, the work by Lusseau points to the need to implement findings by raising awareness among tour operators, and developing better interpretation and education of visitors as to more appropriate forms of behaviour. While much research is often targeted at ensuring the natural capital of areas is not degraded as a result of tourism, the welfare of visitors within peripheral areas is often overlooked. Musa (Chapter 8, this volume) provides valuable research on social impacts on tourists, in particular those related to health and safety when visiting high altitude areas. While experiences of places are mostly formed from the natural capital of a region, equally important in shaping that experience is to be able to enjoy it in good heath and with assurance of safety. Further work is clearly needed here especially if nature-based tourism in peripheral areas is to remain to have a strong activity base, as opposed to one focused on a passive, casual interaction with natural surroundings. Another avenue that requires ongoing research is the development of new ways of thinking in terms of models and frameworks that help to better understand the extent of movement that occurs by visitors as they engage in activities within peripheral areas. The work by Dupuis and Müller (Chapter 7, this volume) provides a useful framework for understanding space–time use of different groups based on preferences and constraints they face. In turn, such research will help shed new light in creating routes and pathways in regions that are best suited for different user groups influenced by the amount of diffusion possible and/or desired. The management implications here are obvious as it will lead to the development of a typology of routes for activities that can accommodate a range of users and preferred activity levels.

Concluding Comments

So what strategies can peripheral regions look to use to maintain nature-based tourism as an option for regional development? The above discussion offers some thinking here. First, not all areas should look to tourism as the only alternative as not all areas are suited as tourism places. Many peripheral regions are dependent on primary industry, and often when tourism isintroduced, the economic contribution that tourism brings to the economy of peripheral communities in terms of jobs, for example, is often much lower than the workforces engaged in traditional resource-based industries, and this point should not be overlooked. Second, if tourism is to be encouraged in whatever form, it must not be seen to take priority over other traditional activities present, and instead the desire should be to promote tourism that is complementary with other resource-based users, after all it would be foolish to place one's eggs in a single basket where the long-term viability of that activity is often in question and where its history is a relatively recent one compared to other resource-based activities. Peripheral regions that are flagging and are not engaged in tourism, however, remain highly vulnerable to change and transformation, and there needs to be awareness that by choosing tourism, change and transformation will occur and this needs to be accepted by communities. One cautionary note is voiced here and this is based on thinking by Wheeller (Chapter 17, this volume) and that is we should not be too quick to change places and impose outside views on what is or is not acceptable behaviour and activity: that nature-based activity should not follow western values and opinions. Third, if tourism is chosen then there is a need to broaden thinking to beyond just eco-tourism as the main type of tourism for peripheral areas, despite its global popularity, but to include resource-based tourism, adventure activities, as well as to develop new products that enhance the uniqueness of a place or add diversity to experiences being offered. It is the difference between places that makes them worthy of visiting and while ecotourism is by far the most preferred option, other types of tourism suited within natural and peripheral contexts should not be dismissed so lightly. Fourth, there is an urgency to ensure that regions develop specific tourism policy that is designed to encourage nature-based tourism in particular, matching the attributes of regions with the characteristics that make nature-based tourism different from other types. Fifth, there is the need to work within the institutional arrangements set up for areas (e.g. permit systems, regional and district plans, specific species plans), and as the chapter by Shelton and Lübcke (Chapter 14, this volume) demonstrated, these can often be complex, and that in the end, management plans for regions are often shaped by the value judgments of managers. Sixth, there is the need to develop strategies that keep control and direction of development in local hands, and as Johnston and Payne (Chapter 2, this volume) state, to be able to promote the social capital needed to give peripheral areas blessed with outstanding natural assets a fighting chance to be successful as opposed to failing. However, despite all efforts to control factors that can shape tourism in peripheral areas, success may have more to do with external factors that regions have no control over such as exchange rates in determining marketplace and levels of visitation as opposed to strate-gies that combat a region's accessibility, or help develop its man-made and human capital to support its stock of natural capital. Nature-based tourism remains a popular option for many peripheral regions, and it is hoped that the contributions provided in the book provides a platform on which further discussion can take place.

References

Boyd, S.W. and Singh, S. (2003) Destination communities: Structures, resources and types. In Singh, S., Timothy, D.J. and Dowling, R.K. (eds) *Tourism in Destination Communities* (pp. 19–34). Oxford: CAB International.

Hall, C.M. and Müller, D. (eds) (2004) *Tourism, Mobility and Second Homes: Between Elite Landscape and Common Ground.* Clevedon: Channel View.

Hall, C.M. and Page, S.J. (2002) *The Geography of Tourism and Recreation* (2nd edn). London: Routledge.

Murphy, P.E. (1985) *Tourism: A Community Approach.* New York: Metheun.

Pearce, P., Moscardo, G. and Ross, G. (1996) *Tourism Community Relationships.* Oxford: Pergamon.

Singh, S., Timothy, D.J. and Dowling, R.K. (eds) (2003) *Tourism in Destination Communities.* Oxford: CABI Publishing.

Index